Mugwumps, Morals & Politics, 1884-1920

Gerald W. McFarland

The University of Massachusetts Press   Amherst, 1975

Mugwumps, Morals & Politics, 1884-1920

Copyright © 1975 by
The University of Massachusetts Press
All rights reserved
Library of Congress Catalog Card Number 74-21242
ISBN 0-87023-175-8
Printed in the United States of America
Designed by Richard Hendel
Drawings by Barry Moser

Publication of this book was assisted by the
American Council of Learned Societies under a
grant from the Andrew W. Mellon Foundation.

Library of Congress Cataloging in Publication Data

McFarland, Gerald W   1938-
    Mugwumps, morals, and politics, 1884-1920.

    Bibliography: p.
    Includes index.
    1. United States—Politics and government—1865 -
1900. 2. United States—Politics and government—
1901-1953. 3. Progressivism (United States politics)
4. Social reformers—United States. I. Title.
E661.M14   320.9'73'08   74-21242
ISBN 0-87023-175-8

Title page illustrations: (top row, left to right)
Low, Curtis, Straus, Deming; (bottom row, left
to right) Gilder, Baldwin, Schurz, Bowker

To my mother,

and to the memory of my father,

Frank E. McFarland

Contents

Preface

This study of the Mugwump record in politics owes much to the extensive reevaluation of American reform and reformers that has taken place since World War II. Indeed, my interpretative task has been one of mining this rich vein of recent revisionist writing in order to update and elaborate the Mugwumps' historical image. Specific sources of my approach are readily evident in three strategies I employed here:

1) Drawing on the example of George Mowry, Alfred D. Chandler, Jr., and others, I have done a career-line analysis of a large group of active Mugwumps. The internal diversity of the Mugwump group is more evident from this broad sample than it has been in histories based largely on a few notable Mugwumps. Further, I have added a comparative dimension to this Mugwump profile by contrasting the Mugwumps' collective socioeconomic traits with those of a parallel sample of regular Republicans.

2) Samuel Hays's strictures against the use of dualistic typologies in historical analysis have been of great value to me. Certainly there has been a tendency, which I discuss at length in my first chapter, to portray the Mugwumps within an either-or framework. They were either myopic conservatives or militant liberals, political opportunists or sincere idealists. Through Hays's writings, however, I first encountered the idea of superseding these dualistic typologies with the model of a spectrum or local-cosmopolitan continuum across which political groups could be arranged according to their degree of commitment to local or cosmopolitan interests. Where, I asked myself, did the Mugwumps fit in this frame of reference? Were they identified with localistic interests, or was their functional role in community life one

which gave them a more cosmopolitan perspective? The answers to these questions helped me clarify the nexus between the Mugwumps' political platform and their socioeconomic characteristics.

3) Taking my lead from Otis L. Graham, Jr., and his book *An Encore for Reform: The Old Progressives and the New Deal*, I traced the Mugwumps' public careers well beyond the chronological limits of previous works, covering their political activities up to 1920. To be sure, there was no Mugwump movement after 1900 any more than there was a discernible effort of surviving progressives to act in concert during the New Deal era. But the Mugwumps' careers in the progressive era elucidate the continuities and discontinuities between mugwumpery and progressivism just as Graham's findings provided new insights about the relationship between the old progressivism and the New Deal.

Many individuals aided me directly or indirectly in preparing this manuscript. Librarians were universally helpful, and one need only consult the list of manuscript depositories in my Bibliography to get an inkling of the debts I owe in that regard. My graduate school mentors, Robert D. Cross and Eric L. McKitrick, encouraged me at an early phase of this project when its rawness was more evident than its virtues.

An on-going relationship with ten young scholars I met while at Columbia University—Lois and James M. Banner, Norman Fiering, Alan Graebner, Otis L. Graham, Jr., Lloyd J. Graybar, Herbert Johnson, James P. Johnson, Linda Kerber, and Daniel J. Leab—gave me intellectual stimulation of the sort that was highly supportive of my research efforts. Other historians—Geoffrey Blodgett, L. E. Fredman, Clyde Griffen, Ari Hoogenboom, and Marlene Wortman—provided, probably without realizing it, helpful insights and vital encouragement at key points along the way.

I reserve a special place for the memory of Adrienne Koch whose inspiring example and friendship were influential beyond what I can express briefly here.

Fellowships or grants from a variety of sources—the Danforth Foundation, the Woodrow Wilson Foundation, the University of Massachusetts (Amherst) Research Council, and the American Council of Learned Societies—were instrumental in enabling me to initiate and complete this project.

I am also grateful for permission to reprint portions, now substantially revised, of my articles "The Breakdown of Deadlock: The Cleveland Democracy in Connecticut, 1884-1894," *The Historian*, 31:1 (May 1969), 381-97, and "The New York Mugwumps of 1884: A Profile," *Political Science Quarterly*, 78:1 (March 1963), 40-58.

At times while working in my Leverett, Massachusetts, study, I became half convinced that the restless spirits of the genteel reformers still roam the New England countryside, plaguing those presumptuous enough to delve into the Mugwump mind. This manuscript is completed, therefore, despite the many distractions provided by those resourceful shades— the herd of horses that ran through the front yard, the bullocks that broke into the garden, the swallows that fell down Milton's chimney, and the innumerable kittens that were constantly under foot.

I mention these friends, colleagues, and mischievous spirits by way of partially discharging my debts to them. They are in no way responsible, through guilt by association, for any errors of fact or interpretation in the final product. Those are solely my doing.

Chapter 1

Schurz

The Mugwump Image in History

The term "Mugwump" has come to have a variety of connotations. To many nonhistorians the word summons up the image of an individual perched on a fence with his Mug on one side and his Wump on the other. Elsewhere the word is used as a synonym for political independence, usually applied to civic reformers who refuse to identify themselves permanently with one political party. When some historians, following Richard Hofstadter's lead, talk about Mugwumps, they are referring to those old-American, white Protestants whose social and political dominance was threatened by immigration, industrialization, and urbanization in the late nineteenth century—a group defined as much by its cultural ties as by its politics. And in the 1960s the notion of mugwumpery as independence was given a generational twist

by a rock music group that adopted "The Mugwumps" as its
name.

In this study, "Mugwump" is used in its more specific, original meaning. Quite simply, those Republicans who bolted
their party during the 1884 presidential campaign to vote for
the Democratic candidate, Grover Cleveland, were called Mugwumps. To these insurgents, being a Mugwump was permanently connected with that particular act of party irregularity.

The lines of debate about the Mugwump reformers and their
role in American politics have changed remarkably little from
the 1880s to the present. The positions of various schools have
become much more refined, of course, and points of emphasis
differentiate recent writings from older ones, but the prepon-
derance of writing about the Mugwumps fits into two broad
schools, which I will label the realist and the idealist views.

Among the Mugwumps' contemporaries, the realist view was
most forcefully expressed by practical politicians. To men like
Roscoe Conkling, James G. Blaine, and Whitelaw Reid, the
Mugwumps were foolish, hypocritical, and self-righteous.
Recognizing that any widespread public acceptance of the reformers' program of nonpartisanship, the merit system, and
independent voting might result in the loss of patronage power
and even of some closely contested elections, the politicos
attacked the Mugwumps without giving quarter. Mugwumps,
they charged, misunderstood the working of popular government even while they wanted its rewards. They were mask-
ing their private desire for power under a vocabulary that
stressed the public good. Mugwumps had pretensions to
practicality, but their policy of independent voting proved
they had completely unrealistic notions of how one achieved
political influence within a two-party system. "Parties are not
built up by deportment, or ladies' magazines, or gush,"

Senator Conkling once asserted in a famous peroration. Many a practical party man, stung by the Mugwumps' attacks on partisanship, expressed similar feelings.[1]

From the idealist viewpoint of the Mugwumps and their allies, however, the reformers were simply sincere and moral- ly concerned citizens who turned to civil service reform and independent voting to fight their age's partisan excesses. Mug- wumps had always depended on the power of the pen to off- set their weakness in numbers and did so again in the histori- cal record. The Mugwumps' cosmopolitan cultural traits and the cohesiveness of their intellectual community, especially in the Boston-Cambridge area, comes across forcefully from an examination of the early writings about Mugwumps and mugwumpery.

Among the Mugwump biographers of other Mugwumps, Joseph B. Bishop wrote on Charles J. Bonaparte, Edward Cary and John W. Chadwick on George William Curtis, and William Dudley Foulke on Lucius B. Swift. In the *Proceedings* of the Massachusetts Historical Society and elsewhere, John F. An- drew was memorialized by Edmund M. Wheelwright, Wheel- wright by Barrett Wendell, and Wendell by Robert Grant. Charles Eliot Norton edited Curtis's speeches and writings and Frederic Bancroft edited Carl Schurz's. Autobiographi- cal writings completed the Mugwumps' literary self-defense. Not uncommonly these reflections included a statement like Thomas Wentworth Higginson's: "I confess that it makes me somewhat indignant to hear such men [as the Mugwumps] stigmatized as mere idealists and dilettantes by politicians who have never done so much to purify and elevate politics as these men have been doing daily for years."[2]

Many of the scholars who initially dealt with the politics of the 1880s were strongly influenced by the Mugwumps. Lord

Bryce's famous analysis of American government, *The American Commonwealth* (1888), was informed by discussions with Mugwump intellectuals (E. L. Godkin, Thomas Wentworth Higginson, Gamaliel Bradford, Sr., and Simeon E. Baldwin) and contained a chapter on municipal government written by Seth Low. Not surprisingly, Bryce's view of Gilded Age politics, that "all has been lost, except office or the hope of it," closely paralleled that of his informants.[3] Similarly, James Ford Rhodes, the Ohio ironmonger-turned-historian, was warmly received by members of the Massachusetts Historical Society, the Mugwump House of Peers, when he moved to Boston late in the 1890s. Rhodes's *History of the United States from the Compromise of 1850*, the first attempt to write a full-scale history of the period from 1850 to 1877, was marked by a critical attitude toward Gilded Age politics and an admiring portrait of reform that no Mugwump would have gainsaid. Finally, the field of Mugwump biography was assiduously worked by two Yankee historians, Bliss Perry and Mark A. DeWolfe Howe, who—though not themselves Mugwumps—knew and admired many of the Massachusetts bolters. Their writings carried an unadulterated version of the idealist school well into the twentieth century.[4]

By the 1920s the impact of progressivism on American historiography was replacing the Mugwumps with other heroes. To Vernon L. Parrington, for example, the great epoch of liberalism in the nineteenth century was from 1820 to 1860. Not until progressivism early in the 1900s did the country have another liberal renaissance. Other writers in the progressive school placed more emphasis on the importance of populism to modern liberalism's development, as did John D. Hicks, but in any case the great watershed was the 1890s, catching the Mugwumps of 1884 on the wrong side of the dividing line. For writers in the Populist-progressive tradition the contrast between progressivism and mugwumpery was clear: progressivism was realistic, hopeful, and activist, while mugwumpery had been pessimistic and negative.[5]

Post-World War II writings on the Mugwumps from the realist perspective reiterated the older indictment of the Mugwumps' impracticality but now often joined to it the charge that they were illiberal. The reformers were "out of step with the rest of society," wrote Ari Hoogenboom in the definitive study of civil service reform (1961). The Mugwumps, according to John G. Sproat in *"The Best Men"* (1968), split the liberal reform movement in 1884 and clung to outmoded "panaceas" like free trade and political regeneration, thus proving their program an "anachronism" that "really had nothing more to offer American politics after 1884."[6] A moderate summary of writing in the realist vein is *Politics in the Gilded Age* (1972) by John M. Dobson who concludes: "The Progressives won their most significant victories while they maintained their ties with the regular parties, not by breaking them as the Mugwumps had in 1884. The early rebels were too hasty, too narrow, and too idealistic."[7]

A few historians, mostly biographers, have continued to treat the Mugwumps from the idealist perspective in the postwar period. Generally admiring of the reformers' political independence, these writers also argue that the realists have underestimated the liberality of individual Mugwumps. According to the biographers of R. R. Bowker, Oscar S. Straus, and Seth Low, Mugwumps did find their way into twentieth-century progressive causes.[8] Of the students of Gilded Age reform, however, L. E. Fredman, *The Australian Ballot* (1968), is the only one to add to this admiration for the Mugwumps' principles an argument that as a group they made a major contribution to the emergence of progressivism.[9]

To the degree I demonstrate that mugwumpery was not a dead end for the reformers and that from the 1890s onward many of them entered progressive causes, my findings might simply seem a refinement of the idealist perspective. Valuable as this might be in correcting some accounts that neglect the politics of mugwumpery after 1884, additional facts do not by themselves break the impasse between the realist and idealist schools. To any evidence that Mugwumps can be identified with progressivism, the answer can be made that equally good evidence links the Mugwumps with outmoded, reactionary ideas—not to speak of wrong-headed and unrealistic political strategy. The metaphor of trench warfare comes to mind: each side constantly digs in deeper, perfecting its defenses. Occasionally the lines of battle move a bit one way or another, but the longer the combat, the less the real movement.

By formulating the historiographical issue in this way and arbitrarily assigning many other issues to the background, I mean to emphasize the dangers inherent in interpretative frameworks based on dichotomies—reform-reaction, idealism-realism, progressivism-conservatism. In fact, post-World War II revisionist studies of progressivism have attacked precisely this type of interpretative framework and thus provide the basis for reevaluating "reform" and "reformers" of the Mugwump variety as well.

The landmark revisionist study of progressivism was Richard Hofstadter's *Age of Reform* (1955). Drawing on earlier work by George Mowry and Alfred D. Chandler, Jr., Hofstadter reworked the traditional portrait of progressivism, retouching it in more conservative tones. He explicitly connected the Mugwumps with the progressives, referring to the latter as the "Mugwump type" and characterizing them as a group that was on the defensive in the new industrial society: "Their wealth and power were being dwarfed by comparison with the new eminences of wealth and power. They were less important and they knew it." According to Hofstadter, disaffected men of this type turned to politics, seeing progressivism as a way of returning themselves to dominance in American life.[10]

In the 1960s revisionism continued apace. Robert Wiebe, in *The Search for Order* (1967), agreed with Hofstadter in making the source of progressivism urban, middle-class professionals and businessmen, but he turned Hofstadter's argument that this group's status was declining upside down, making the progressives into members of a vigorous "new middle class." For Wiebe, the progressives were reshaping the social order to fit their priorities—specialization, education, and bureaucratic order. Noting differences from the older Mugwump type, Wiebe also pointed out that both progressives and Mugwumps had a faith in efficiency, expertise, and non-partisanship.[11] According to radicals like Gabriel Kolko and James Weinstein, these were the predictably "conservative" values of a corporate economy. Such reforms might be characterized as "liberal," but only if one understood that they were elitist in origin and directed at social control rather than social change.[12]

Taken by itself the discovery of progressivism's conservative side has limited value in understanding Mugwump reform, particularly if viewed from a political perspective in which liberalism represents good and conservatism equals reaction. The result is another dualistic typology. The way to avoid being locked into such dichotomies, according to another postwar revisionist, Samuel Hays, is to place political groups

on a spectrum running from those with localistic and neighborhood loyalties to those with dominantly cosmopolitan
and national commitments. Applied to the progressive era,
Hays's thesis produced a story in which municipal reform
was less the triumph of goodness and liberalism than the victory of cosmopolitan, upper-class citizens over representatives of an older, ward-based power structure.[13]

The relevance of the local-cosmopolitan framework to the
Mugwumps becomes evident in the work of Geoffrey Blodgett and Robert Wiebe. In an essay entitled "Reform Thought
and the Genteel Tradition" (1970), Blodgett argues that a
major cause for the Gilded Age reformers' lack of political
success was their having sought "a national, cosmopolitan
function in a social matrix which remained profoundly local
in the roots of its organization."[14] Wiebe suggests in *The
Search for Order* (1967) that the progressive era marked the
triumph of cosmopolitanism in American life, the localistic
society of 1877 having been gradually superseded by the
nationalized one of 1920. Progressivism, interpreted in this
way, might well have the older cosmopolitanism of Blodgett's
genteel reformers as one of its roots.

Post-World War II revisionism, therefore, whatever its
limitations turn out to be as an interpretation of progressivism,
has opened the way for a reexamination of Mugwump reform.[15]
The old realist-idealist impasse may be circumvented by focusing on the Mugwumps' functional role within the community.
Thus, the historian's task is not so much to determine whether
the Mugwumps were really fighting for the good of all the
public as to define the position within the local-cosmopolitan
spectrum from which the Mugwumps arrived at their version
of what the public good was. Cosmopolitanism may represent
a link between the Mugwumps and the progressives, but as the

revisionists point out, cosmopolitanism need not be equated with liberalism. Moreover, a nexus between nineteenth- and twentieth-century cosmopolitanism does not imply that the two were identical, for they existed in radically different social contexts. Indeed, a comparison of the old and new cosmopolitanism may well result in a heightened awareness of the distinctions between the Mugwumps and the progressives.

Historiography has a way of becoming an inkblot test for the historians, reflecting the crucial concerns of the historians' age as well as the significance of the subject under study. One Mugwump characteristic, noted by realists and idealists alike, was the Mugwumps' determination to maintain their independence. They defended it against a variety of threats: the partisans' demands that they submit to the discipline of party regularity and also the more impersonal forces of industrialism's social disciplines—standardization, centralization, and bureaucratic order. To be sure, Mugwumps accepted those elements of the emerging urban-industrial society that suited them, but with their characteristic individuality they also rejected much that was new. For the twentieth-century progressives, absorbed as they were with the new, the Mugwumps' response seemed proof positive that the old bolters were reactionaries living in the past. Post-World War II revisionists, though more critical of progressivism, generally shared the progressives' affirmative view of modern corporate society and saw the Mugwumps as its opponents.

Having lived in a pre-industrial age, the Mugwumps had a personal awareness that something was lost as well as gained with the emergence of modern America. For the most part this awareness was lacking among twentieth-century Americans until recently. Today, however, modernity's obituary is being written by those who declare that our times are a "post-modern" era, thus placing the Mugwumps' resistance to elements of modernity in a new light. Present-day Americans cannot, of course, share the Mugwumps' pre-industrial experience and may find their specific response to industrialism uncongenial. But today's renewed ambivalence about urban-industrial society creates a certain sense of kinship between the Mugwumps' age and ours, making an evaluation of Mugwump reform once again a timely task.

Chapter 2

Curtis

Two Gilded Age Portraits:
Bolters & Blaine Men

In the history of American reform, the year 1884 might appropriately be remembered as the year of the Mugwumps. It
was in that year that these gentlemen reformers, traditionally
Republicans, repudiated their party's presidential nominee,
James G. Blaine, and supported the Democratic candidate,
Grover Cleveland. During the sometimes bitter campaign,
the bolters and Blaine's backers flailed away at each other
without asking for quarter. Contemptuous of the anti-Blaine
dissidents, GOP regulars followed the lead of Charles A. Dana
(editor of the *New York Sun*) in labelling them "Mugwumps"
—an Algonquian Indian word meaning "great men," thus im-
plying that the bolters were rather too proud of themselves.
Just what all the fuss was about becomes evident from a review of the Mugwump insurgency's background and a

comparison of the bolters' composite portrait with the socio-economic profile of their rivals, the Blaine men.

In the years immediately after the Civil War many conscientious Republicans came to believe that slavery had been replaced by spoils politics as the "greatest danger threatening our republican institutions."[1] From the mid-1870s onward men who held this view called themselves Independent Republicans and attempted to purge their party of spoilsmanship. Their ultimate threat was that as a self-defined "party of the centre" they were prepared to shift support from one party to the other depending on the parties' performances on issues.

The threat of bolting was rarely carried out before 1884. Even in the case of the ill-fated Liberal Republican protest against Grant in 1872, a sizeable percentage of the future Independents who initially joined the movement abandoned it after Greeley received the Liberals' nomination. In 1876 and 1880, the Independents called pre-convention meetings to urge reform and righteousness on the Republican party. In the end, however, the party's Independent wing did not determine the Hayes and Garfield nominations so much as it acquiesced in them, convinced that it could do no better. For all the eminence of some of its leaders, therefore, the Independent Republican movement was notable for its weakness, for the sporadic quality of its activism, and for the lack of permanent institutions or organizations representing its interests.[2]

Several reform associations presaged the Mugwump bolt by departing from the unorganized Independent Republican style of protest. The National Civil Service Reform League, the Massachusetts Reform Club, and the Brooklyn Young Republican Club were all founded in the early 1880s. They reinvigorated the reform cause by recruiting members, winning some significant political victories, and establishing its on-going organization strength.

Considering the fact that reformers had been advocating civil service reform since the end of the Civil War, it is remarkable that the first civil service reform association was not founded until 1877. Even then the New York Civil Service Reform Association, as it was called, almost immediately disintegrated. Something of the anti-institutionalism that had plagued pre-Civil War antislavery societies persisted among the civil service advocates, many of whom were former antislavery activists. Also, many of the reformers were reluctant to break with the Republican party. The result was an anomalous situation in which the Independents distrusted the GOP's spoils element but timidly avoided truly independent, pressure-group politics.

By 1880 the sentiment for depending on the Republican party was declining. The New York association was reconstituted, and within a year similar groups were organized in other cities, a National Civil Service Reform League established (August 1881), and the initial issues of the *Civil Service Record*, the monthly publication of the Boston and Cambridge association, had appeared.[3] The more the momentum for reform built up, "the more shrill were reformers' protests over public immorality."[4] In 1883 a national civil service law, the Pendleton Act, passed Congress, and the New York and Massachusetts legislatures adopted similar bills. Fed by such successes, the reformers protested Blaine's nomination with undiminished aggressiveness.

The Brooklyn Young Republican Club was more local in its aims than the civil service associations. Organized in 1881, it was composed of Republicans who hoped to promote municipal reform in Brooklyn. In 1881 and 1883 the club supported

Seth Low as the Independent Republican candidate for mayor. Low won both elections and successfully instituted two programs dear to the hearts of the future Mugwumps—a nonpartisan municipal government and a business administration of city affairs.

These two closely related ideas reflected the view that there was no Democratic or Republican way to pave streets, build sewers, or educate children. In effect the reformers were denying that parties based on national issues had a valid role to play in municipal government. The issue, as Low put it in 1883, reduced to the simple question of whether the "municipal spirit or the party spirit" would prevail.[5] In 1884 many of Brooklyn's "young Republicans" did not bolt, an indication of their loyalty to the party and to Blaine as well as their conviction that independent voting was appropriate in local elections only. But a sizeable group of men left the Brooklyn Young Republican Club and joined the anti-Blaine protest, seeing it as the logical extension of their efforts to combat municipal partisanship.[6]

Massachusetts Independents were slower to organize than their New York counterparts, partly because regular party channels were more open to reformers in the Bay State. In New York powerful Democratic and Republican machines ground away at each other, neither willing to tolerate sorties by reformers into the political arena. In Massachusetts during the pre-1884 period, however, a number of future bolters— among them Charles R. Codman, Henry Lee, and Thomas Wentworth Higginson—won elective office in districts dominated by Independent Republicans.[7]

Nevertheless, by 1882 the organizational impulse took hold among the Bay State reformers, and they established the Massachusetts Reform Club. Although the club's first campaign

was for Theodore Lyman, a political independent, in his race
against a Republican incumbent in the Ninth Congressional
District, this was not viewed by the club as a bolt from the
Republican party. Indeed, in 1883, the reform clubbers cooperated with the regular Republican organization to defeat
a mutual enemy, Governor Benjamin Butler, who was seeking
reelection. Before the 1884 campaign, then, the Massachusetts
Reform Club members were nearly all loyal Republicans who
tried to implement their platform—"civil service reform and
independent action in politics"—by bringing pressure to bear
on their party.[8]

Blaine's nomination in 1884 came at a time when the political fortunes of the GOP's reform wing were on the upswing.
Instead of strengthening the reformers' allegiance to the Republican party, a number of victories—the election of an independent Massachusetts congressman and a vigorous reform
mayor in Brooklyn, along with the passage of state civil service laws in Massachusetts and New York—encouraged restive-
ness with party discipline. With their numbers augmented and
better organized than previously, the reformers became more
militant. The Mugwump bolt, far from being a product of
despair, was an outgrowth of this new-found confidence.[9]

The paramount issue in 1884, the Mugwumps insisted, was
a moral rather than a political one. According to the bolt's
spokesmen, "the platforms of the two parties do not essentially differ" on such political questions as the tariff and the
civil service.[10] Voters nevertheless faced a crucial choice,
based on the character of the two candidates.

Blaine, the Mugwumps believed, was a spoilsman. Cleveland
was not. Blaine had been implicated in a shady bond deal while
Speaker of the House of Representatives. Cleveland had made
the statement that "a public office is a public trust" his watch-

word. Blaine typified the machine politics that had marred post-Civil War political life. Cleveland? Admirers said they loved him for the enemies he had made, supposedly among party hacks. While the contrasts between the candidates were not nearly so stark as the Mugwumps made them seem during the heat of the campaign, the bolters felt their anger with the Republicans was completely justified. Of the party that nominated a man it had previously passed over partly because of his tainted public reputation, one bolter concluded, "We have not left the party; it is fairer to say that the party has left us."[11]

The bolters' political strategy in 1884 created a long-lasting cleavage between Mugwumps and the Republican reformers who backed Blaine. Although the Mugwumps asserted that reform would best be served by bolting, many members of the Republican party's reform wing disagreed. Senator George Edmunds of Vermont and Senator George F. Hoar of Massachusetts, political figures admired by many Independents, ridiculed the idea that bolting would increase the Mugwumps' influence. It would almost certainly have the opposite effect, they contended. One reform-minded Republican put his rationale for sticking with the party succinctly: "I do not greatly admire Blaine," he wrote, "but I do admire things that are practical and expedient."[12]

Whether or not to bolt and whether Blaine or the Democratic party posed the greater threat to reform were issues that split friends and families. Senator Hoar's nephews, Samuel and Sherman, joined the bolt against the advice of their uncle and their father, former United States Attorney General E. R. Hoar. The famous minister of Plymouth Congregational Church in Brooklyn, Henry Ward Beecher, backed Cleveland, but his sister, Harriet Beecher Stowe, and her husband, Calvin, stayed firm with Blaine. Joseph H. Choate, a

noted New York lawyer, remained loyal to the party, though
his older brother William was active in the New York City
Mugwump campaign. Mark Twain, a Mugwump, labored long
and unsuccessfully to persuade his friend William Dean Howells to join him in bolting.[13]

The division in the Independent Republican ranks produced
considerable acrimony. Mugwumps reserved a special scorn
for "Independents" such as Theodore Roosevelt and Henry
Cabot Lodge who refused to act independently when the chips
were down. For their part Roosevelt and Lodge writhed with
annoyance at the Mugwump imputation that they had sold
out. Neither ever forgave the bolters for these attacks. Senator Hoar likewise saved some choice bits of political invective for the Mugwumps, condemning them as "the vilest set
of political assassins that ever disgraced this or any other
country."[14]

During the campaign Republican strategists did everything
they could to discredit the Mugwump dissidents. In state after
state respected individuals identified with the old Independent
Republican movement were drafted to remonstrate publicly
with the bolters. The insurgents, Blaine's supporters, charged,
were deserting the party in its hour of need. In a good example
of just such a letter, Yale's president, Theodore Dwight Woolsey, wrote, "The independents who have broken away from
the party have lost part of my respect. . . . If they had
staid in the party, whatever danger now befalls it from a low
class of men inclined to enter it would have been counter-
acted."[15]

Just what moved the Mugwumps to bolt in the face of such
pressure becomes more evident from a close study of the movement's membership. What follows is a composite portrait of
nearly one thousand Mugwumps from various states. This is

supplemented by an even more detailed analysis of the socio-economic profile of approximately four hundred bolters from the "New York City area"—that is, Mugwumps who lived or worked in what today comprises New York City. Comparison of this profile with a composite biography of a roughly equal number of New York City Republicans throws the salient Mugwump characteristics more sharply into relief. (See Appendix A for lists of names, tables of findings, and an explanation of sampling procedure.)

The Mugwump protest was composed almost entirely of men residing in the northeastern United States. When the National Conference of Independents and Republicans was held in New York City on July 22, 1884, 467 delegates registered. Of the registrants 284 were from New York state, 33 from New Jersey, 84 from Massachusetts, 35 from other New England states, 19 from Pennsylvania, and only 12 from all other states combined.[16]

While the proportion of New Yorkers at the meeting was doubtless exaggerated somewhat by the gathering being located in their state, there is ample testimony in Mugwump materials to the difficulty of winning anti-Blaine recruits outside the New York-New England area. Lucius B. Swift, an Indianapolis civil service reformer, remarked that "although in the East Independents were plentiful enough, in Indiana a Mugwump was very rare."[17] In Illinois the Chicago Independents led by Edwin Burritt Smith and Franklin MacVeagh could collect only about two hundred Mugwump names in the city. They held a meeting but stated that "we did not wish any reporters to be there because they would ridicule the smallness of our numbers."[18] A representative from New Jersey said that even in his state, close as it was to the center of the bolt, there were few indigenous Mugwumps, most of

the New Jersey bolters being either Yankee transplants or
men who had business and professional connections in New
York City.[19]

Two explanations advanced by the Mugwumps themselves
provide clues to the bolt's geography. First, outside of New
York and Massachusetts there were virtually no pre-existing
Independent groups to form an organizational base for the
Mugwump movement. In most states the problem, as one
local leader put it, was "organizing men not known to one
another [and] not brought together by the influence of
neighborhoods" in which reform activity had firmly established roots.[20]

Secondly, the bolt did not prosper where local newspaper
support was lacking, and outside of a few eastern cities there
were few Mugwump newspapers. In Connecticut the bolt was
strongest in New Haven where the *New Haven Morning News*
was owned by Henry W. Farnam and Simeon E. Baldwin and
edited by their fellow bolter, Clarence Deming. Hartford had
no Independent newspaper, and, relatively speaking, the anti-
Blaine campaign languished there. In New York City the Mugwump protest received a powerful assist from the *New York
Times* and the *New York Evening Post*. Boston's *Herald* and
Transcript provided similar encouragement and publicity in
eastern Massachusetts, as did the *Springfield Republican* in
the western part of the state. Outside of these few cities the
situation was more as Edwin Burritt Smith of Chicago described it: "We had no newspaper backing except what we
might have from the East."[21]

Within the New York-New England region the Mugwump
spirit flourished mainly in urban settings. In Massachusetts
the anti-Blaine insurgency centered in the Boston-Cambridge
area, three-fourths of the Bay State bolters living within ten

miles of Boston Common. Nearly two-thirds of the Connecticut Mugwumps were from either New Haven or Hartford. A similar proportion of the New York bolters lived or worked in New York City and Brooklyn. Most of the remaining Empire State Mugwumps came from other large cities—Albany, Buffalo, and Syracuse—the smallest of which was Syracuse with 51,792 inhabitants.[22] Even in states in which there were few Independents, most came from cities—Chicago, Indianapolis, Newport, Providence, and Philadelphia.

Small town Mugwumps were relatively rare birds, and those who did exist felt a sense of isolation. One bolter from Sharon, Connecticut (population 2,580), wrote his state's anti-Blaine organization, "I fear you must think me very remiss in the matter of this appeal to voters [to bolt the Blaine ticket], but you must make allowance for . . . the difficulty of getting the ordinary country man to put his name down to anything that he fears may offend his neighbor."[23] Similar responses from non-urban districts were received when the Massachusetts Mugwump committee conducted a survey of the Protestant clergymen in the state. Especially after news became public that Cleveland had an illegitimate son, there was a great reluctance to switch from Blaine to the Democratic candidate, even among men who were unenthusiastic about Blaine.[24] Clearly, small town, pietistic New England remained a bastion of party regularity nearly impervious to Mugwump appeals.

The Mugwumps were not late comers to urban life. Rather, they were often men who had been born in a city in the years before the Civil War. The year 1860 may serve as a reference point for assessing the urban background of the bolters. In that year only 15 percent of the American people lived in cities having more than 10,000 residents. At birth approximately

half of the Mugwumps lived in cities of that size, though nearly all Mugwumps were born well before 1860.[25] Urban origins
were even more prevalent among the New York City area
bolters, more than 60 percent of whom were born in such
large urban centers as New York City, Brooklyn, Boston, and
Baltimore.[26]

Veteran reformers lent their reputations to the bolt, frequently serving as its spokesmen. Like George William Curtis,
editor of *Harper's Weekly*, these men had figured prominently
in Republican party politics for twenty years or more, often
having participated in the GOP's formative phase before the
Civil War. E. L. Godkin and Horace White of the *New York
Evening Post*, Thomas Wentworth Higginson, once an antislavery agitator, Charles Francis Adams, Jr., the railroad expert whose grandfather and great-grandfather were presidents
of the United States, and Carl Schurz, the German expatriate
and former Civil War general, United States senator, and secretary of the interior, were representative of this group. For
these men the Mugwump insurgency was strongly reminiscent
of the pre-Civil War antislavery crusade. As one such reformer wrote after attending a Mugwump meeting: "The addresses
by Curtis and Higginson . . . were full of the same thoughts and
sentiments we used to feed on in old Anti-Slavery times. Curtis was magnificent, and as I sat there and saw him and heard
him, it seemed to me that it was Charles Sumner back again,
pleading for truth and righteousness as against the corruptions
and wickedness of the times."[27]

Most Mugwumps were younger than these old hands at reform.
Nationally the bolters divided almost equally between those less
than forty years of age and those forty and older.[28] In the New
York City sample the median age was thirty-eight, reflecting
the youthful constituency of the local Mugwump committees.

The young New Yorkers had become a force within the Independent Republican movement late in the 1870s. In 1879 R. R. Bowker, a thirty-one-year-old publisher, led the so-called Young Scratcher protest against the nomination of Alonzo B. Cornell, a member of Roscoe Conkling's Stalwart faction, for governor of New York. Urging anti-machine Republicans not to bolt but to scratch (that is, to delete Cornell's name when casting the official Republican ballot), Bowker initiated the anti-Cornell fight only after older reformers, notably George William Curtis, had refused to take the lead.[29]

In the 1880s the impetus for reform continued to shift to men like Bowker who had come of age since the Civil War and who had not been bruised by the rough-and-tumble politics of the Grant era. Older liberals were quick to sense the change. As one tariff reformer who had cut his ties with the GOP during the Liberal Republican bolt of 1872 wrote Carl Schurz, "a different class of men have come up since we were in the thick of the fight."[30] Thus reinforced, reform campaigns acquired a youth motif that persisted through the decade.[31]

The younger Mugwumps often explained their bolt as a rejection of the "old politics" rooted in Civil War issues. To these men the Republican party had ossified through nostalgia for the war years, and "weary of the continued reference to the past" the new recruits to reform came to "long for some new issue."[32] R. R. Bowker, an articulate spokesman for the new generation of reformers, wrote in 1876, "I am one of a considerable class whom the politicians overlook and who are likely to overlook the politicians. We were boys during the war, which, historically glorious, is politically a dead issue to us."[33] To be sure, even in the 1880s the Republican party's war record still provided it with a great reservoir of moral capital that it could tap at election time, but among men of the Bowker sort appeals not to desert the GOP for Cleveland and the "party of treason" had lost much of their persuasiveness by 1884.

Three individuals—Bowker, Henry W. Farnam, and George Fred Williams—typify the importance of men under forty to the Mugwump bolt. Bowker, thirty-six in 1884, was the oldest of the three. In addition to the Young Scratcher campaign, he had figured prominently in pre-convention Independent Republican activities during 1880 and in the movement to elect Seth Low mayor of Brooklyn in 1881. From 1878 onward the publisher of *Publisher's Weekly*, Bowker was never content to be simply a joiner. He participated actively in free trade, civil service, ballot, and tenement house reform efforts and the movement to establish a national association for librarians, as well as the campaign for international copyright laws. In 1884 Bowker's "tact and good judgment" were recognized by the Mugwump national committee, which relied heavily on him to organize its affairs and to bring in additional bolters from among his friends and contacts in the New York City area.[34]

Farnam was an economist who went to Yale as an undergraduate and later taught at his alma mater for nearly four decades. His ownership of the *New Haven Morning News* gave the bolt crucial support in Connecticut. Like Bowker, Farnam drew others into the reform cause and had a wide range of reform interests, including settlement house and labor reform in addition to the more familiar Mugwump causes of civil service and tariff reform. Farnam, with two lawyer friends —Simeon E. Baldwin and James F. Colby—handled most of the day-to-day work of the Mugwump state organization in Connecticut.

Williams, as the workhorse of the Massachusetts anti-Blaine movement, performed much the same role. A dynamic young lawyer at the beginning of a long career in politics, Williams soon became impatient with the leadership of the older Independents, particularly those who counselled the younger bolters to remain completely nonpartisan and to shun membership in the Cleveland-led Democratic party.

Occupationally, the Mugwumps were about evenly divided between professionals (lawyers, professors, physicians, and ministers) and businessmen (merchants, manufacturers, bankers, and brokers). If white-collar workers are included with the business contingent and editors and publishers with the professionals, the division between the two groups of New York City Mugwumps was almost exactly equal.[35]

Exceptions to the dominantly professional-entrepreneurial status of the bolt's membership were not numerous. Among the New York City area sample, the only Mugwumps whose occupations do not appear to be at least in the white-collar class (itself only 6 percent of the sample) were two "painters," one "polisher," and possibly an "engraver." Two other men worked for the Long Island Railroad—Warren Place as a transfer agent and Frank Texido as a freight agent.

The near absence of blue-collar or lower middle-class occupations from the lists of active Mugwumps is substantiated by information from other states. In Connecticut, among all the Mugwump petitions, only four signatures—two of "factory foremen," one of a newspaper "pressman," and another of a "telegraph operator"—deviate from the professional-entrepreneurial profile. One member of the New Haven Committee of Twenty-Five, the Mugwump campaign organization in 1884, was Porter C. Moulton, a "skilled laborer" and a former Knight of Labor who often addressed Mugwump rallies. Such efforts to cross social and occupational lines were usually marked by discomfort on both sides, however, as illustrated by the fact that the gentlemen reformers were ill at ease with Moulton's "tactless" remarks and edited them when reporting their meetings.[36]

There were considerable variations of wealth and social eminence among the Mugwump professionals and entrepreneurs. At one end of the scale were the millionaires, who comprised perhaps as much as 5 percent of the most active Mugwumps. Jackson S. Schultz (leather-goods manufacturer) and George Jones (owner of the *New York Times*) in New York City, James J. Goodwin (president of Connecticut Mutual Life Insurance Company) in Hartford, and Henry Lee Higginson (an investment banker) in Boston were examples of extremely successful businessmen who supported the bolt. Approximately one-third of the Mugwump millionaires inherited their fortunes, and most of the others amassed their wealth well before 1884.[37] That the wealthy and socially established bolters were not just a thin veneer on the movement was suggested by the fact that more than one-sixth of the anti-Blaine men in New York City were listed in the *Social Register*.[38]

Nevertheless, most Mugwumps, for all that they lived in the better residential sections of their cities and prospered professionally, were not idle rich men living off their investments. The vast majority of them were working professionals and executives whose business commitments required attention and frequently limited the amount of time they were willing or able to devote to political affairs.[39] There were also those, though they were definitely a minority, whose professions or small mercantile establishments provided them with only modest incomes. Among these men restricted finances had often forced them to make less desirable career choices—

going to work at an early age or dropping out of college.

An exceptionally high educational status set the Mugwumps apart from the mass of Americans in their time. Only 2.72 percent of the Americans between eighteen and twenty-one years of age were enrolled in institutions of higher learning in 1880. The median number of years in school for people born in 1865 (by which time all the Mugwumps were born) was eight.[40] Among the Mugwumps, however, college education was the rule rather than the exception.

In the New York City sample there was sufficiently extensive biographical information available on 255 bolters to provide some indication regarding education. Slightly less than one-fourth of these (56) either reported no educational information or indicated that their education was limited to the grammar school or high school level. The remaining three-fourths of the sample had at least some college experience. Of these men 41 percent (83 or about one-third of the entire educational sample) had a second, professional degree—usually a bachelor of law, sometimes an M.D. or Ph.D., and occasionally a B.D. or D.D.[41]

The New York City Mugwumps attended a few colleges with great regularity—in order of frequency Columbia, Harvard, Yale, College of the City of New York, and New York University. More bolters received degrees from Columbia Law School alone than attended all colleges other than the five just-mentioned institutions. Some classes at these fine schools, especially in the mid-1870s, were crowded with future Mugwumps. Twelve bolters graduated from Columbia Law School in either 1877 or 1878, and of these, two—Thomas Fenton Taylor and Henry S. Van Duzer—were 1875 graduates of Harvard, a class that included Gorham Bacon, George F. Canfield, and William W. Richards of New York as well as four future members of the Bay State anti-Blaine contingent.

Club memberships further confirm the distinctly intellectual predilections of the Mugwump group. In New York City
Mugwumps gravitated toward the University Club and the
Century Association, both organizations whose aims were
more literary and intellectual than political. In a bellicose
Republican club, the Union League, the thirty-five Mugwump
members were in a decided minority and were unable to prevent the club from giving its endorsement to Blaine in 1884.
Many years later one Mugwump recalled that a regular Republican had suggested to him that resignation from the Union
League was the logical next step for the Mugwump apostates
to take.[42]

By contrast, the intellectual clubs were sanctuaries for rene-
gade Republicans. The National Conference of Independents
and Republicans at which the bolters endorsed Cleveland was
held at the University Club. In 1884 seventy-three Mugwumps
were members and four were on the executive committee, including the publisher Henry Holt, who was one of the club's
founders. Similarly, sixty-one of the Mugwump sample belonged to the Century Association, wryly characterized by
Mark Twain as "the most unspeakably respectable club in the
United States, perhaps."[43]

In sum, a variety of traits—urban birth, college education,
and professional status—placed the Mugwumps in a relatively
small segment of the American population. Although veteran
political reformers gave the anti-Blaine protest invaluable
public leadership, the Mugwump bolt was not a rear guard
action by tired old men, but a movement whose ranks were
swelled by numerous, enthusiastic young recruits. The point
is not that all young, professional, and college-educated men
in the larger cities of New York and New England became

Mugwumps, for a great many did not, but that nearly all the Mugwumps came from this rather restricted group.

The Mugwumps' composite traits are highlighted further by contrasting them with the socioeconomic profile of the non-bolting Republicans, using samples of 470 Blaine men and 429 bolters drawn from New York City campaign sources. (A complete list of the individuals in both samples may be found in Appendix A.) For example, the Mugwumps were younger on the average than the Republicans for whom age data could be found. During the 1884 campaign the insurgents' accent was on youth. The regulars appealed to the wise old heads, an emphasis that shows up in the active Republicans' median age of forty-eight as opposed to the Mugwump group's median age of thirty-eight.

Occupationally, 50 percent of the Mugwumps were in professions, while not quite 30 percent of the regulars were in those fields. Although the sample of regulars was greater by about 10 percent, the Mugwumps outnumbered them in nearly every professional field—law, medicine, publishing, and teaching—the ministry being the only exception. The broad cultural reasons that explain this exception were captured in a condensed way by Reverend Burchard in his famous alliteration about the Democrats as the party of "Rum, Romanism, and Rebellion." Of course, not all clergymen shared this pietistic low-Protestant prejudice against the Irish Catholics who formed the backbone of Cleveland's party in New York City. Among the traditionally Republican ministers who had been inclined to bolt, however, there was a scramble to leave the Cleveland camp once the candidate's premarital indiscretions became known.[44] Thus, while men in most professions continued to oppose Blaine on the issue of public morality, the issue of private morality led many clergymen to castigate Cleveland and sanctify Blaine.

Several facts suggest that the Republicans were drawn from a more representative group within the general population than were the Mugwumps. The number of active regulars holding white-collar jobs was almost double that of the active Mugwumps in the same occupational category. Also, the regulars' religious profile more closely approximated the profile of all New Yorkers. Blaine's supporters frequently came from the larger low-Protestant denominations—the Methodists and the Presbyterians. The anti-Blaine men were overwhelmingly members of the Episcopal, Congregational, and Unitarian churches, that is, of relatively smaller and often higher-status denominations.

As for education and place of birth, the regulars were closer to the American average for their time in those categories as well. Sixty percent of the New York City bolters were born in urban environments and 40 percent in small town or rural settings. The figures were almost precisely the opposite for the regulars, only 38 percent of whom were city-born and 62 percent of whom were born on farms or in small towns. Similarly, more than twice as many regulars as Mugwumps stopped short of a college education. To be certain, many of the regulars, many more than the national average, received some college training, but the proportion of college-trained regulars (45 percent) was much below that of the Mugwumps (78 percent).

The contrasts between the profiles of regulars and Mugwumps reflect a divergence between an old and a new pattern in professional and associational life. Among the Republicans who went into professional fields, a much higher proportion gained their legal training in an old-fashioned way, reading law rather than following the typical Mugwump lawyer's path of attending

law school.[45] Also, the regulars greatly outnumbered the Mugwumps in the old-line Union League (108 Republicans and
35 Mugwumps) and were thinly represented in the University
Club (17 Republicans and 73 Mugwumps) where a college
degree constituted a prerequisite for admission. The charge
of the younger Mugwumps that the Blaine men adhered to an
older style of things gains credibility from these facts.

In the category of wealth, however, the above generalization must be reversed, for in that area it was the Mugwumps
rather than the Republicans who were tied to an older life
style. The Republican millionaires outnumbered the Mugwumps
both in absolute numbers (sixty-one to twenty-seven) and proportionately within the total samples (13 percent to 6 percent).
Furthermore, the "Money Kings" who gathered at Delmonico's
to honor Blaine late in the campaign were representatives of
a new economic order. Some of these men had inherited
their wealth (18 percent compared with 33 percent of the
Mugwump millionaires), but they were much more likely to
be self-made millionaires like Andrew Carnegie, Charles
Crocker, Henry M. Flagler (of Standard Oil), Jay Gould, and
Russell Sage. The companies they represented were often the
giant national corporations that had emerged since the Civil
War—Carnegie Steel, Standard Oil, Armour Brothers, Western
Union Telegraph, and the Southern Pacific and Union Pacific
railroads, to name but a few examples.

A theme that bulked large among the Republicans was that
of an organizational-corporate ethic. Two-thirds of the Republicans were businessmen or white-collar workers, and many
of these were identified with the expanding world of industrial
capitalism. The great entrepreneurs among the Blaine men led
the way in transforming the structure of American business
from local-regional lines to an economy of nationally integrated

corporations. Charles Crocker (who consolidated the Southern
Pacific and Central railroads in 1884), Herman O. Armour (who,
with his brother Philip, revolutionized the meat-packing industry), and Henry H. Rogers (a Standard Oil executive who promoted many corporate consolidations including the Amalga-
mated Copper trust in 1899) were examples of this element in
the Blaine camp.

Such entrepreneurs held something of a middle ground in
politics. Grover Cleveland's election posed no particular
threat to their interests; therefore, they were not thick-and-
thin Republicans of the Stalwart sort. Nevertheless, they
were hard headed and realistic. The Republican party and
Blaine were known quantities. By habit Republicans and
having experienced the party's relative dependability, such
practical men found little to attract them in the Mugwump
manifestoes about public morality.

In the complex of loyalties that sustained Republican orthodoxy in 1884, the Civil War still carried weight. Age figured
importantly here. In both New York samples there were men
between thirty-seven and sixty-nine years of age in 1884 who
had served in the military during the war, but the proportion
of regulars who belonged to this Civil War generation was much
higher than that of the Mugwumps—197 of 231 regulars (85 percent) to 121 of 224 Mugwumps (54 percent). The number of
veterans was both absolutely and proportionately higher among
the Blaine men than the bolters. Only 31 of 121 Mugwumps
(26 percent) were veterans; whereas 73 of 197 regulars (37 percent) had done military duty. The war was a direct, personal
experience for many of the regulars. For the younger Mugwumps it was mainly a childhood memory.[46]

Military service provided first hand experience, through
length of service and promotions received, with the rewards

of organizational discipline. In general, the Republican veterans served longer periods than the Mugwumps. About an equal number in each group had military careers of less than two years in length, but proportionately almost twice as many Mugwump veterans were in this group, which served only briefly. A higher percentage of the regulars enlisted for the duration of the war, a few even staying in the service until well after the war was over—Wager Swayne remaining until 1870, Horace Porter until 1872.

The Republican veterans also achieved significant advancements within the ranks by a ratio about half again that of the Mugwumps. Anson G. McCook served from 1861 to 1865, rising from captain to brigadier general (brevetted). The future Republican senator Warner Miller rose from private to lieutenant colonel. Reverend John R. Paxton was promoted from private to second lieutenant between 1862 and 1865, and Charles H. T. Collis, who served for the duration, was successively a private, sergeant, captain, major, colonel, brigadier general, and major general. Some Mugwumps had service records of comparable length, and a few—notably Francis C. Barlow and Christian T. Christensen—won extensive promotions, but these were exceptional cases. The military motif, emphasizing loyalty, steadfastness, and discipline, that figured so prominently in post-Civil War politics had a close parallel in the Civil War experience of many Republicans but was rarely a factor in the careers of the New York Mugwumps.

For the regular Republicans, party loyalty had proven itself as one of the most rewarding forms of organizational discipline. In the New York sample of Blaine men, fifty-nine, or approximately one-eighth of the total, held public office between 1880 and 1885. These offices ranged from that of

United States senator (Warner Miller and William M. Evarts), postmaster general (Walter Q. Gresham), and minister to France (Levi P. Morton), down to clerk of the county court (Thomas Riker), customs inspector (Samuel Minnes), and deputy marshall in the Post Office (John H. Grimes).

Among the Mugwumps, at most fourteen (3 percent) of the New Yorkers held office in the period from 1880 to 1885, only one of which (Seth Low as mayor of Brooklyn) was elective and just one other (Carl Schurz, secretary of interior from 1877 to 1881) was a position of much significance. Those Mugwumps who had held high governmental posts in the past had been out of office since the middle of the 1870s —Francis C. Barlow (attorney general, New York, from 1870 to 1873); Benjamin H. Bristow (secretary of the treasury from 1874 to 1876); Daniel H. Chamberlain (governor of South Carolina from 1874 to 1876); and Edward Salomon (governor of Wisconsin from 1862 to 1864).

It is possible to overemphasize the distinctions between the Mugwump and Republican profiles and lose sight of the striking contrasts within the Republican camp. Socially, for example, Republican blue bloods—Stephen Van Rensselaer Cruger, Gouverneur Morris, Jr., and Elihu Root—had more in common with the socially prominent, old-family Mugwumps than they did with the Post Office clerks who backed Blaine. Similarly, Republican reformers like James W. Hawes and Walter Howe seem closer politically to the bolters than to Stalwart politicos of the John "Chonney" Brodsky and Henry C. Perley sort, though Hawes, Howe, Brodsky, and Perley all voted for Blaine and the Mugwumps did not.

Put in other words, the Mugwump and Republican groups overlapped in every category—age, education, occupation, place of birth, and social prominence. Proportionately,

Republican representation in the *Social Register* was lower
than that of the Mugwumps. However, regulars such as John
Jay, Joseph H. Choate, and William M. Evarts had social distinction and family backgrounds equal to any Mugwump's.
Likewise, both groups included many men whose families
dated back to the early settlement of America, though a larger
percentage of Mugwumps came from distinguished old families. The Republicans more frequently had not achieved
prominence until the individual's own generation.[47] Clearly,
though, the demarcation between the two profiles is a matter
of tendencies and proportions rather than absolute divergence.

Differences there were, however, and these go far to explain
why the two groups divided politically in 1884. From the
regulars' proportionately higher representation in elective and
appointive offices, it might seem that the bolt was simply a
struggle between "in" and "out" factions of the GOP.[48] Un-
questionably a man's prospects within the party influenced
his decision whether to bolt, but this was not the sole consideration at work. All the Independent Republicans, for example, shared in the losing battle against Blaine's nomination.
Yet Theodore Roosevelt, no party insider in 1884, backed
Blaine, and John F. Andrew of Massachusetts, like Roosevelt
a young state legislator and delegate to the national convention, chose to bolt. Factional allegiances, therefore, were
just one element in the Republicans' corporate and organizational ethic. Business connections, club memberships, and
even military experience also reinforced the conviction that
voting for Blaine was much the best thing to do. Another set
of characteristics—youth, a high degree of formal education,
inherited social status, and a proclivity for the professions—
predominated in the Mugwump profile and provided the underpinnings for the Mugwump ethic.

Chapter 3

Bowker

The Mugwump Ethic & the 1884 Election

The Mugwumps' credo of political independence was rooted in motivational sources every bit as compelling as those that shaped the regulars' loyalty to organizational imperatives. Like the Republicans who combined old patterns—unwavering party allegiance and informal educational training—with careers based on the new force of corporate capitalism, the Mugwumps also blended traditional and modern traits. The bolters' family heritage and established social status linked them with the past. They were also tied to newer forces, however, by their active participation in post-Civil War efforts to redefine the status of professionals nationally in accordance with the demands of an emerging industrial order.

Among the traditional traits influencing the Mugwumps' ethic, family background bulked large. The family heritage of many Mugwumps was closely identified with habits of community leadership. Typical biographical statements about the fathers of Mugwumps read as follows: "leading politicians"; "diplomat"; "president of Wesleyan College"; "country storekeeper, farmer, and justice of the peace"; "elected reform mayor of New York in 1844"; and "a noted publisher." The Mugwump families had long viewed themselves as an elite of respectable and principled citizens. From their early youth, therefore, the future Mugwumps were instilled with the idea that they had a role to play in the life of the community and nation.

The importance of education to the Mugwumps' reform impulse can scarcely be overemphasized. College education provided more than a preparation for entering a vocation. The Mugwumps' college years were an experience that further shaped their understanding of their role in the community. Young men listening to George William Curtis, for instance, making a commencement address entitled "The Public Duty of Educated Men," doubtless found his main point to be a familiar one. Public duty, Curtis insisted, required "constant and active participation in the details of politics . . . on the part of the most intelligent citizens" to prevent public affairs from falling "under the control of selfish and ignorant or crafty and venal men."[1] The Mugwumps' years of political activism, many of which were largely unrewarding, make little sense without an appreciation of their feeling that they were obligated, as educated men, to attempt "the education of all classes in the community to their duties of citizenship."[2]

In their vocational choices, the Mugwumps had typically manifested a preference for professions that had a quasi-public quality. The bolters' private pursuits, in other words, had long been closely tied to the public life of the community.

As professional men and owners of businesses, they were among the first to feel the demoralizing consequences of the post-Civil War debauch of spoilsmanship. Mugwump importers like Thomas C. Sloane protested the rampant thievery they found among free-booting Customs House officials in the 1870s.[3] George Jones, owner of the *New York Times*, reportedly turned down a 1 million dollar bribe to curb his paper's attacks on the Tweed Ring. Thomas Nast, illustrator for *Harper's Weekly*, reached a large audience with his hard-hitting caricatures of Tweed and other spoilsmen. The Mugwumps' readiness to adopt the role of guardians of civic morality was not determined entirely by the quasi-public responsibilities of their occupations, but their professional duties did tend to reinforce attitudes previously inculcated through family and educational experience.

Similarly, the Mugwumps' relatively secure economic status contributed to their reform ethic. Although it would be incorrect to characterize them as an elite of wealth alone, wealth supported their view of themselves as an elite of the "best men" in many ways—by enabling them to put off working until they completed college, for instance. Perhaps even more important, their established economic status gave them a measure of psychic security that was fundamental to the Mugwump spirit. To men who were born into comfortable circumstances, the acquisition of more wealth did not always seem an adequate personal goal.[4] Hence the Mugwump contempt for the money grubbers and the indulgent rich who contributed little to the community's well-being.[5] Secure economic status, then, prompted Mugwumps to enter public affairs and facilitated their political independence by freeing them from the necessity of being beholden to any party or partisan leader.

In the years immediately after the Civil War a new ingredient, which I will call the professional impulse, was added to the historic mix of traits that supported the Mugwump ethic. In part this professional impulse sought to check the decline of hierarchy and specialization in such fields as the ministry, law, and medicine.[6] In the 1840s and 1850s relatively restrictive rules for admission to and practice of these occupations had been undercut by a popular attack on deference to the learned professions. One consequence was that qualifications for professional training and standing were greatly loosened. Compulsory medical licensing was abolished in many states, and requirements for admission to the bar were made less dependent on formal legal training and approval by a professional elite.

The success of the assault on traditional professional patterns was not simply a product of the widespread egalitarianism in antebellum thought. There was also internal dissension in every profession as professionals themselves sought new authorities and verities, whether legal, medical, or theological. In the pre-Civil War period "the content of professional knowledge was neither stable nor securely progressive."[7] Thus, the medical community failed to provide cohesive leadership even in such clear emergencies as epidemics in cities and was unable to muster the political resources to retain compulsory licensing laws for physicians. Similarly, many lawyers accepted the abolition of formal distinctions between different types of legal specialists and acquiesced in the New York Constitution of 1846, which made judicial positions elective.

Among the Mugwumps the memory of an older style of professional life replete with lengthy formal training, requirements for acceptance from men of proven distinction, and clear-cut lines of occupational status was often a matter of family ties. During the early nineteenth century, for instance, the bolters' ancestors were usually high Federalists or Brahmin Whigs who prided themselves on advocating high standards of professional training and practice at a time when those standards were beginning to come under attack. The Mugwump families, in other words, had long harbored very un-Jacksonian notions that made their members less willing than most Americans to accept the pre-Civil War decline of professional status.

Just as industrialization led to the nationalization of business, so too the structure of American professions was dramatically altered in the last quarter of the nineteenth century. In the post-Civil War period the climate of professional opinion again shifted but this time toward a reemphasis on training, standards, and professional distinctiveness. The impact of applied science, the growth of graduate schools in all fields, and the demand for technicians and experts in giant industries and expanding urban centers accounted for this trend as much as the presence of an old professional elite. As Merle Curti points out, "scholars would not have organized and zealously attended annual meetings of their learned societies or published their technical monographs had not the new urban and industrial civilization made all this specialization and professionalization possible."[8] The drive to restore the stature of the professions, therefore, was not merely traditional values asserting themselves but a case of traditions being reshaped in a radically altered social and economic milieu.

Before 1870 only a few professionals had grouped themselves in national associations. The American Medical Association, founded in 1847, and learned societies established by statisticians (1839), ethnologists and orientalists (1842), geographers (1852), and etymologists (1859) were the primary exceptions. Otherwise, professional groups were either local ones, such as the Massachusetts Historical Society, or generalized organizations such as the American Association for the Advancement of Science (1848), which included all the scientific disciplines, and the American Social Science Association (1865).[9] The latter tried to encompass all study relative to "the development of Social Science, and to guide the public mind" in a sweeping range of fields—"the best practical means of promoting the Amendment of Laws, the Advancement of Education, the Prevention and Repression of Crime, the Reformation of Criminals, the progress of Public Morality, and the adoption of Sanitary regulation."[10]

The process of establishing professional associations accelerated in the post-Civil War period, peaking in the 1880s. According to Merle Curti, "at least seventy-nine local and national learned societies were formed in the eighteen-seventies, 121 in the 'eighties, and forty-five in the 'nineties."[11] This trend was more than quantitative, for it also brought vastly increased specialization and a greater emphasis on national groupings. Repeatedly the word "American" introduced the names of the new organizations, whether they were composed of philologists (1869), public health experts (1872), librarians or chemists (1876), lawyers (1878), historians (1884), economists (1885), copyright advocates (1886), or psychologists (1892). Mugwumps participated actively and prominently in this associational movement.

Among lawyers, one of the crucial steps toward professionalization was the establishment in 1869 of the Association of the Bar of the City of New York. In the midst of the Erie Ring and Tweed scandals, a group of leading attorneys proposed the new association as one way of checking the "dangerous rottenness of our judicial system . . . . caused by the wholesale use of Erie money in corrupting the bench and bar."[12] Their goal was nothing less than a restoration of the legal profession's public standing. After mentioning the "social vicissitudes" caused by the Civil War and the "social demoralization which confront[s] us on every side," the lawyers asked, "What has been the effect of all these things on the Bar? Many say, its glory and dignity are gone, that it has ceased to be a noble profession and is merely a trade with the rest. We do not admit this charge."[13]

Mugwumps played a considerable role in the association's early years. Four of the association's first executive committee of sixteen were future Mugwumps—Stephen P. Nash, James C. Carter, Francis C. Barlow, and William G. Choate. At least fifty-six of the bolters eventually joined the organization. In 1884 James C. Carter was its president, and five other Mugwumps were on its executive committee. Many other members of the association shared the belief that Blaine's nomination was a symbol of the very "social demoralization" they had intended to combat in founding their organization fifteen years earlier. In a public statement opposing the Republican candidate, the Mugwump lawyers asserted that because Blaine "had sold his official power and influence for railroad bonds . . . the rights of every citizen, even the humblest, would be endangered by his election."[14]

According to the men who established the Association of the Bar of the City of New York, professional standards had once been maintained in legal circles largely through an informal consensus among practicing lawyers. When the bar's "members were fewer and a longer probation was required for admission to its ranks," the association's founders contended, "the tradition of the profession served, to some extent, to answer the purpose of a corporate organization."[15] By the

1870s, however, easier admission standards and the legal profession's great numerical expansion had overburdened these informal channels of communication. The custom of professional self-regulation through friendship and daily contact was definitely outmoded.

The founders of the American Bar Association (ABA) also thought of their association as an institutional arrangement for restoring the sense of community and occupational identity that had existed in the pre-Jacksonian bar.[16] Incorporated in 1878 by approximately fifty lawyers from various states, the ABA adopted a program with both intellectual and social elements "to advance the science of jurisprudence, promote the administration of justice . . . , uphold the honor of the profession . . . , and encourage cordial intercourse among [its] members."[17] Benjamin H. Bristow, former secretary of the treasury and a future Mugwump, was a signer of the organizational call and served as the group's second president from 1879 to 1880. Simeon E. Baldwin, ABA president in 1890 and original editor of the ABA's *Journal*, was in charge of local arrangements for the initial meeting. Moorfield Storey, president of the ABA from 1895 to 1896, was yet a third distinguished Mugwump lawyer to preside over the organization during its first twenty years. Other bolters—Charles J. Bonaparte of Maryland, Talcott H. Russell of New Haven, James B. Thayer of Cambridge, and E. C. Sprague of Buffalo—were early members.

The American Public Health Association (APHA), founded in 1872, soon acquired a truly national membership, though at its inception it was sponsored mainly by New Yorkers. Efforts to upgrade New York City's health administration achieved little success until the mid-1860s when the Metropolitan Health Bill of 1866 was passed. One of the bill's

sponsors, Dr. Stephen Smith, felt this was just a beginning of
work that needed to be done. He especially regretted the lack
of an organized body to promote the extension of the law to
other municipalities and to familiarize the public with recent
advances in "sanitary science," as public health advocates
liked to call their field. In order to achieve much influence
in civic affairs, public health workers would have to be clearly established as members of a reputable professional spe-
ciality. To this end, Dr. Smith invited a number of interested
New Yorkers to join in founding the APHA.[18]

Initially, the American Public Health Association was quite
small, but within seven years it had grown to about six hundred members. Its annual publication, *Reports and Papers of
the American Public Health Association*, despite a cumbersome
title, served as an important device for communicating up-to-
date information to its members and for promoting sanitary
regulations nationally. Among the dozen or so future Mugwumps who were active in the association during its early
years, Dr. Francis Bacon was an incorporator and member of
its first executive committee. New York's sanitary commissioner, Jackson S. Schultz, was also an officer. Elwyn Waller,
a chemist at Columbia College, and George E. Waring, Jr., a
civil engineer who later received national attention for his
reform work as street commissioner in New York City, presented papers at early association meetings.

Although APHA membership was by no means restricted
to doctors, its credo clearly made it an ally of those physicians
who felt their own profession needed to put its house in order.
In a self-conscious effort to improve the medical profession's
public image, the APHA described its supporters as "educated
and public-spirited men," the "best of physicians," and "the
most earnest and philosophical of public teachers." Individuals

of this sort would apply the "formulas of science" and work from an "exact and comprehensive knowledge of facts" in dealing with community health problems.[19] Conversely, an old-fashioned (but still prevalent) "empiricism" would have to be eliminated from medical practice, for if the profession was to receive the public's respect, there was little room in the field for the "irregular" physicians—nature healers, "Indian" doctors, and dosing parsons—who had proliferated in the pre-Civil War period.[20]

The founders of the APHA also condemned partisan politics as having no positive role to play in public health work. Not only was the association to be "free of official and governmental relations," but its objective was a nonpartisan health system controlled by experts in the field instead of men selected largely for their loyalty to a political organization.[21] Here the emerging professional consciousness of the Mugwump doctors led them to adopt ideas closely parallel to other Mugwump programs—civil service reform and Seth Low's "Brooklyn Idea" of a business administration of city government.

The themes of science, specialization, and professional status appeared in the literature of nearly all the postwar learned societies, even the American Library Association (ALA), established in 1876. In the early post-Civil War period there was no uniform method of cataloguing books, no trade journal to inform librarians of recent publications, and little in the profession's goals that reflected the modern tasks of librarians. Indeed, one Mugwump active in the ALA's early days argued that the nineteenth-century librarian saw his task as keeping books, not loaning them, and remembering what he had collected, not organizing it in such a way that it would be available to others.[22]

A definite improvement in the profession's conditions was evident by the American Library Association's sixth annual meeting in 1883. R. R. Bowker had begun to publish the *Library Journal* and *Publisher's Weekly*. Numerous proposals were being offered for architectural improvements that would make the use of libraries easier. Also, a system of orderly book classification had been developed by Melvil Dewey, ALA secretary from 1876 to 1880, editor of the *Library Journal* in the same years, and organizer of the first library school in the country in 1887. The librarian's field was coming of age, and again Mugwumps figured importantly in fostering this maturation process. Along with R. R. Bowker, Charles C. Soule (Boston publisher of law books) and Josephus N. Larned (Buffalo librarian and ALA president from 1893 to 1894) were early officers of the organization. F. W. Christern, a New York City dealer in foreign books, was an original member.

In the academic profession the late nineteenth century marked the beginning of the age of the university, and research, specialization, and graduate training were the hallmarks of the universities. Although some graduate degrees had been initiated at Yale, Harvard, and Columbia before 1875, a new era for work beyond the bachelor's degree began in 1876 with the opening of Johns Hopkins, the first institution primarily for graduate study. Graduate enrollment nationally expanded from 198 students in 1871 to 2,383 in 1890 and to 9,370 by 1910.[23] The greatest growth was yet to come, but in these earlier years pioneering programs, many introduced from German models, had become firmly established.

Among the Mugwump professionals, those in college teaching were a sizeable group. Although their numbers were much smaller than those of bolters in law, the professors were the second largest group of professionals nationally in 1884 among the Mugwumps. Friend and enemy alike recognized the strong influence of academicians on the anti-Blaine movement. In the Republican press, the bolt was contemptuously dismissed as "nothing but a blank charge, rammed home by college professors and fired off by free-traders."[24] In most university and college towns throughout the East, Mugwump professors were conspicuously enlisted in the anti-Blaine cause. J. Franklin Jameson, then a young history instructor at Johns Hopkins, reported that his university was a veritable Mugwump preserve. At Cornell, at least a quarter of the faculty signed Mugwump petitions. Even in Indiana, where Mugwumps were few and far between, David Starr Jordan, the head of the natural science department at Indiana University, reported that he was a Mugwump "like the majority of university men of Republican antecedents."[25]

Professional associations were one by-product of the rise of the university, and Mugwumps figured prominently in the establishment of these learned societies. William H. Nichols, a Brooklyn chemical manufacturer, was an incorporator and the first treasurer of the American Chemical Society (established 1876). Another Mugwump, Elwyn Waller, served as the group's first librarian as well as a member of its board of directors. At least twenty Mugwumps were listed as members of the American Historical Association within a year of its founding in 1884.[26] Some—Herbert Tuttle and Moses Coit Tyler of Cornell and J. Franklin Jameson of Johns Hopkins—were initiators of the drive to organize the historians.

The story was much the same among philologists, modern language scholars, archeologists, and psychologists. Professor William D. Whitney of Yale was chosen first president of the American Philological Association upon its organization in

1869. The Reverend Joseph Anderson of Waterbury, Connecticut, Professor Francis Child of Harvard, and President Franklin Carter of Williams College were other Mugwumps who joined together in support of "the general promotion of philological studies."[27] Carter also was an early leader of the Modern Language Association (established 1883), serving as its first president. Similarly, Charles Eliot Norton, the distinguished Harvard classicist, was the first president of the Archeological Institute of America, remaining in office for ten years, 1879 to 1890. In the field of psychology, George T. Ladd and William James were among the original thirty or so members of the American Psychological Association. Ladd was its second president. James was its third.[28]

Most of the incorporators of the American Economic Association (AEA) in 1885 were men like Richard T. Ely who strongly disapproved of the conventional laissez-faire economics espoused by E. L. Godkin and William Graham Sumner. But even among the rebels against the older liberal creed, a few Mugwumps appeared—William James, Clarence Bowen, Joseph W. Harper, Robert Treat Paine, and Stuart Wood. Wood was the AEA's vice president from 1889 to 1890, and another Mugwump, Henry W. Farnam, later served a term as its president.

Something must be said specifically of the Mugwumps from business-oriented occupations who supported the emerging professional ethic. It was not unusual for individual Mugwump businessmen to become active participants in the professional movement. Stuart Wood, the Philadelphia manufacturer and vice president of the American Economic Association, and William H. Nichols, the chemical manufacturer and treasurer of the American Chemical Society, have already been mentioned. R. R. Bowker, Charles C. Soule, and F. W.

Christern were Mugwump businessmen who joined the American Library Association. Jackson S. Schultz, a wealthy leather-goods manufacturer with a long-standing interest in municipal sanitation problems, was an early member of the American Public Health Association. Daniel H. Wells, a Hartford insurance man, became president of the Actuarial Society of America.

Beyond these individual expressions of interest in the formation of learned societies, there was a broad sympathy on the part of many Mugwump businessmen for the spirit of professionalism. Seth Low, the Brooklyn merchant-turned-mayor (and later college president), made "business" administration the watchword of his theory of municipal government. In so doing he invoked a theme that was attractive to Mugwump professionals and businessmen alike—namely, the idea that men trained in business or the professions were more fit to administer municipal affairs than were career politicians. Professionalism, moreover, was central to Low's business ideal. During his two terms as mayor he attempted to professionalize Brooklyn city government by instituting a municipal civil service system and by appointing department heads for their qualifications as experts rather than for their partisan loyalties.[29]

The Mugwump devotion to the business ideal came full circle when, after years of advocating bureaucratic and legalistic reforms in political affairs, Mugwumps applied the same values to the sphere of business. The American Copyright League, for instance, was organized in 1883 to promote laws safeguarding copyrights against what Robert U. Johnson of *Century Magazine* called "literary piracy." Notably, the organization's drive was spearheaded by Mugwump publishers and editors who had in the previous decade resisted free-booting in political life by advocating civil service reform, municipal nonpartisanship, and independent voting.[30] Thus, while it is possible to discuss the business ideal, the professional impulse, and independent politics separately, the interdependence of the three is clearly evident in the careers of individual Mugwumps like R. R. Bowker—a Young Scratcher, a businessman interested in copyright law reform, and a forceful advocate of professionalizing the field of library science.

On the surface, the extensive professional movement under review here may seem to have little connection with the Mugwumps' immediate reasons for bolting in 1884. Younger bolters simply seemed to have lost patience with appeals to work from within the party when their efforts in that direction bore so little fruit. Young and old Mugwumps alike hoped that their favorite programs—civil service reform and tariff reduction—would be fostered by Cleveland's election. Economic considerations influenced some of the insurgents. Mugwump manufacturers contended that the protective tariff on raw materials placed eastern businessmen like themselves at a disadvantage competitively relative to businessmen in newer industrial regions that were closer to American sources of raw materials. New York merchants resented the GOP machine's role in the harassment to which importers had been subjected under the old Custom House system, which exacted heavy penalties for minor errors in estimating the value of shipments.

Basic to most reasons for joining the bolt, however, was the Mugwumps' public ethic, their conception of themselves as guardians of public morality. The professional impulse reinforced the chief elements of Mugwump political behavior— their devotion to political activism without fully embracing party politics; their use of moral terminology ("duty," "trust,"

and "respectability") rather than the language of interests
and practicality; their distrust of men who were absorbed
with seeking partisan advancement or personal wealth; and
their aloofness from the mass of voters who could not be ex-
pected to practice the disinterestedness that Mugwumps admired. Of course, the Mugwumps' "disinterestedness" was
in the interest of men who, like themselves, were cosmopolitan, well-educated, and socially secure. In this respect their
private and public values coincided. Scientific objectivity
and specialization became their watchwords in business and
professional life, just as nonpartisanship and expert administration was their program for reforming politics.

It was the threat that Blaine seemed to pose to this emerging professional and bureaucratic order that was at the heart
of the Mugwump rebellion. As the "Plumed Knight" of Republican party politics, Blaine seemed to the dissidents more
the defender of partisan interests than the champion of efficient public service. To be sure, many Mugwumps were soon
disappointed with Cleveland because he was also a partisan.
But to focus on this obvious disillusionment is to miss the
more subtle social forces at work in the Mugwump protest.
The tenuousness of the Mugwumps' cultural position in 1884
was not alone that their family background and established
economic status linked them with traditional ways. They
were also members of a new elite seeking to establish its
barely formulated values of professionalism and specialization in public affairs.

There is a strong resemblance between the Mugwumps of
1884 and the new middle class that Robert Wiebe says emerged a decade or more later. The qualities that Wiebe attrib-
utes to the new middle class seem very much Mugwump traits
—their faith in the "public man" who was to be above partisan

motives; their proposals for a government bureaucracy dominated by experts; their abandonment of "compulsive identification with a political party"; and their promotion of professionalism through occupational associations. Also, the new
middle class "not only concentrated in the cities but generally
appeared first in the older, larger, and more industrially developed ones, mostly in the Northeast"—an apt description of
Mugwump origins as well. Indeed, the Mugwump protest's
numerical and geographical limitations tend to confirm that
as of 1884 the new middle-class consciousness scarcely existed outside of a few locations on the eastern seaboard.[31]

For all these similarities, mugwumpery in 1884 was not
identical to twentieth-century progressivism. The new middle
class had not come of age, even though the Mugwumps were
to a degree its progenitors. Elitist notions, assumptions of
moral superiority, and distrust of the mass of American voters
—all traits still evident among the progressives—were more
prominent among the Mugwumps. Even in the 1880s, during
the earliest phase of the new middle class's development, the
Mugwumps were predominantly members of only one of its
components, that of the professionals. Wiebe's second type
of progressive—the specialist in business, labor, and agriculture
—was less frequently found in the Mugwump ranks. Moreover,
for all that the Mugwumps advocated a rudimentary program
of bureaucratization in government administration, most did
so with the assumption that the result would be an austere
government, serving the needs of its citizens by performing a
few functions well. Efficiency and honesty, not expanded
services, were its hallmarks.

By no means all the men who pioneered in the professional
movement after the Civil War joined the Mugwump insurgency.
As the division in the Independent Republican camp exemplifies

so well, even some men whose reform ideas closely paral-
lelled those of the Mugwumps did not unite with them in
opposing Blaine. But with the professional class just beginning to coalesce and with both party platforms so ambiguous,
this failure to achieve unity was scarcely surprising. Even in
the progressive era, when the new middle class had reached
a greater degree of maturity, its members divided over what
party—Republican, Bull Moose, or Democratic—provided the
best agency for reaching its goals. After all this is said, however, what remains impressive is how thoroughly Mugwump
sentiment dominated the locales and institutions in which the
new middle-class consciousness was most evident in 1884—
the universities with graduate programs, the professional
associations, and intellectual circles in the Northeast.

If the cultural underpinnings of the Mugwump bolt were
not yet fully manifest in 1884, the political significance of
their protest was no less unclear. The 1884 election hinged
on the narrowest of margins in the key state of New York.[32]
Cleveland carried the day there by a mere 1,149 votes. Since
the Mugwumps had gotten thousands of signatures on their
anti-Blaine petitions, they could claim that their bolt swung
New York, and with it the election, to Cleveland. Other observers, however, pointed to a variety of factors that had
hampered Blaine's campaign—the presence of an independent
Prohibition party candidate in the field, former Senator Roscoe Conkling's refusal to back Blaine, and Reverend Burchard's allusion to the Democrats as the party of "Rum,
Romanism, and Rebellion" to mention but a few. More
recently, one historian has challenged the notion that these
special campaign incidents decided the contest, arguing that
the trend of elections since the Civil War had been against
the Republicans and that this broad tendency, not incidents

during the campaign, accounted for Blaine's defeat.[33]

Measured by mass electoral statistics alone, the impact of the Mugwump bolt was indeed slight. However, this criterion must not be applied without attention to the impression the anti-Blaine movement made on its contemporaries. National politics in the 1880s were marked by a near stalemate in party strength. With every presidential race determined by small fluctuations in party power in a few swing states, the importance of restive political factions was greatly exaggerated.[34] Practical politicians watched shifts in voter allegiance warily, believing that even a small defection might have potentially major effects, and the vehemence with which Republican leaders attacked the Mugwump malcontents was just one example of how seriously such rebellions were taken. Cleveland, for his part, believed the bolters had contributed to his victory, and he committed himself to federal civil service reform partly out of a desire to hold the reformers in his winning coalition. Thus, the slim margin of Cleveland's victory and the crude methods for calculating electoral trends in the 1880s combined to give the Mugwump bolt an impact wholly out of proportion to its raw numerical strength.

For the bolters themselves, the anti-Blaine insurgency was a departure of considerable significance, involving more than a little political risk. Many were original Republicans. Others were energetic young men like R. R. Bowker, Henry W. Farnam, and George Fred Williams who were deeply and idealistically committed to public life. Until 1884 these men— comprising a small but vocal body of important editors, professionals, and businessmen—had devoted themselves to making the Republican party the vehicle for their reform ideas. In abandoning Blaine to support Cleveland, they were not simply instigating another election-year demonstration against what the party of Lincoln seemed to them to have become. They were also abandoning the established reform strategy of working from within the GOP.

This apostasy was implicitly a political gamble, as non-bolting reformers were quick to point out. In a single act, the Mugwumps might well be throwing away what leverage they did have within the post-Civil War party system. To be sure, idealistic dissatisfaction with the major parties had historically found expression in election-year rebellions, and sometimes the major parties had later adopted the programs and ideals of the rebels. But whether the Mugwump bolt would become a means for achieving greater influence in national affairs or whether it would simply become a march into political oblivion, there was no way of saying in 1884.

Chapter 4

Quincy

The Cleveland Coalition & After

The Mugwumps' independent posture in 1884—symbolized by the figure of a defiant fence sitter with his Mug on one side of the fence and his Wump on the other—had liabilities as a basis for long-term political effectiveness. It left the bolters in a particularly ambiguous position relative to the incoming administration, having endorsed Cleveland without committing themselves to his party. As of the beginning of 1885 the consensus among Mugwumps was that they should act as friendly neutrals, supporting whatever reforms the president-elect might propose but ready to rebuke him and his party should either go astray. The full range of Mugwump opinion was broader, however, some bolters insisting on the purity of absolute independence and others advocating an open entente with the president on civil service reform.[1]

For all the precariousness of their position, the Mugwumps achieved some successes in the early years of the Cleveland regime. The president-elect delighted the reformers by endorsing civil service reform shortly after his election.[2] He also flattered the leading bolters by giving their views an attentive hearing.[3] A few of his major appointments caused consternation in Mugwump circles, but others pleased the reformers—particularly his selection of the Yankee blue-blood, William C. Endicott of Massachusetts, as secretary of war and his appointment of Charles S. Fairchild, a New York reformer, as assistant secretary of the treasury.[4] Mugwump optimism about the possibilities for infiltrating the Democratic party with reformers and reform ideas reached a peak in 1886 when the Massachusetts Democrats named a bolter, John F. Andrew, as their gubernatorial candidate.[5]

Eventually, civil service reform proved unsatisfactory as a basis for Mugwump-Democratic cooperation. Purist Mugwumps like Carl Schurz infuriated Cleveland by being relentlessly critical, quick to condemn faults, and wary of seeming too generous with praise.[6] Those Mugwumps, epitomized by George Fred Williams, who wanted to establish more harmonious relations between the president and the reformers condemned the uncompromising independents for undermining cooperative efforts.[7] Democrats, irate at Cleveland for his supposed parsimony in distributing patronage to loyal partisans, struck at the reformers. In New York machine Democrats under Governor David B. Hill's leadership urged Cleveland to repudiate the Mugwumps as unreliable allies.[8] Connecticut state boss William H. Barnum swiftly checkmated a move by the Mugwump-dominated Tariff Reform League to convert Democrats to reform.[9] Andrew's candidacy in Massachusetts failed to win over the state's rank-and-file Democrats,

who were apparently hostile to the Yankee reformers and
their civil service principles.[10] Caught between carping criticism from Mugwumps and rebellious rumblings among regulars, Cleveland gradually made concessions to the stronger
force, his fellow Democrats. By 1887 frustration over the
civil service issue had brought the entente between Cleveland
and the Mugwumps to the verge of complete disintegration.[11]

At this critical juncture tariff reform emerged as the basis
for a Mugwump-Democratic rapprochement. Although some
leading Democrats were protectionists, the bulk of the party
favored a lower tariff. Among the Mugwumps the only dissent
from giving a high priority to tariff reform came from civil
service purists unwilling to see their pet issue deemphasized.
Otherwise, every major segment of the bolters—businessmen,
intellectuals, and professionals—supported tariff reform.

Mugwump businessmen were convinced that the protective
tariff protected someone else. As representatives of New
England-based industries—iron products, woolen and leather
goods, and India ink—they were dependent on imported raw
materials.[12] Should the duties on raw wool, leather, pig iron,
and coal be lowered or eliminated, northeastern businessmen
of their sort would be able to compete more successfully with
rivals in other regions. Jackson S. Schultz, for instance, noted
that he had joined the Republican party on antislavery grounds
in the 1850s, but that by 1884 he felt war issues were fading
and was again attracted to his earlier Democratic preferences
by that party's economic platform.[13] Roland Hazard, president of a diversified woolens firm in Rhode Island, was an
articulate opponent of duties on raw wool, arguing that these
tariffs hurt his company's competitive position without particularly benefitting domestic wool producers.[14] The New
Haven hardware manufacturer Joseph B. Sargent contended

that protection favored the "coal and metal oligarchs" of Ohio, Pennsylvania, and Michigan at his expense.[15]

Another group of Mugwumps came at tariff reform less from a dollar-and-cents viewpoint than a philosophical perspective. These men—editors, professors, and publicists—included some of the best known Mugwumps: E. L. Godkin, William Graham Sumner, Horace White, and Edward Atkinson. Their economic thought was heavily derivative, combining as it did the old-fashioned liberalism of John Stuart Mill and David Ricardo with the Protestant justification of work and Herbert Spencer's application of Darwinism to human society. Theirs was a classical laissez-faire definition of freedom and individualism. The good of the community was best sustained by negative government. Poverty was explained as immorality. Great disparities of wealth were attributed to the inevitable workings of natural economic laws. Tariffs were rejected as flagrant evasions of free competition, special privileges created through legislative fiat.[16]

An important element in the tariff reform credo was its attack on monopolistic concentrations of wealth as by-products of protectionism. Leading Democratic reformers like David Ames Wells, for instance, asserted that the economic health of the nation depended on the productivity of workingmen, not on the existence of a few people with colossal fortunes. Yet tariffs, he argued, taxed working consumers and "favored or created trusts" and "private fortunes"—a criticism that men of divergent backgrounds found compelling.[17]   Porter C. Moulton, one of the few Mugwumps who was also a laboring man, made much the same point as Wells: "High protection . . . furnishes the food upon which trusts and monopolies live."[18]   One result, according to R. R. Bowker, was that the Republican tariff policies that created trusts also created a "new slavery" for American labor. "Who get the benefit of the Trust?" asked Bowker. Answer [the article being entitled "A Short Catechism on Trusts"] : "The capitalists who organize it. Who get left? Answer: The wage-earners and the people generally."[19]

Although derived from laissez-faire economic thought, this rudimentary criticism of corporate wealth served as something of an introductory course in the malfunctions of an unregulated capitalist system and led some Mugwumps to abandon the orthodox liberal's absolute denunciation of social and economic legislation. As a Yale undergraduate, for example, Henry W. Farnam had been impressed by William Graham Sumner's ideas, but upon reading Sumner's "What Social Classes Owe to Each Other" in 1883, he declared it full of platitudes.[20] Farnam soon expanded his reform ideas beyond civil service and tariff reform, which fit with his mentor's thinking, to include labor legislation, which definitely did not. Thomas G. Shearman came to his "radical" ideas, as he called them, from even more improbable beginnings than Farnam, having been a lawyer for the Erie Railroad in the days of Gould and Fisk. Yet Shearman's subsequent study of the tariff led him to make a broad attack on plutocracy and unjust taxation in the United States, and he became, in common with a handful of other Mugwumps, a convert to Henry George's single tax scheme.[21] Another small group of Mugwump tariff reformers adopted the evolutionary socialism of Edward Bellamy.[22] A tiny minority within the Mugwump group as a whole, these single taxers, Bellamyites, and advocates of social legislation nevertheless suggest something of the diverse support tariff reform received in the 1880s.

In December 1887 Cleveland supplied the impetus for an alliance of Mugwumps and tariff reform Democrats by making his annual message to Congress a call for tariff revision. In January 1888, less than a month later, the Young Men's Democratic Club of Massachusetts and the New York Reform Club were founded. The Rhode Island and the New Haven Reform clubs were established later in the year as reform energy spread to lesser centers of Mugwump activity. In 1888, as in the earlier burst of organized reform effort from 1880 to 1883, a high proportion of the reform club members were men in their thirties. Cleveland's Mugwump backers, however, surrendered some of their predecessors' prickly independence to work side by side with Democratic reformers.

The most striking evidence of a tactical departure among the Mugwumps was furnished by those who joined the Young Men's Democratic Club of Massachusetts (YMDC). Unlike the older Massachusetts Reform Club, which had functioned as an august, nonpartisan debating forum, the YMDC was avowedly a campaign club organized to supplement the work of the State Democratic Committee. The YMDC also distinguished itself from previous Mugwump-Democratic ententes by winning the allegiance of Irish as well as Yankee Democrats. With the approval of two sympathetic Irish bosses, Patrick Maguire and John F. Fitzgerald, numerous O'Gradys, Donovans, and Sullivans swarmed into the club's ranks.[23] This "combination of Harvard College and the slums of Boston," as one observer described the YMDC, became New England's most powerful body of Cleveland Democrats and an avenue to political preferment for many Bay State Mugwumps.[24]

Cleveland's followers in New York, faced with hostile Democratic factions in control of both the state and city party organizations, were forced into a different course from that of their Massachusetts brethren. With the indefatigable

R. R. Bowker and two reform Democrats, Everett P. Wheeler and John DeWitt Warner, taking the lead, a New York Reform Club open to members of all political parties was established. Its format was that of a social club with moderately high dues (twenty-five dollars), a clubhouse, and a monthly meeting. Public debates and a variety of publications were the club's main methods for reaching the general public.[25] The pattern, in other words, was that of the old Massachusetts Reform Club, not of the openly Democratic YMDC. Reformist more than Democratic in 1888, the New York Reform Club nonetheless had a thoroughly partisan raison d'être—educating voters to back Cleveland and his tariff reform proposals.[26]

When New Haven's reformers finally organized themselves in May 1888, they followed the course of their New York colleagues, establishing a New Haven Reform Club. Many of its incorporators were Mugwumps—Henry W. Farnam, Talcott H. Russell, Henry B. Sargent, and Henry C. White. Consistent with the New Yorkers' example, however, a contingent of important tariff reform Democrats were enlisted as members— Norris G. Osborn, editor of the *New Haven Register*, James E. English, a former governor of Connecticut, and Edward E. Bradley, a former state legislator. James P. Pigott, an Irish Catholic serving in the current legislature, accepted a position on the club's executive committee.[27] Although many Mugwumps indicated their desire to uphold Cleveland's tariff reform ideas by belonging to the Reform Club, most were not yet willing to accept membership in his party, dominated as it was in the state by William H. Barnum and his cohorts. But one former bolter, Simeon E. Baldwin, decided that the time for such mugwumpish caution was past and announced that he was joining a Democratic campaign club.[28]

Despite the labors of the newly established reform organizations, the gains for reform were few in 1888. Cleveland's national campaign failed to develop enough momentum to carry him back into office. Among the Mugwumps the pro-Cleveland faction was dismayed when doctrinaire civil service reformers either endorsed the Republican candidate, Benjamin Harrison, or lethargically backed the president's reelection campaign.[29] Locally, John F. Andrew's election to Congress from Massachusetts was one of the few bright spots for reform. Another came in Brooklyn where William J. Coombs, like Andrew a tariff reform Democrat of Mugwump antecedents, also won a congressional seat. But these limited gains did not provide much encouragement for those who hoped to establish a coalition of Mugwumps and Democrats. Unwilling, as one such individual put it, to "sit on the fence and growl perpetually," the young Mugwumps waited impatiently for more positive developments.[30]

Events soon pushed the Mugwump fence sitters into the Cleveland Democracy and paved the way for its greatest successes. The Harrison administration's policies—higher tariffs, concessions to the silver interests, and heavy-handed spoilsmanship—made even the civil service purists willing to give Cleveland a second chance.[31] Mugwump and Democratic opinion also coincided on a variety of issues below the national level, enabling them to forge a working partnership in some New England states. These coalitions were so successful, in fact, that by the late 1880s the deadlock that had long characterized party battles in the Northeast seemed to be breaking down in favor of the Democrats.[32]

The GOP's response to cultural issues in the period inadvertently contributed to the Democratic revival. Temperance sentiment posed just such a problem for the Republican leaders because it was increasingly popular with their party's rank-

and-file. In Connecticut, for instance, the Prohibition party polled only 0.4 percent of the state's vote in 1880 but won 3.8 percent of the vote in 1886, mostly in traditionally Republican districts.[33] Fearful of losing further "dries" to the Prohibitionists, the GOP endorsed local option prohibition in 1886 and pressed several high license and temperance measures through the legislature in 1887. In both Connecticut and Massachusetts the party sponsored prohibition amendments only to have them rejected by two-to-one margins in statewide referendums held in 1889.[34] Clearly, the Republicans had taken the unpopular side in a troublesome cultural dispute, while the Mugwumps and Democrats, who had figured prominently in the opposition to prohibition, were the gainers.[35]

Mugwumps and Democrats also found common ground in the campaign for the weekly payments bill of 1887 in Connecticut. A Mugwump manufacturer, Joseph B. Sargent, was one of the earliest and most persistent advocates of legislation requiring weekly payment of workers' wages. From 1882 onward he made yearly trips to the state capitol to testify for the proposal before legislative committees. Then in the mid-1880s Henry W. Farnam's *New Haven Morning News*, the major organ of Mugwump opinion in the state, swung its support behind the idea.[36] And to make the circle of Mugwump-Democratic cooperation complete, Democratic state conventions endorsed the proposed legislation in 1886 and 1887. Although a Republican legislature passed the weekly payments bill in 1887, credit for promoting the measure belonged to the Mugwumps and Democrats.

Ballot reform was another issue contested on the state level during the 1880s. Mugwumps favored the secret, or "Australian," ballot system largely because it reduced the possibilities for coercion of voters at the polls and vested responsibility for printing ballots with the state rather than with political parties. In Massachusetts the reform was popularized almost single-handedly by a Mugwump, Richard Henry Dana III, and passed into law in 1888.[37] Elsewhere in the Northeast, particularly in New York and Connecticut, the Mugwump struggle for ballot reform evoked more acrimony and required more concerted effort on the part of the reformers.

The New York ballot reform bill was drawn up in 1887 by members of the Commonwealth Club, an organization of professionals and businessmen committed to civil service reform and the secret ballot. Horace E. Deming and George Walton Green, both young lawyers active in the Mugwump bolt, served as chairman of the legislative drafting committee and club secretary, respectively. During the final days of the reform bill fight William J. Coombs, a Mugwump-turned-Cleveland Democrat, was the club's president. Other familiar Mugwump names, among them Carl Schurz and R. R. Bowker, were sprinkled throughout the club's roster.[38]

Since resistance to the Commonwealth Club's ballot proposal came mainly from Democrats led by Governor David B. Hill, the story of ballot reform in New York is less an example of statewide Mugwump-Democratic cooperation than a case study of how civic group coalitions with large Mugwump contingents pressed for their goals. The bill drafted by Deming was introduced in the legislature by Charles T. Saxton, a Republican state senator, and passed in 1888, only to be vetoed by Hill, who charged that the plan would add hoards of political "adventurers" to the ballot at public expense.[39] The reformers thereupon escalated their campaign publicity, sending allies to Albany to testify for the bill. A united front organization, the New York Ballot Reform League, was established to coordinate the work of all clubs favoring the bill—the Commonwealth Club, the Manhattan Single-Tax Club, the Irish-American Republican Club, the New York Reform Club, and others. Horace E. Deming became the league's chairman. Twice more Hill beat off efforts to pass the Saxton Bill, conceding nothing until representatives of the Ballot Reform League arranged a conference between the Governor and Saxton. A compromise bill, considerably weakened from the original, finally passed in 1890 with Hill's blessing.[40]

The Connecticut Secret Ballot Act of 1889, like the earlier weekly payments bill, was a stepping-stone toward a Mugwump-Democratic alliance in the state. Connecticut Democrats, cognizant of their minority position in state politics, took up the secret ballot idea partly as a means of harassing the Republican leadership. After initial efforts for the reform failed, the Democratic state convention of 1888 passed a resolution accusing GOP legislators of repeatedly setting aside the people's hopes for a secret ballot system.[41] When the legislature passed a reform law the next year, Governor Morgan G. Bulkeley, a Republican strongman with no fondness for "Mugwump" reforms, vetoed the bill and insisted that it be revised to make the provisions for secrecy voluntary. In this weakened form the bill passed the legislature—once again a situation in which Connecticut Mugwumps and Democrats had worked together and eventually won some legislative concessions from the Republicans.[42]

The midterm elections of 1890 confirmed the growing effectiveness of the Cleveland coalition. For the first time since the Civil War, New England Democrats won a majority of the region's congressional seats: in Massachusetts there were 7 Democrats where there had been only 2 in 1888, in Rhode Island 2 where there had been none, and in Connecticut

3 instead of 1. Nationally, the new House of Representatives was composed of 235 Democrats and only 86 Republicans, a staggering majority of 149 for Cleveland's party.

The Young Men's Democratic Club of Massachusetts rode high with the tide of Democratic success. Three of the club's victorious congressional candidates were former Mugwumps—Sherman Hoar and George Fred Williams joining their fellow bolter John F. Andrew in the House of Representatives. Two other Mugwumps were defeated in bids for House seats, Charles R. Codman losing in a heavily Republican district and William Everett failing in a canvass against Henry Cabot Lodge. The election of another YMDC man, William E. Russell, as the first Democratic governor since Benjamin Butler more than balanced these setbacks, however. Even one of the new GOP congressmen was a former Mugwump, Joseph H. Walker of Worcester.

The triumph of the Bay State Democrats had its parallel in Connecticut where the Cleveland Democracy, after many years in the making, finally coalesced. With the death of William H. Barnum in 1889, the influence of his faction diminished within the state party, and tariff reform Mugwumps felt the way was clear to organize an outright Mugwump-Democratic campaign club. Early in 1890, therefore, a call was issued for the first meeting of the Connecticut Democratic Club (CDC), and a former Mugwump, Simeon E. Baldwin, was elected president of the club.[43] Its membership represented a union of former Republicans and old Democratic wheelhorses pledged to a common cause—civil service reform, tariff revision, and Cleveland. Hereafter, the CDC's spokesmen announced, "reform" and "Democratic" could be used interchangeably.[44]

Under the impetus provided by the CDC, a quiet revolution

took place within the state's Democratic organization. The old-line Democrats under Barnum's successor, Alexander Troup, were pushed aside during the 1890 election. The state convention endorsed tariff reform and nominated a CDC man, Luzon B. Morris, for governor. Morris won the subsequent election by a majority of about thirty votes, but the results were disputed, and the incumbent Republican governor refused to let Morris or his Republican rival take office. Morris was vindicated in 1892, when he ran again and won the gubernatorial campaign by a comfortable margin. In 1890 two other CDC members, Lewis Sperry and Robert E. De Forest, were elected to Congress, while a third Democratic reformer, David Ames Wells, lost a close race in another district. With these developments the balance of power shifted decisively in the Connecticut Democracy and to a lesser degree in the state government also into the hands of Cleveland Democrats.

Although the pattern of Mugwump-Democratic cooperation was not so thorough outside of Massachusetts and Connecticut, it was still sufficient to produce some gains for the Cleveland Democrats. In Rhode Island the state's two Republican congressmen were unseated by their Democratic opponents in 1890. The Rhode Island Reform Club did valuable work in the campaign under the leadership of Roland Hazard and two other tariff reform Mugwumps who had become Democrats—Benjamin F. Thurston, managing editor of the *Newport Daily News*, and Richard B. Comstock, a lawyer who would be elected to the state legislature in 1892 and serve as a Wilson elector in 1912.[45]

The New York Reform Club also labored effectively in 1890. Working with regular Democrats to insure the nomination of tariff reformers in New York City congressional districts, the club brought about the nomination and election of one of its incorporators, John DeWitt Warner. William J. Coombs was reelected from his Brooklyn district by an increased majority, while overall the Democrats gained seven new seats in New York's congressional delegation.

Following their victories in 1890, Cleveland's supporters turned their attention to forestalling any possible threat to his renomination and reelection in 1892. The most immediate danger seemed to be the growing congressional sentiment in favor of legislation providing for free and unlimited coinage of silver. The New York Reform Club responded by stepping up its efforts to solidify public opinion behind a gold standard.[46] When the newly elected Fifty-second Congress assembled, sound money men, including the former Mugwumps serving in the House, succeeded in defeating the free coinage proposal.[47] Meanwhile, another threat arose as anti-Cleveland forces rallied to David B. Hill's banner and planned on holding the New York State Democratic convention unusually early in 1892 in hopes of starting a rush to Hill. But the Cleveland men again counterattacked, condemning the "snap convention" maneuver and organizing a rival meeting of "anti-snapper" Democrats.[48] By March 1892 the Hill movement was blocked throughout the Northeast, and Cleveland's nomination was assured.[49]

Many Mugwumps who had remained Independents since 1884 openly became Democrats in 1892, completing their long journey from the GOP into the Democratic party. Throughout the Northeast the old bolters now channeled their energies into work for Cleveland's party. In the Bay State the Young Men's Democratic Club replaced the Massachusetts Reform Club as the most influential reform organization. In Connecticut the Connecticut Democratic Club superseded the Tariff Reform League and the New Haven Reform Club. Even the old nonpartisan reform associations caught the spirit of the times. The Massachusetts Reform Club had from its inception treated both parties with an icy aloofness. In late 1891, however, an independent-minded member made pointed references to the club's increasingly Democratic leanings.[50] Similarly, when the New York Reform Club first organized in 1888, its ranks included reformers of every partisan stamp— Republican, Democratic, and Independent. But only six years later, a Mugwump member complained that the club had gradually lost its nonpartisan character and had become a "tail to the Democratic kite."[51]

The Democratic kite flew high in 1892, carrying a slightly frayed Mugwump tail behind. Nationally Cleveland was swept back into office with a Democratic majority in both houses of Congress. In the East William E. Russell won a third consecutive term as governor of Massachusetts, an unprecedented feat for a Democrat in the post-Civil War era. Luzon B. Morris became Democratic governor of Connecticut, and the Connecticut Democratic Club successfully backed its favorite Irish Catholic reformer, James P. Pigott, for Congress. Less happily, three incumbent Mugwump congressmen from Massachusetts were defeated for reelection, victims of a slight revival of Republican strength in the state. Some storm clouds were also visible in the West and South where Populist and free silver sentiment was gaining, but these harbingers of trouble ahead were easily overlooked in the aftermath of Cleveland's solid victory.

As of 1892, therefore, Cleveland's Mugwump allies still had cause to remain sanguine about their past record and future prospects. Cleveland had been largely an unknown quantity in 1884, but his later adoption of views closely parallel to theirs on the tariff and currency seemed to confirm the wisdom of the Mugwump bolt. Often accused of impracticality in political affairs, the Mugwumps had managed several difficult political transitions: first, moving from the Republican party into a civil service entente with Cleveland, and secondly, when Democrats found civil service reform too much to abide, moving into the tariff reform wing of the Democratic party. Moreover, quite in contrast to their reputation as unorganized and undisciplined allies, the Mugwumps had helped establish and maintain a variety of influential Cleveland reform clubs in the Northeast.

The results of the Mugwumps' shifting strategy and of their organizational efforts were also gratifying. So successfully did the Cleveland men contribute to the revival of their party in New England that the balance of power there seemed to shift decisively to the Democrats in 1890 and 1892. During these halcyon years of the Cleveland Democracy, Mugwumps in Massachusetts, Connecticut, and Rhode Island worked within, not just with, the regular Democratic party organization as state and national committeemen. The former Independents also made the Democratic party a viable agency for their personal political aspirations, as even a partial listing of Mugwump officeholders suggests: John F. Andrew, William Everett, George Fred Williams, and Sherman Hoar from Massachusetts and William J. Coombs from New York served in Congress; and two former bolters were elected Democratic mayors—Samuel R. Honey in Newport and Joseph B. Sargent in New Haven. Thus, for a time, the tariff reform side of the Cleveland Democracy's program allowed for an effective coalition of Mugwumps with both Yankee and Irish Democrats.[52]

The Mugwumps' influence in national politics depended on special circumstances, which disintegrated rapidly during Cleveland's second term. Until 1892 the strength of the two parties had been balanced to the point of near deadlock, and under these conditions the Mugwumps gained considerable leverage politically even though they comprised only a faction within one wing of the Democratic party. In 1894 and 1896, however, the electorate reacted sharply to the depression of those years and delivered a resounding vote of no confidence in the Cleveland Democrats. As of 1892 the governors of New York, Connecticut, and Massachusetts were all Democrats. By 1894 they had been replaced by Republicans. In 1890 there had been twelve Democratic congressmen from Connecticut, Rhode Island, and Massachusetts. A slight resurgence of GOP strength reduced the number to nine by the next Congress, but the 1894 elections left John F. Fitzgerald as the only New England Democrat in Congress. The old party equilibrium was smashed by the Republican landslides of 1894 and 1896, and the GOP emerged from the mid-1890s with an electoral majority that was to last for decades.[53]

The Mugwumps' response to the politics of depression differed from that of most groups in the Democratic coalition of the early nineties. Many rank-and-file Democrats, hard hit by the economic crisis, abandoned the Democracy in 1894. In wards with a high proportion of either Irish or Cleveland Democrats, however, the party's losses in 1894 were relatively small. The Irish Democrats remained loyal to the party because of its position on cultural issues, especially its attacks on the GOP's proclivity for anti-Catholic nativism. The old stock, middle- and upper-class Democrats, on the other hand, stayed with the party because as of 1894 they were largely untouched by the depression and continued to prefer Cleveland's politics to any available alternative. But in 1896, after Bryan's free silver forces captured the Democratic party, Cleveland's Yankee and Mugwump admirers abandoned it in droves, thus making their departure two years after that of most Democratic voters who turned against the party.[54]

Mugwump approval of Cleveland's second administration was by no means unqualified. Civil service reformers in particular were angered by the president's heavy-handed use of patronage in order to win repeal of the Sherman Silver Purchase Act in 1893.[55] Adding insult to injury, former Mugwumps led the way in carrying out Cleveland's patronage strategy—Josiah Quincy as assistant secretary of state and Winslow Warren as collector of the Port of Boston. A cry went up against Mugwumps acting as spoilsmen. "Joe Quincy has out-heroded Herod," charged one Republican reformer.[56] The Massachusetts Reform Club and National Civil Service Reform League meetings in 1893 and 1894 reverberated with attacks on the administration.[57] Even so steadfast a Cleveland admirer as Richard Watson Gilder, editor of *Century Magazine*, expressed dismay at the havoc the repeal fight played with civil service principles.[58]

With Cleveland's goals—repeal of the Sherman Silver Purchase Act and passage of a tariff reform act—the Mugwumps had no argument. Thus, although Massachusetts Reform Club members greeted most references to the president with stony silence, there were still bursts of applause when his name was mentioned in connection with assaults on the free silver heresy.[59] During the congressional debates over tariff revision, the one remaining Mugwump in the Massachusetts Democratic delegation was William Everett, the hypersensitive son of Edward Everett, the famous orator. As the tariff bill progressed through Congress, Everett conveyed to fellow reformers his distress at the drift of things—the "bitter pill" of voting for the House version with an income tax rider attached to it, the spectacle of a "wretched Senate" removing most of the lower duties from the bill, and the final blow of finding the bill so unsatisfactory that he could not bring himself to vote for the conference version.[60]   Although most Mugwumps greeted these setbacks with fewer histrionics than Everett, they shared his and the president's disappointment with the Wilson-Gorman tariff.

From the Mugwump viewpoint, there was a ready explanation for the unbroken chain of electoral defeats that struck the Democratic party beginning in the fall of 1893. The blame, they believed, lay with the anti-Cleveland Democrats, both silverites and protectionists, who in resisting the president during the repeal fight and tariff debate had left "the Democratic majority broken and disorganized" in Congress.[61] The failure to redeem the party's pledge for reform, Winslow Warren asserted, was "a sad case of suicide." It was an "opportunity" thrown away, Richard Henry Dana III concluded. Little wonder, observed George Walton Green, that "the popular verdict was prompt and decisive" in 1894.[62] While this analysis was largely a reflection of their private dissatisfaction and ignored the stark reality of the depression's impact, it was a view of things that enabled the Mugwumps to remain faithful to the Cleveland Democracy well into 1896.[63] As one admiring Mugwump concluded, history would not acclaim Cleveland for "statesmanship" or "tact," but it would rank his leadership high because of his "diligence," "steadfastness," "rigid economy," and "dogged insistence on national good faith in the face of furious hostility and faint-hearted support."[64]

Bryan's nomination in 1896 worked a change in the Mugwumps' political allegiances every bit as dramatic as that which had taken place from 1884 to 1892. Originally, of course, the Mugwumps had been Republicans. By 1892 an estimated

75 percent called themselves Democrats and an even higher
number, roughly 90 percent, voted for Cleveland.[65] In 1896,
however, many Cleveland men left the Democratic national
convention in disgust after a futile attempt to stem the tide
of free silver feeling. "No respectable man could afford to
remain," wrote one such individual.[66] The urgent need now
seemed to be to secure the defeat of the Bryan Democrats
and their wrong-headed currency proposals. Yet McKinley,
with his persistent advocacy of a protective tariff, was hardly
an attractive alternative. The strategic problem in 1896, as
one puzzled Cleveland man put it, was "how to beat Bryan
and not vote for McKinley."[67]

In the end, most Mugwumps saw no way of accomplishing
both these goals. Approximately 60 percent voted for McKinley, and roughly 30 percent backed the National (Gold) Democratic ticket of Palmer and Buckner. Less than 10 percent
(five of sixty-five) supported the regular Democratic ticket
headed by Bryan.[68] Although many of the Mugwumps who
switched to the Palmer ticket later returned to the Democratic
party, those who switched to the GOP often became permanent defectors. Thus a long-range reshuffling of Mugwump
party allegiances dated from 1896. In that year, and in most
national elections thereafter, the Mugwumps divided their
loyalties along quite consistent lines. As indicated by Table
4.1, 55 to 60 percent of the Mugwumps voted Republican
and 40 to 45 percent voted Democratic in every election from
1896 to 1916 excepting 1908 and 1912.[69]

As with all things Mugwump, the paths by which they came
to vote for McKinley in 1896 varied considerably. A tiny
handful, perhaps 10 percent of the Mugwump sample, had
continued as active Republicans after the 1884 bolt, with two
of them—Congressman Joseph H. Walker and Governor Roger

Table 4.1

*Mugwump Party Preferences in
National Elections, 1896-1916*

Year	Percent voting Republican	Percent voting Democratic	Number in Sample
1896	58%	42%*	50
1900	60%	40%	47
1904	59%	41%	34
1908	88%	12%	24
1912	46%**	54%	28
1916	56%	44%	16

*The Democratic percentage for 1896 combines Bryan (10 percent) and Gold Democrats (32 percent).
**The Republican percentage for 1912 combines Taft (21 percent) and Roosevelt (25 percent) voters.

Wolcott of Massachusetts—becoming politically prominent in the 1890s. Others—Charles J. Bonaparte and William Dudley Foulke may serve as examples—were civil service purists who had voted for Cleveland Democrats, but who had never trusted Democrats in general. After 1896 men of this sort found it quite comfortable to return to active membership in the GOP. Henry W. Farnam and Oscar S. Straus represented another distinct group—men who had been enthusiastic Cleveland Democrats until 1896, but who subsequently left the party, Straus converting to Republicanism, Farnam calling himself an "independent" while generally voting Republican.[70] Finally, McKinley's Mugwump supporters in 1896 included tariff reform Democrats who, as Charles R. Codman said of himself, had "no great faith in the courage or insight" of the Republican leaders, but who backed McKinley as the "safest" way of insuring Bryan's defeat.[71]

Approximately 40 percent of the Mugwumps voted Demo-

cratic in 1896, most of them acting with the anti-Bryan or
National Democratic party. A large contingent of Mugwumps
—among them R. R. Bowker, Louis D. Brandeis, and George
Haven Putnam—enlisted actively under the Gold Democrat
banner. Although the party was obviously a temporary haven
for men who had nowhere else to go, or nowhere they cared
to go anyway, the anti-Bryan campaign was not taken lightly.
To one adherent, at least, the Gold Democrats' program was
"the best presidential platform ever presented in this country."[72]
The Mugwumps who favored Bryan were, by contrast, pain-
fully aware that they were a "hopeless minority" in New England.[73] Only two Mugwumps—George Fred Williams and
Joseph B. Sargent, both men influenced by the Bellamy Nationalist movement—played prominent roles in the Bryan campaign. With sentiment in the total Mugwump sample running
easily ten to one against Bryan, news of his defeat was greeted
with relief by most of the old bolters.

In 1898, four years after the initial rout of the Cleveland
Democrats, the Mugwumps returned to the national spotlight
in a short-lived campaign against imperialism. Notably, the
anti-imperialist crusade was the last time the Mugwumps acted in a solid organizational phalanx. Fittingly, it also reunited
them temporarily with some of the Independent Republicans—
George F. Hoar, George F. Edmunds, and William Dean Howells—with whom they had parted company politically in 1884.
Theodore Roosevelt and Henry Cabot Lodge, both avid inter-
ventionists, were clearly exceptions to this tendency.

Anti-imperialism was undeniably an epilogue, however.
Even though it returned the Mugwumps to their cherished
role of keepers of the nation's conscience, it brought them
back in their old, independent posture without an effective
base in either party organization. In a musical metaphor, anti-

imperialism was a brief coda in which the themes of Mugwump reform were presented once more in a variation keyed to foreign affairs.

The roll call of anti-imperialist meetings from 1898 to 1900 read like a reunion of the bolters of 1884. The New York Anti-Imperialist League numbered among its members E. L. Godkin, Carl Schurz, R. Fulton Cutting, and Richard Watson Gilder. In Philadelphia George G. Mercer, a Mugwump lawyer, was president of the anti-imperialist society. The New England movement was even more dominantly Mugwump, with William James, Thomas Wentworth Higginson, Gamaliel Bradford, Sr., Samuel Bowles, William Graham Sumner, Charles R. Codman, Moorfield Storey, Edward Atkinson, Charles Eliot Norton, and many other former bolters working for the cause. The Chicago Mugwumps, Franklin MacVeagh and Edwin Burritt Smith, so isolated as bolters in 1884, also rallied to the anti-imperialist banner.[74]

The old reformers attacked imperialism along familiar lines, drawing on their perennial concerns with orderly public conduct, individual freedom, and civic morality. The expansionist debauch, they charged, like the materialistic spirit of post-Civil War politics, was degrading the nation morally and politically. Informal empires of economic influence were one thing, tolerable and perhaps even desirable, but colonial rule of other peoples would certainly corrupt America's republican way of life. A government founded on representative principles could not safely abandon them in foreign affairs. In international relations, as in international trade (drawing here on a theme from their free trade credo), a harmonious interdependence of groups and nations must prevail over force, whether that force took the form of tariff protection or colonial rule.[75]

The alternative of admitting the conquered peoples to equal participation in the American system was, the Mugwumps believed, not a practical solution to this democratic dilemma. They were convinced that the racial and cultural backgrounds of the Filipinos and Puerto Ricans would prevent them from achieving a level of political sophistication equal to that of white Americans. And inequality, the Mugwumps feared, would inevitably lead to domination of the dark-skinned peoples by their white conquerers.

The racist overtones of this judgment reflect badly on the larger liberality of the anti-imperialist crusade.[76] Nevertheless, it would be a mistake to dismiss the foes of imperialism as "racists" pure and simple. Many, according to one authority, can be labeled "racist" only by stretching the term considerably.[77] Moreover, few of them shared the imperialists' penchant for racial domination, usually expressed in justifying annexation as the noble work of a white master race. Doubts about the potentialities of dark-skinned peoples, indeed, were less fundamental to the Mugwumps' critique of imperialism than their skepticism regarding the annexationists' moral and political wisdom.[78] In the latter feeling there was a good deal of prescience, for what the Mugwumps feared did happen: Filipinos and Puerto Ricans were denied the chance to work out their own political futures, with unfortunate consequences for the conquered peoples and their conquerors.

Politically the anti-imperialists failed at every step. They were unable to prevent the war with Spain, to prevent annexation of the Philippines and other conquered territories, and to prevent the imperialist administration from winning reelection in 1900. To be sure, anti-imperialism's strength was in the moral dimension—in calling attention publicly, often in the face of vehement patriotic backlash, to the total inconsistency

of imperialism and American ideals. Yet the sad fact was that
their concerted moral attack on the administration did not
culminate in a successful political offensive in the election of
1900. Again, a fusion of politics and morals eluded them.

In fairness, the correct strategy for the anti-imperialists was
not obvious, given the candidates between whom they had to
choose in 1900. If the Mugwump dilemma in 1896 had been
how to defeat Bryan without seeming to endorse McKinley's
protectionist ideas, the comparable puzzle in 1900 was how
to defeat the McKinley-Roosevelt ticket without seeming to
support Bryan's economic program. Many at first joined Carl
Schurz and Moorfield Storey in trying to circumvent the problem by initiating a third-party movement.[79] As prospects
for the third-party alternative faded, the anti-imperialist Mugwumps decided, most of them with considerable reluctance,
to vote for Bryan—the number who did so exceeding by a
margin of four to one that of anti-imperialist Mugwumps who
backed McKinley.[80] Mugwumps critical of the majority position and anti-imperialist Republicans such as Senator George
F. Hoar, ridiculed the idea of voting for Bryan, comparing it
to jumping "out of the frying-pan into the fire."[81] The pro-
Bryan men admitted that voting for Bryan was a "most dis-
tasteful thing." Yet in their defense they doggedly asserted
that the Democratic leader was right on the campaign's pre-
eminent issue, anti-imperialism, and therefore deserved their
votes on moral grounds.[82]

The debate over imperialism did not radically alter the Mugwump group's party allegiances, which from 1896 onward
showed a slight preference for the GOP over the Democracy.
The debate did have an impact on the political loyalties of
individual Mugwumps, however. For Republicans like Seth
Low who supported the war, the issues it raised provided one

more justification for continued adherence to the GOP.[83]
Some Cleveland Democrats disenchanted with Bryan's leadership drifted yet further from the party in reaction against the
Commoner's belated swing to anti-imperialism. This was the
case, at least, among moderate anti-imperialists who accepted
annexation once it was a fait accompli (e. g., Franklin Mac-
Veagh), as well as among war supporters (Richard Welling).[84]
By contrast, the anti-imperialist campaign provided the impetus for the return of many Cleveland Democrats to their
party, including such able individuals as Charles R. Codman,
Samuel Bowles, Josiah Quincy, and Winslow Warren. The
solidly anti-imperialist sentiment among Bryan's Mugwump
backers and the continued support other Mugwumps gave
McKinley were simply more evidence that the Cleveland
Democracy's breakup had produced an irreparable cleavage
in the ranks of the old bolters. Whatever direction their political careers might take in the twentieth century, their response to the new century would not be determined by membership in a unified Mugwump movement.

Chapter 5

Low

State & Municipal Mugwumpery

Mugwump orthodoxy underwent marked modification in the 1890s. This transformation was scarcely apparent at the national level, where Mugwumps continued to admire that archfoe of innovation, Grover Cleveland. In state and local politics, however, Cleveland's Mugwump allies often identified themselves with the era's incipient progressivism. This is not to say that the Mugwumps were the primary instigators of state and local progressivism in the 1890s, for in many cases they were not. But that they participated in progressive causes at all is remarkable, given their defensive reaction nationally to the crisis of the nineties.

Having referred to some causes as "progressive," let me hasten to add how conscious I am that the term may have very loaded connotations, especially in the light of recent historical writing and its stress on the "conservative" side of "progressive" reform.[1] My emphasis in this chapter and those that follow, however, is not on the word's connotative association with "liberalism" as opposed to "reaction." Rather, I mean to use "progressive" in a largely denotative way, that is, to identify Mugwump activities that anticipated or embraced concerns—municipal reform, social legislation, and the settlement house movement—commonly linked with twentieth-century progressivism.

During the Cleveland Democracy's heyday in the early 1890s, an incipient progressivism was evident in Massachusetts. During William E. Russell's three terms as governor from 1891 to 1894, the state became a pace setter in legislative reform. As one historian has observed: "In most matters identified with Progressivism after 1900, Massachusetts had earlier taken an advanced position."[2] Geoffrey Blodgett, in his fine book *The Gentle Reformers: Massachusetts Democrats in the Cleveland Era*, has described this "imaginative response" to industrialism in all its particulars.[3] They do not need repetition here beyond a brief summary to suggest the part that Mugwumps played in the Bay State's reform era.

The list of legislative accomplishments from the Russell years is an impressive one. Even before Russell took office, his Democratic allies were responsible for the Lobby Regulation Act of 1890. Prompted by George Fred Williams's dramatic attacks on legislative lobbying practices, the bill was steered through the legislature by Josiah Quincy, who adroitly managed things so that the anti-lobby furor would not reflect badly on any prominent Democrats.[4] During 1891, Russell's initial year in office, the poll tax was abolished. In 1892 the Corrupt Practices Act, which required political parties to file public statements of their campaign income and expenses, was

the end product of another legislative drive sponsored by
Quincy.[5]   Governor Russell's proposals for reorganizing the
state's executive branch along the centralized lines suggested
by Seth Low's "Brooklyn Idea" did not win approval, however.[6]

In economic legislation the Bay State Democrats also anticipated progressive concerns. An anti-sweat shop bill passed in
1891, prohibiting the "sale of clothing and garments made
outside the State in tenements and unsanitary shops"—a provision that had a pro-labor sound even while it protected local
manufacturers from some out-of-state competition.[7] Also in
1891 the Mugwump Bellamyites—Thomas Wentworth Higginson, Sylvester Baxter, and George D. Ayers—won approval
for their proposal that municipalities be permitted to manu-
facture and sell gas and electricity.[8]   Finally, Quincy, a student
of British labor legislation and a member of the House committee on child labor, proposed no less than a "dozen separate
labor laws." Most of them dealt with factory conditions, but
one 1892 law also regulated the working hours of women and
minors, restricting them to a fifty-eight hour work week.[9]

After the disastrous midterm election of 1894 the Yankee-
Irish coalition of the Russell years disintegrated in the state,
surviving only in Boston, the bastion of Massachusetts Democracy. There Josiah Quincy, with the aid of an Irish Democratic
boss, Patrick Maguire, was elected mayor in 1895 and reelected in 1897. Aware that younger Irish leaders such as James
Donovan and Martin Lomasney had no love for the Maguire
idea of a Yankee-Irish coalition, Quincy maneuvered astutely
to shore up the entente's waning strength. Under his administration municipal baths were established in Boston's industrial sections, and the city sponsored free lectures, concerts,
and recreational activities for its citizens. The city also

enforced wage and hour standards in municipal projects, both
to encourage a higher quality of work and to provide a yardstick for measuring private labor practices in the same fields.
A municipal socialism of the European sort was introduced,
with many tasks that previously had been handled by private
contractors—repair projects, municipal printing, and electrical
work—now being performed by city departments.[10]

The prominent role played by a few Mugwumps during the
Russell and Quincy regimes should not be taken as proof that
most Bay State Mugwumps were in the vanguard of these
state and local reform movements. Early in the 1890s, of
course, Mugwumps filled the ranks of the YMDC and supported the Russell administrations wholeheartedly. But only a few
of the old bolters—Josiah Quincy, George Fred Williams,
Thomas Wentworth Higginson, and Sylvester Baxter—turned
up regularly as active advocates of the economic legislation
of the Russell years. Aside from the tariff and currency questions, therefore, economic issues did not determine the Mugwumps' loyalty to Russell and the Cleveland Democracy.

Quincy, as mayor, received little Mugwump support. By
the time he took office in 1896 Bryan's nomination was near
at hand, and many Mugwumps thereafter shunned everything
Democratic. There was still a great deal of bitterness in the
Mugwump circle because of Quincy's activities as a spoilsman
during the second Cleveland administration. Furthermore, few
of the Mugwumps, Sylvester Baxter being the most prominent
exception, were enthusiastic about Quincy's brand of municipal socialism. To the Mugwump mind, Quincy's programs
simply increased the municipal budget and created a multitude
of new city jobs for patronage-hungry Democrats. The result
was that when Quincy sought the aid of Yankee reformers,
he was more likely to turn to young professional social workers

like Robert A. Woods and Joseph Lee than to his former Mugwump associates.[11]

The Massachusetts Mugwumps who rejected Bryanism or
who had their doubts about Quincy's policies nevertheless
sometimes made significant contributions in public affairs
during the 1890s. Charles Francis Adams, Jr. served on the
Park Commission with Sylvester Baxter and felt that his work
in planning Boston's metropolitan park system ranked high
among his achievements in a long career of public service.[12]
Louis D. Brandeis, with Moorfield Storey one of the few Boston lawyers to support George Fred Williams' assaults on the
lobbyists, increasingly took a public advocate's role against
corporate monopolies and the abuses of unregulated business.
In 1900 Brandeis established the Public Franchise League, a
watchdog organization intended to scrutinize public franchises
and to maintain public control over them. Samuel Bowles,
Mugwump editor of the *Springfield Republican*, was one of
the league's consistent backers.[13] Even more commonly the
old reformers expanded their mugwumpery to include programs of structural reform—the secret ballot, corrupt practices
legislation, and increased executive powers. Moorfield Storey,
Richard Henry Dana III, Solomon B. Griffin, and Gamaliel
Bradford, Sr. were leading activists among the Mugwump political reformers.

The shift in the Massachusetts Democracy from Yankee to
Irish control nevertheless took its toll in the Bay State Mugwumps' enthusiasm for politics. Once Massachusetts had stood
practically alone among the Mugwump states in offering independents access to political careers through Mugwump enclaves. But fewer and fewer such enclaves were available as
the 1890s progressed. Thus, although some Massachusetts
reformers shed their Mugwump skins and became municipal

progressives, the new political climate in Boston did not encourage such transformations. Ironically, just as the Bay
State Mugwumps lost their verve, the New York bolters gained strength. After years of being poor relations, seemingly
unable to cooperate successfully with party regulars, the New
Yorkers made a striking adaptation to the demands of municipal politics.

Beginning early in the 1890s the New York reformers repeatedly indulged in their favorite pastime—pulling the Tammany Tiger's tail. With the impetus provided by a variety of
new reform organizations, the tiger-baiters defeated the machine in 1894 and 1901. Although the machine Democrats
both times returned to power in the next election, the municipal reform campaigns produced an "Age of Reform" in New
York City well before progressivism surfaced in national politics.[14]

The anti-Tammany campaigns were in large part an extension of the Mugwump impulse to municipal affairs. Mugwumps
comprised a major element within the organizations that bore
the brunt of the reform battle—the City Club (organized 1892),
the Good Government clubs (1893), the Committee of Seventy (1894), and Citizens' Union (1897). Approximately
10 percent of the City Club and Citizens' Union membership
at their inception were Mugwumps from the New York City
sample of 1884. A considerably smaller proportion were men
from the 1884 sample of regular Republicans, an indication
that municipal reform drew regulars and Mugwumps together
again, but that many loyal party men were not so ready to
join the reform alliance as were the Mugwumps.[15] In method
as well as membership, the anti-Tammany crusades were
municipal mugwumpery. Whether in the form of the City
Club (a relatively exclusive social club with political aims)

or in the efforts of Citizens' Union to form a nonpartisan municipal party, the reform groups operated outside of, rather than within, established Republican and Democratic organizations.

Before the 1890s Tammany had been attacked on a number of occasions without much permanent effect on its methods or political power. During the years just after the Civil War, Tammany under William Marcy Tweed and his cohorts systematically plundered city funds through kickbacks, bogus contracts, and padded budgets. A citizens' campaign in 1871 and 1872 (in which future Mugwumps such as George Jones, Thomas Nast, and Edward Cary played important roles) drove the Tweed Ring from power.[16]

Tammany, however, soon returned to control of the city under a new boss, "Honest" John Kelly. In the 1880s Kelly's regime also was assaulted by the so-called County Democracy, a group of reform Democrats that included Abram S. Hewitt, William C. Whitney, and William R. Grace. By the time of Kelly's death in 1886, his leadership had been weakened by revelations of widespread graft among the Board of Aldermen and by Grace's victory as candidate for mayor in 1884. Kelly's successor, Richard Croker, nevertheless quickly reestablished Tammany's dominance within the city's politics. Clearly the Tammany tiger was a cat with many lives. The machine's power was firmly based in services rendered to the voters. The reformers, by contrast, weakened their claims to public support by a tendency to focus on political uprightness to the virtual exclusion of the electorate's social and economic needs.[17]

As Tammany's strength revived and the County Democracy faded in the late 1880s, the field of municipal reform was left by default to the City Reform Club (CRC), an organization

quite inadequate to the task. The CRC was established in 1882
by a group of socially prominent young men interested in municipal affairs. Theodore Roosevelt was an original member.
After his election to the state legislature, however, Roosevelt
was forced to resign from the club because its by-laws forbade
any member from compromising his political independence
by holding a party or a public office.

This delicacy about office-holding, together with the club's
small size and elite membership, served to reinforce the popular view that the City Reform Club was a haven for political
dilettantes. The *New York World*, for one, described the club
as "composed of young men well acquainted with the turns
in Central Park drives." It went on to mock the appearance
of the City Reform Club "dudes":

> When the Chairman, Mr. S. J. Colgate, who appeared in full
> evening dress, including a white butterfly necktie, rapped for
> order, those present, thirty-eight in number, stopped eyeing
> each other in wonderful admiration and faced front. Four-
> teen were in full-dress suit, thirty-six carried canes and twenty-
> two had their hair furrowed down the centre.[18]

Literally and figuratively the CRC epitomized "kid-glove
politics."

The importance of the City Reform Club was not its immediate impact on the city, which was slight, but rather its
influence on the reformers. Originally numbering from two
to three hundred members, the CRC dwindled in size until
in 1887 it was reorganized as an executive committee of fewer
than twenty men.[19] But for those who remained the club
served as a training ground for later fights against Tammany
Hall. Members prowled the city on election day, tracking
down election-law violations and ferreting out examples
of police vice.[20] The long-range effect of this apprenticeship

was evident in a Mugwump like Richard Welling, one of
the club's incorporators and for a time its president.
Welling was perhaps exceptional in the longevity of his
career in reform, participating actively in every major municipal reform movement from the 1880s to the La Guardia
era. But the records of other club members who applied
their CRC experience to the anti-Tammany crusades of
the 1890s is further testimony to the continuity of reform.[21] It was also a CRC member who first developed
the practice of printing the annual voting record of New
York assemblymen and senators, an educative service to
voters later taken up by Citizens' Union and continued
to this day.[22]

The People's Municipal League (PML), established in 1890,
was another organization typical of an early stage in the evolution of municipal reform. Its founders, many of them CRC
men, hoped to broaden the base of urban reform in New
York by drawing large numbers of citizens into a "voters'
league." Although distinct from the City Reform Club in
proposing a non-elite membership pattern, the PML was like
the CRC in espousing a program of municipal mugwumpery—
civil service reform, municipal elections separate from national
campaigns, and a businesslike administration of city government. In effect, the cure most Mugwumps prescribed for
municipal problems early in the 1890s was nonpartisanship,
at least the elimination of national partisan influences from
local affairs. The reasoning behind this program was stated
simply by an original PML member: "City government is
business . . . [and] questions of National or State politics
have no proper place in elections to local office or in the conduct of local affairs." [23]

One of the foremost figures in the league was a Mugwump
lawyer, Horace E. Deming. Forty years of age in 1890, Deming

already had more than a decade of reform experience behind
him. He had joined the Young Scratcher movement in 1879,
backed Seth Low for mayor of Brooklyn, and served on the
Mugwump national committee in 1884, acquiring additional
documentation of Blaine's questionable railroad bond deal-
ings. Deming was instrumental, through his friendship with
Albert Shaw, the scholarly editor of the American *Review of
Reviews*, in getting national magazine coverage for the People's
Municipal League.[24] The league, however, never participated
significantly in New York City electoral battles but rapidly
developed into a national organization. Again Deming took
a leading role, suggesting in 1894 that a National Municipal
League (NML) be formed and helping to see the project
through later in the year.[25]

Neither the national league nor its New York branch ever
became the mass-membership organizations envisioned by the
PML's founders in 1890. The National Municipal League was
more accurately "a clearing-house for the exchange of municipal ideas."[26] Principally a body of experts who collected
statistics and published books on city problems, it was an important channel of communication among urban reformers
at a time when the study of municipal problems was in its
infancy. Functioning something like a national professional
association for municipal reformers, the National Municipal
League proved far more durable and influential than the City
Reform Club, which it resembled in its early program. By
flexibly revising its program to incorporate new ideas, the
NML remained a force for reform well into the twentieth
century.[27]

The persistence of Tammany Hall corruption contributed to
the eventual resurgence of municipal reform feeling in New
York City. After the election of Tammany sachem Hugh J.

Grant as mayor in 1888, Richard Croker's Democratic stal-
warts carried on what political wits called "politics for
revenue only." From 1889 to 1894 the city was rocked
by a series of revelations of graft and malfeasance reminiscent of Tweed days.[28] In rapid succession a grand jury
investigation of the Sheriff's Department revealed numerous examples of kickbacks and bribery (individual cases of
which involved sums up to $20,000), and Tammany-run
protection schemes were uncovered by a State Senate inquiry. Despite these exposés Croker's Democratic machine
at first showed no signs of weakness. Tammany mayors
were elected in 1890 and 1892 by majorities of 23,199
and 75,587 votes, respectively.[29] These were flush years
for the Democrats, whether of the Tammany or the Cleveland variety.

The attack on Tammany rule gathered force between 1892
and 1894. Early in 1892 Reverend Charles H. Parkhurst of
the Madison Square Presbyterian Church assailed Tammany
for its connection with organized vice in the city. With some
help from the City Reform Club, but primarily on his own
initiative, Parkhurst substantiated his accusations with hard
facts. Under the stimulus provided by Parkhurst's revelations
and his continued attacks on the machine, Republican State
Senator Clarence Lexow introduced a bill during the 1894
legislative session to provide funds for investigating police
graft in New York City. Governor Roswell Flower vetoed the
appropriation, but the New York Chamber of Commerce advanced enough money to pay for the inquiry.[30]

When the Lexow Committee uncovered everything the reformers had hoped and feared it would—bribery, pay for no
work, and contracts to party favorites at ludicrously high fees
—the Chamber of Commerce urged the formation of a committee

of distinguished citizens to combat civic immorality. A call
was issued in September 1894, inviting the city's residents to
band together "irrespective of party" to "organize a citizens'
movement for the government of the city of New York, entirely outside party politics, and solely in the best interests
of efficiency, economy, and public health, comfort, and safe-
ty."[31] A Committee of Seventy was soon gathered to spear-
head the anti-Tammany campaign.

The committee's membership comprised a formidable array
of influential citizens: J. Pierpont Morgan, Abram S. Hewitt,
Jacob H. Schiff, and William E. Dodge, among others. The
group's chairman was Joseph Larocque, a Mugwump and a
former president of the city's Bar Association. Other bolters
—John Claflin, Abraham Jacobi, Percival Knauth, and George
Haven Putnam—were among the seventy.[32] Whether Mugwump, Democrat, or Republican, the anti-Tammany men were
ethnic and social rivals of the groups that formed Tammany's
power base. Predominantly Yankees and Protestants (with
a dash of Germans and Jews added), they represented a cosmopolitan, business, and professional segment of the city's
population. Their goals of efficient and economical city government offered cold comfort to Tammany's ethnically diverse and ward-based political following.[33]

As the campaign of 1894 progressed, the reformers spelled
out their aims more broadly and drew support from other
organizations. The Committee of Seventy's circulars announced hopes for bringing the city cleaner streets and improved
pavements, nonpolitical management of police affairs, improved schools, and more public parks, playgrounds, baths and
lavatories "to promote cleanliness and increased public comfort."[34] Among the organizations that joined the reform
coalition were the City Club, the Good Government clubs,

Parkhurst's City Vigilance League, the German-American Reform Union (abbreviated GARU or GAROO, and by less
sympathetic observers, GAZOO), the Society for the Prevention of Crime, the State (anti-Hill) Democracy, and the County
Democracy.[35]

The City Club and its associated societies, the Good Government clubs, were forceful additions to the reform alliance.
The City Club had been founded as the result of a fortuitous
combination of circumstances in 1892. The City Reform
Club men were looking for a method of expanding their influence and membership. Dr. Parkhurst was giving dramatic
publicity to the need for civic action; and, at this propitious
moment, Edmond Kelly, a lawyer with unusual zeal for public service, offered his time and energy to the formation of a
new reform association.

Kelly originated the idea of a dual-level approach to reform,
combining a citywide social club for patrician reformers with
precinct-level campaign clubs for workingmen. The first part
of his plan he derived from the City Reform Club men who
wanted to reorganize their group as a permanent social club
for municipal reformers. The City Club, as the new group was
called, was complete with all the luxuries of a Knickerbocker
or Union League club—a clubhouse with dining and smoking
rooms "suitably furnished" and providing "service . . . such
as our members are in their own houses accustomed to."[36]
The supposed advantages of such a club were twofold: it
would provide some continuity with previous reform efforts,
and it would draw wealthy and socially prominent advocates
of municipal reform together on a regular basis.[37]

In both these goals the City Club was apparently a success,
and the appeal of the social club format was proven by the
establishment of "City Clubs" in many cities—Boston, St.

Louis, Milwaukee, Chicago, and Philadelphia.[38] Many prominent men not previously active in municipal reform found
the City Club a congenial means of participating in city affairs. James C. Carter, the club's first president, was a Mugwump, a former president of the New York City bar association, and the lawyer who argued for the constitutionality of
the income tax before the Supreme Court in 1895. Two
millionaire brothers, William Bayard and R. Fulton Cutting,
were representative of the politically conscious men of wealth
who joined the club, both brothers being prodigious in their
philanthropic and reform activities. These men, along with
other Mugwumps, dominated the club's councils and imbued
the organization with their ideas of nonpartisan city government.[39]

Kelly, however, feared that left to their own devices the
City Club members would be "too few, too dainty, and too
rich" to overcome Tammany.[40] In order to supplement the
City Club's membership of three hundred or so prominent
men, Kelly set out to organize "workingmen's drinking clubs"
to be called Good Government clubs, one for each election
district in the city. These groups were to give the nonpartisan,
business-government movement its numerical base. As Kelly
explained: "Under this plan the City Club was not to be an
isolated and friendless group of vainly protesting citizens, but
by affiliation with other clubs was destined to acquire that
force of numbers at the polls which alone the practical poli-
tician understands and fears."[41]

Good Government Club "A" was formed early in 1893, and
by the municipal election of 1894 twenty-three more had been
established. Each club had at least fifty members. Although
the reformers pointed with pride to the fact that one club
elected a butcher and an iron moulder as its vice presidents,

Kelly's hopes that the Good Government clubs would be work-ingmen's organizations were for the most part not realized.[42] By and large the Good Government clubs, their members satir-ically labeled "Goo Goos" by the *New York Sun*, simply ex-tended the City Club's recruiting among professionals and businessmen. Nevertheless, they augmented the City Club's strength significantly, more than two thousand Goo Goos serving as poll watchers in the 1894 city election.[43] In addi-tion, the growth of reform's organized strength was an aus-picious development and a tribute to Kelly's ingenuity. The reformers were at last trying to fight Tammany on the ma-chine's own ground of mass membership and precinct-level organization.[44]

The "triumph of reform," as E. L. Godkin called it, came in 1894, aided by the conjunction of several favorable politi-cal trends. One was the reemergence of anti-Tammany feel-ing and organizations among the Mugwumps and other native-born business and professional men drawn into the ranks of the City and Good Government clubs. Another was the pre-cipitous decline of popular support for the Democrats in 1894 among less well-off voters hard hit by the depression. Finally, the GOP leadership, seeing an unusual chance to defeat the city Democrats, cooperated with the Committee of Seventy campaign and endorsed the fusion candidate, William L. Strong, a life-long Republican, rather than fielding a separate candidate. With these forces working in his favor, Strong carried more than three-fourths of the city's thirty assembly districts, dramatically reversing the results of the 1892 elec-tion in which the Democrats had swept every single district.[45]

Both Mugwumps and the men from whom they had broken politically in 1884, the Independent Republicans, were active in Strong's administration (1895-97). Of Blaine's backers, the most conspicuous representative was Theodore Roosevelt. Appointed commissioner of police with the injunction to clean up the graft-ridden department, Roosevelt launched into his duties with characteristic flamboyance, conducting surprise inspections of night police patrols and roaming the city in hopes of catching delinquent patrolmen unawares.[46] Determined to eliminate graft at its source, Roosevelt pressed particularly hard for the enforcement of Sunday closing laws for saloons, feeling that illegal sales of alcoholic beverages had become one of the major sources of kickbacks and bribes for police protection and lax law enforcement. Evidence on this point is slim, but Mugwumps very likely sympathized with the goal of eliminating graft, even though most of them would have preferred a more moderate closing law enforcement policy than Roosevelt pursued.[47]

Indeed, the aspect of Strong's administration that won the Mugwumps' applause was not Roosevelt's campaign to eliminate police graft, but the work of George E. Waring, Jr., as chief of the city's street cleaning department.[48] Waring, a Mugwump in 1884, was a highly respected sanitary engineer and an early member of the American Public Health Association. He made every effort to turn his department into a practical example of the APHA's objective of nonpartisan, expert-controlled public health administration. To the reformers' delight he fired "unqualified" holdovers from the Tammany regime but also demonstrated his nonpartisanship by retaining those Democratic appointees who proved to his satisfaction that they would work efficiently under his direction. "Colonel" Waring had served in the Civil War, and his penchant for military discipline showed up when he organized annual departmental parades at which his men, nicknamed "Waring's White Wings," marched dressed in white, ostensibly to boost their morale and self-image. According to Waring's contemporaries, however, the great accomplishment of his leadership was not parades but the simple fact that many miles of city streets where trash had remained untouched in the Tammany period were now cleaned and kept clean.[49]

Other Mugwumps served the city in various capacities during the Strong years. George Walton Green, a Cleveland Democrat and lawyer, was appointed aqueduct commissioner in 1895. Lewis L. Delafield, another lawyer, became secretary of the Rapid Transit Commission, and Austen G. Fox served as a special counsel appointed by the district attorney and the Committee of Seventy to investigate the Police Department. Frederick G. Ireland was appointed to the municipal Civil Service Commission. Richard Watson Gilder and Roger Foster (both state appointees) conducted a searching investigation of tenement house conditions and wrote the Tenement House Act of 1895. Foster continued on as special counsel to the city Board of Health in prosecuting violations of the reform housing act. To these participants in what the editor of the *Review of Reviews* called "Our Civic Renaissance," the Strong regime seemed to bring many worthwhile accomplishments, among them cleaner streets, the tenement house legislation, improvement of the city's school and public park system, and the reduction of municipal graft.[50]

This was, of course, a reform's eye view of reform and one with which many disagreed. Members of the Reverend Parkhurst's City Vigilance League and the city's evangelical Protestant clergy might cheer Roosevelt's crackdown on Sunday closing law violations, but Germans who loved their beer and saloon keepers, brewers, and small businessmen who benefitted from the lucrative Sunday trade were greatly annoyed. As early as 1895, in fact, some German members of the fusion coalition made it plain that they preferred Tammany's relaxed "continental Sunday" to reform's Puritanical sabbath. Similarly, Street Commissioner Waring might boast that he had rid the city of the "annoyance" of private trucks left standing on city streets overnight, but to many draymen and businessmen who had to rent private parking facilities, Waring's policy was a nuisance—and expense to boot.[51] Radicals complained that Gilder's new tenement law was completely insufficient, while wealthy vestrymen of Trinity Episcopal Church were indignant with Gilder's commission because it exposed their large investment in substandard housing.[52] And so it went: partisans of local school control were displeased by Strong's school program, which replaced locally elected representatives with a Board of Education appointed at large by the mayor; Republicans felt the administration was too independent; Independents thought it too Republican.[53]

The next mayoralty election was in 1897. If anything, the stakes in the contest were higher than ever, largely because it was the first election under the Greater New York Charter, which unified a large geographical area into the modern metropolis with its five boroughs—Brooklyn, Bronx, Manhattan, Queens, and Richmond. The year 1897 was also the first test of the reformers' long-standing demand that municipal elections be held in off-years, that is, years when no presidential or congressional campaigns were in progress. Supposedly this would promote voting that was independent of national party labels, though the chief beneficiaries in 1897 were likely the Democrats who, ironically enough, were in a better position in 1897 than in 1896 when they had to carry the burden of Bryan's unpopularity in the city. Freed of Bryan's candidacy, Tammany was able to concentrate on issues that would return its drawing power to normal, much as it had used off-year elections in 1895 to recoup some of its losses from 1894.[54]

By the 1897 election the reform coalition of 1894 was in total disarray. The large German community, an important element in the earlier fusion victory, had been soured on anti-Tammany politics by the closing law issue. Strong recognized his weakened position and declared that he was not a candidate for reelection. The Good Government Club faction, annoyed by the "partisan" Strong regime, was busily reconstituting itself in a new organization, Citizens' Union, and demanding that municipal candidates be independent of both national parties. The organization Republicans, meanwhile, were basking in confidence born of their electoral victories of 1896 and were in no mood to make concessions to the troublesome independents. The upshot was that the Republicans and independents went their separate ways. Citizens' Union chose Seth Low, the former mayor of Brooklyn and president of Columbia University since 1890, as its candidate, and the Republicans selected their own nominee, Benjamin F. Tracy.[55]

Although the failure to achieve fusion with the Republicans did not greatly trouble the more independently minded Citizens' Union men, Low himself believed a united front campaign would have greatly increased his chances of winning. He never tired of reiterating his belief that the Republicans, as the minority party in the city, were natural and virtually indispensable allies of the independents. "In a community like the city of New York," Low wrote, "where the political majority is so one-sided, it is safe to say that success can never be had except when Independents and the minority party work hand in hand."[56]

Despite these obstacles, Citizens' Union made a strong showing in 1897. Low ran second in a three-man contest in which the Tammany candidate received about 20,000 fewer votes

(233,997) than the combined total of Low's vote (151,540) and that of the Republican nominee (101,864). A fourth candidate, Henry George, died late in the campaign, removing an independent Democrat who might have cut Tammany's strength and given Low the victory. Undismayed, R. R. Bowker wrote Low to say that "nearly 30%" of the vote was excellent, considering that Citizens' Union was a brand new organization running an independent ticket in a city in which vote "outside party lines" was usually only about 10 percent.[57]

The Mugwumpish independence displayed by Citizens' Union in 1897 was not surprising, given the strong Mugwump strain in its membership. Formed early in 1897, the union chose a bolter, R. Fulton Cutting, as its first chairman. The men who made the initial formal contact with Low (himself a Mugwump) about his possible candidacy were Cutting, Carl Schurz, and Joseph Larocque—all three Mugwumps. Numerous other Mugwumps—R. R. Bowker, Horace E. Deming, John K. Creevey, Henry W. Maxwell, William H. Nichols, and William A. White— friends of Low from his days as mayor of Brooklyn, led the fight to secure his nomination in that borough.[58] Richard Watson Gilder headed the union's press and literature committee. In the association's Committee of Organization for 1897 old bolters outnumbered Republicans from the 1884 samples by twenty-six to nine.[59]

The Citizens' Union program was also municipal mugwumpery, emphasizing that "good city government cannot be secured through the agency of existing parties, organized upon National and State issues."[60] An overly strict adherence to this faith in an independent municipal party doubtless undermined efforts at fusion and contributed to Low's defeat in 1897. Yet many Mugwumps shared Horace White's conviction that "the separation of municipal affairs from national politics" was the "essential" principle to which the Citizens' Union owed its existence.[61]

Although these familiar Mugwump themes figured prominently in the early Citizens' Union credo, the organization also represented something of a departure from old anti-Tammany campaigns. Unlike the Committee of Seventy, Citizens' Union was organized as a permanent reform association, and after Tammany's victory in 1897, the reformers kept hammering away at the renewed indiscretions of Croker's machine. In addition, the Committee of Seventy was an elite body of handpicked community leaders, while Citizens' Union was a municipal party that had an open membership and held open platform and nominating conventions.

In 1901, after much discussion, Citizens' Union again named Low as its candidate for mayor. With a boost from President Roosevelt, who intervened behind the scenes, Low also won the Republican endorsement, which he had lacked in 1897.[62] Less prickly about their independence than earlier, the reformers also built a true fusion ticket in 1901, nominating Democrats for several major posts—Edward Grout, controller; Charles V. Fornes, president of the Board of Aldermen; and William T. Jerome, district attorney. Voters swept the Citizens' Union slate into office by a comfortable margin, and the next day one happy reformer recorded in his diary that it had taken him two hours to walk to work what with "stopping to shake hands with everyone."[63]

In both 1897 and 1901 Citizens' Union campaigners mixed traditional appeals to throw the rascals out with endorsements of an incipient progressivism in social matters. Consistent with the precedent set by the Committee of Seventy in 1894 of appealing for cleaner streets, better public schools, and other public services, the Citizens' Union campaigns gave a high

priority to social benefits for voters in the city's poor districts.
In 1897 the first six campaign pamphlets issued by the union
dealt with services rather than corruption—public baths and
lavatories; clean streets; public schools; housing; small parks
and recreation piers; food and shelter; and care for the sick,
the destitute, the aged, and the insane. Some found this emphasis on social services a bit strong. For example, one Citizens'
Union Mugwump reported that "the concessions we have made
to the Labor Men"—such as having endorsed an eight-hour day
for municipal employees—were causing defections among the
more conservative reformers.[64]

During the 1901 campaign the public service side of the
fusion platform was, if anything, given even greater emphasis.
The Citizens' Union election handbook stated flatly: "Mis-
management, favoritism and dishonesty must go. But this is
not enough. *We must have positive benefits for the people.*"[65]
Workingmen were promised a "judicious increase of direct
employment of labor by the city in its public works" and an
effort to pay these employees "the prevailing rate for an 8-
hour day."[66] As chairman of the Citizens' Union committee
on speakers and meetings, Richard Welling was sensitive to the
need for sending men like Jacob Riis to speak in laboring districts. Aware also that "we want to reach the foreigner,"
Welling noted in his diary that "the lower East Side is *the
place to go.*"[67] Felix Adler, a Mugwump with many contacts
in the Jewish community, had earlier done his part by sending
in the names of two East Side Russian Jews with an interest
in reform. As in 1897, settlement workers were enlisted as
speakers in 1901, and this, together with fusion's endorsement
of Jerome, who had a following among East Side residents,
further strengthened the Citizens' Union ticket with immigrants and working-class voters.[68]

At times the Citizens' Union election drive suffered from a
split personality. Fusion speakers pledged extended services
to working-class audiences downtown, while promising economical government to the middle-class voters uptown. The
wealthy Mugwump publisher, George Haven Putnam, later
wrote that the Citizens' Union open membership was generally
a source of strength, though it had the disadvantage of drawing in some "cranks." However to Henry G. Seaver, also a
Mugwump but a single-taxer with more radical views than
Putnam's, the fusion organization was not crankish enough.
Citizens' Union leaders, Seaver asserted, were too interested
in getting "a pure man for mayor" and not enough committed
to changing basic economic conditions within the city by insisting on policies such as municipal "ownership of transportation and other utilities."[69] Tensions were undoubtedly raised
within the fusion camp by competition between these varied
constituencies, but it is important to recognize that all these
groups had some place in the Citizens' Union coalition. Indeed,
the need for the coalition's constituent groups to coexist, if
fusion were to succeed in 1901, helped generate sincere efforts
to cross class and residential lines, especially on the part of
uptown Mugwumps who tried to articulate some of the social
needs of downtown working-class voters.

One of the foremost spokesmen for social progressivism was
R. Fulton Cutting, a Mugwump who served as chairman of the
Citizens' Union in both 1897 and 1901. A patrician by birth
and disposition, Cutting was descended from Robert Livingston and Robert Fulton and had inherited a large fortune
through his family connections. He built a cluster of mansions
for himself and his daughters near Fifth Avenue in the East
Eighties. In public manner he was reserved, always wearing
formal evening attire to night meetings. Every inch an aristo-

crat, Cutting was also representative of those rich New York
Episcopal laymen who, under the influence of Social Gospel
Christianity in the 1890s, came to advocate public social ser-
vice on both pragmatic and idealistic grounds.[70]

In a speech given just after Low's 1901 victory, Cutting denounced past reform movements for savoring "more of Oli-
garchy than Democracy." Patronizing appeals for civic morality had met with limited success, he believed, because reformers made no effort to make city government important to the
average voter.[71] Street Commissioner Waring's great popular-
ity grew out of service, his department bringing a beneficent
arm of the government into every tenement district almost
daily. As an advocate of Social Gospel Christianity, Cutting
predicted that the twentieth century would produce a broad
trend toward expanded government social and economic programs: "There is a swelling tide of human brotherhood that
seeks to express itself through Democratic institutions and the
religion of the Twentieth Century is destined to employ Government as one of its principal instrumentalities for the solution of social issues."[72]

The Low administration followed much the same pattern
as the Strong regime had seven years earlier. There were again
some excellent appointments, and substantial improvements
were made in a variety of areas—the city's finances and its
health and water departments.[73] But the reform administration had its share of troubles. Low's first choice for police
commissioner proved unequal to the task of reforming the
graft-ridden department, a goal that had been high on Low's
list of election pledges. Further, Low's vacillation on the enforcement of excise laws offended partisans of both stricter
and less stringent application of Sunday closure laws. The
mayor also moved too slowly in fulfilling other platform

promises, leaving the reformers bickering among themselves about the results or lack of results under reform. By 1903 the evangelical fervor of the 1901 fusion campaign ("The City for the People!") was lost, and Low was not reelected.[74]

Low's defeat did not immediately bring a return of the days of Tweed and Croker, for both reform and Tammany had changed in the decade since 1892. Croker, who had led the Democrats to two defeats, was forced to step down as boss, and his successor, Charles F. Murphy, was careful not to underestimate the public's desire for good government. In 1903 he outmaneuvered the reformers by naming their 1901 fusionist Democrats, Edward Grout and Charles V. Fornes, on the regular Democratic ticket. The next two mayors, George G. McClellan and William J. Gaynor, were nominally Tammany men during elections, but they conducted themselves with some independence once in office. The public had grown accustomed to a certain level of competence and sensitivity among city officials, and Tammany under Murphy's leadership did not ignore this fact.[75]

The great transformation, however, was among the reformers and in their methods. Many of the Mugwump municipal reformers stopped trying to improve civic life by defying the rules of politics. In 1901 they challenged the boss on his own ground, that of political organization, and won. Instead of simply vindicating their own political purity by bolting a bad candidate, they organized their own political machine, Citizens' Union, and met the tiresome, daily problems of keeping it running. Thus, elite organizations like the City Reform Club were superseded by a mass-membership municipal party. Moreover, the union's appeal was not based solely on demands for a moral revolt against the boss and the machine, for now the reformers also promised to outdo the machine in offering social services to the electorate. Little wonder that the decade from 1892 to 1902, as experienced by a veteran of many municipal campaigns, was a period of the reformers' "development from abysmal ignorance toward sophistication."[76]

Chapter 6

Gilder

The Mugwump Social Reformers

During the 1890s some of the central figures in the Mugwump movement adopted an activist approach to social reform that would hardly have been recognizable as mugwumpery to the orthodox liberal of the previous decade. This activism seemed to depart sharply from earlier Mugwump social programs and to be inconsistent with the bolters' negative attitude toward social legislation nationally. The departure, however, was not so sharp nor the inconsistency so great as it appeared. Indeed, the Mugwump social reformers based even their most innovative proposals on the need to defend long-standing Mugwump values—professionalism, individualism, and the educated man's responsibility for civic well-being. These and other Mugwump themes, therefore, were a source of continuity between the Mugwumps' old and new social programs and the common

ground underlying their response to both local and national
politics.

One of the earliest efforts to deal with urban conditions,
the municipal sanitation movement, illustrates the links between the Mugwumps' social reforms and their professional
impulse. When the Civil War draft riots brought home the
dangers of unameliorated slum conditions, the New York City
reformers set out to improve the health and sanitary environment of slum residents. A Metropolitan Health Bill was passed by the state legislature in 1866. It had been proposed by
Dr. Stephen Smith, the founder of the American Public Health
Association, and drafted by Dorman B. Eaton, a lawyer best
known for his career in civil service reform.[1] The first president of the Board of Health under the new law was Jackson
S. Schultz, a leather-goods manufacturer whose interest in
public health dated from a trip to England in 1860—one of
many instances in which Mugwump reformers drew their in-
spiration for reform from British example.[2] As board president from 1866 to 1868, Schultz brought constant pressure
to bear on street cleaning contractors in an effort to keep the
city's streets refuse-free. Thereafter, every reform administration attempted the hygienic approach to slum problems and
had its dynamic Mugwump leading the crusade for clean
streets, Ripley Ropes under Seth Low in Brooklyn and George
E. Waring, Jr. under Mayor Strong in New York City.[3]

Another early method Mugwump philanthropists and social
reformers utilized was the voluntary charity organization.
Consistent with their credo of public responsibility, Mugwumps
joined the charitable societies in full force. In Buffalo, for
instance, every Mugwump in the 1884 sample was a member
of the Buffalo Charity Organization.[4] Commitment, of course,
did not necessarily mean understanding. In the post-Civil

War era Americans were still in the process of discovering the
nature and extent of urban poverty. Thus the usefulness of
the charity organizations was circumscribed by a tendency to
identify immorality as the source of economic failure.[5] The
charity organizations also drew a distinction between the "de-
serving" poor—those who were physically disabled and incap-
able of earning a living—and the "able-bodied" poor, those
able to work but apparently unwilling to do so. All too often
unskilled and illiterate persons unable to find work were refused assistance, despite great need, because they fell into the
"able-bodied" category.

For all their major deficiencies, the charitable organizations
attempted some programs that foreshadowed later social reforms. The Brooklyn Union for Christian Work, with Seth
Low and Henry Ward Beecher among its leading members,
provided working-class people with a reading room, evening
classes in crafts and languages, a sewing room for girls, and an
employment bureau. The New York Association for Improving the Condition of the Poor, during William Bayard Cutting's
presidency in 1884, advocated governmental social programs—
public parks, free bathhouses, public laundries, and improved
sanitation.[6] Another type of group—the Associated Charities
of Boston and the New York Charity Organization Society—
made its goal coordination of the disparate organizations working in the charity field.[7] These coordinating societies also collected a mass of statistics on social conditions, in a small way
foreshadowing the progressives' love of facts. But in the nineteenth century these statistics did more to educate the middle
class about poverty than to alleviate the problem itself.

Gradually the Mugwumps turned from the moral preach-
ments of the charity organizations to housing reform as a means
of preventing social degeneration in slum areas. From the 1870s,

when Alfred T. White built his first model tenement projects
in Brooklyn, until the New York Tenement House Commission
of 1901, the primary vehicle for the Mugwump housing reformers' efforts was the model tenement movement. The reformers' hope was quite simply that by demonstrating the prof-
itability of good housing through model tenement projects
they would encourage private entrepreneurs to adhere to higher building standards in tenement districts.

Higher standards were certainly desperately needed in late
nineteenth-century slum housing. Under regulations that prevailed until 1902, tenements frequently covered as much as
90 percent of a lot's ground area. Some rooms had no windows, and the only ventilation for many other rooms was provided by windows opening onto an air column between the
midsections of adjacent buildings. The buildings touched at
the front and back to form a "dumbbell" shape. Landlords
were not required to provide running water, fireproof stair-
cases, or toilets and, therefore, rarely did so. A contemporary
concluded that tenements were "a perpetual source of physical
and moral danger."[8]

The leading spokesmen for model tenement reform was
Alfred T. White of Brooklyn, a wealthy fur importer. He
flatly rejected the then "very general misconception that poor
people preferred such surroundings as they had, and did not
desire either sunshine or fresh air, and would not care for
better rooms or domestic privacy."[9] He set out to construct
model tenements with adequate facilities for sanitation, cook-
ing, heat, lighting, and fire protection. After a trip to England
to study the model housing built under Octavia Hill's direction in London, White began his first structures in 1877, ex-
perimentally adopting a whole block rather than just a narrow
lot as the basic housing unit.[10] Built on the outer part of the

block, White's model tenements were in no place more than two rooms wide from front to back. In this way every room had adequate ventilation, and the backs of the structures opened onto a sizeable park in the center of the block.[11]

White had three aims. He wanted to demonstrate to skeptics that working-class people desired good housing. He also felt his model tenements would establish a yardstick by which tenement construction standards and the need for regulatory legislation could be evaluated. Finally, he was determined to prove that owners of well-built tenements could make a profit from their operation, a goal that earned for White's Brooklyn project the nickname "philanthropy for five-percent."[12]

The idea of getting individual builders to change their ways through the profit motive was perhaps the weakest point in White's program. According to Roy Lubove, a modern critic of White's thought, the trouble was that "the model tenement represented no challenge whatever to economic orthodoxy." Thus, White and his fellow reformers placed great reliance on good will, reason, and voluntarism, even though privately financed model tenement ventures were inadequate to the task of reconstructing slum neighborhoods. Lubove concludes that the Mugwump model tenement advocates channeled reform energy away from much needed legislative remedies and in so doing very likely slowed the progress of housing reform.[13]

Voluntarism, while a significant aspect of the reformers' thought, was by no means the sum and substance of their thinking. White, for instance, had few illusions about the power of private action alone to eliminate the social ills of slum districts. As early as 1877 he called for government intervention in the field of housing: "The need of immediate legislation," he wrote, "to control the erection of new houses on sanitary principles, to compel the needed alterations in existing houses and to demolish such as cannot be rendered fit for habitation, is clear."[14]   Coming twenty-five years before effective housing legislation passed in New York, White's words were a far-sighted plea for action. By the turn of the century other Mugwumps—Richard Watson Gilder, R. Fulton Cutting, and Robert Treat Paine—joined White in emphasizing the need for corrective legislation.[15]

In the 1870s and 1880s, however, the idea of reform through example still had great appeal for the Mugwumps. White's theories were soon applied in New York by a model tenement company known as the Improved Dwellings Association. With William Bayard Cutting as its president, the company completed its first tenements in 1882.[16] R. R. Bowker again demonstrated his sensitivity to developing trends in reform circles, publishing an article in *Harper's Monthly* on the housing reform work of Octavia Hill in London and of Alfred T. White in Brooklyn.[17] Shortly thereafter, a group of prominent New Yorkers founded the Tenement House Building Company. Unlike its predecessors, the new model tenement corporation chose to construct its dwellings in congested slum areas like Cherry Street rather than on uptown or suburban lots, but otherwise it followed closely the pattern prescribed by White.[18]

Boston had its counterpart to White in the person of Robert Treat Paine. Coming from one of those seemingly innumerable clans of Bay State Mugwumps—Danas, Quincys, Adamses, and Bradfords—descended from Puritan forefathers, Paine graduated from Harvard and studied law with two of Boston's most prominent lawyers, Richard Henry Dana, Jr. and Francis E. Parker. Retiring from active practice in 1870 at the age of thirty-five, Paine twice sought elective office in the mid-1880s, winning one term in the Massachusetts General Court but losing a bid for a seat in Congress.[19]

Paine's principal civic contribution was in philanthropy, not politics. He was instrumental in founding the Associated Charities of Boston and also in constructing a large number of model tenements in Boston's South End. Throughout his career he backed many projects for workingmen—the campaign for bimonthly payment of workers' wages; a bank that offered low-interest loans to laborers; Trinity Settlement House; and the People's Institute, a meeting place that freely opened its doors to labor union speakers. The prominent Boston settlement worker Robert A. Woods said that although Paine was a patrician whose demeanor was anything but democratic, he nevertheless had "a large share in changing the whole standard of social responsibility in this community."[20] Like the Cutting brothers and Seth Low of New York, Paine was a Social Gospel Episcopalian—not a reform type that would dominate liberal circles after the New Deal, perhaps, but a type that played a major role in the incipient social progressivism of the 1890s.[21]

A significant step toward realistic tenement house legislation in New York came in 1894 when the governor appointed Richard Watson Gilder chairman of a commission to investigate slum housing conditions in New York City.[22] The poet-editor of *Century Magazine* responded with enthusiasm. He personally went to every tenement fire to determine its cause and found that though tenements comprised only 31 percent of the city's buildings, they accounted for 53 percent of the city's fires.[23] With the help of his fellow Mugwump Roger Foster and other members of the commission, Gilder compiled statistics on slum housing construction and on the race, nationality, and income of tenement residents. An exposé of dismal conditions in tenements owned by Trinity Church, a wealthy Episcopalian congregation, gave dramatic publicity to the Gilder Commission's findings.

This and other revelations enabled the indefatigable Gilder to cajole the legislature into passing a modest reform proposal. Higher standards of fireproofing, sanitation, and ventilation were required in structures built after the law went into effect. The work of completely revising New York's housing code and of virtually eliminating the "dumbbell" tenement was to await the efforts of the Tenement House Commission of 1901 under Lawrence Veiller and Robert W. De Forest. But the Gilder Commission had shown the way.[24]

One immediate product of the commission's report was a final effort at model tenement reform. The City and Suburban Homes Company, as it was called, organized with the object of proving that "decent tenement houses can be built and maintained with a return upon the money invested."[25] This prospectus, echoing as it did the goals first espoused by Alfred T. White two decades before, produced the best financed and most sustained model tenement building program on record. With Gilder, White, Bowker, and the Cuttings among the company's major stockholders, the new venture eclipsed all previous model tenement companies in scale and duration, lasting into the 1930s.[26]

Even as model tenement reform reached its culmination in the City and Suburban Homes Company, advanced social reformers were shifting their energies into the social settlement movement. Model tenement projects, like municipal sanitation campaigns, had the disadvantage of being largely mechanistic reforms, which left the slum dwellers' basic social and economic patterns untouched. By contrast, the settlement reformer's goal was often nothing less than neighborhood reconstruction, accomplished through educating immigrant residents of city slums to traditional middle-class American values of cleanliness, industriousness, and self-government. To be sure, the most eminent settlement leaders—James B. Reynolds, Robert A. Woods, Jane Addams, and Lillian Wald—were young men and women who belonged to the rising generation of progressive reformers.[27] But numerous men who had been active in Mugwump politics—R. R. Bowker, Richard Watson Gilder, R. Fulton Cutting, Seth Low, Robert Treat Paine, and Henry W. Farnam—actively identified themselves with the settlement house movement.

The settlement house idea was another English import that flourished in America. In the late 1860s some English college students had begun to spend part of their time residing in London's East End slum districts. By so doing they hoped to learn first hand the problems of lower-class people and perhaps to help the slum dwellers raise their standard of living. Most importantly, the scheme was a form of mutual education intended to break down the barriers between educated middle-class people and the lower classes. In the mid-1880s the first English settlement, Toynbee Hall, was established, and shortly after visiting there in 1886 a young Amherst College graduate, Stanton Coit, opened the first American settlement, Neighborhood Guild, on New York's Lower East Side. R. R. Bowker provided publicity for the fledgling movement in May 1887, publishing an article on his visit to Toynbee Hall.[28]

Settlements proliferated rapidly thereafter, some of the more important being Jane Addams' Hull House (1889) in Chicago, Robert A. Woods' Andover House (1891) in Boston, and Lillian Wald's Henry Street Settlement (1893) in New York City. Everett P. Wheeler, a Democrat, civil service reformer, and Social Gospel Episcopalian in Bowker's circle of friends, made his pilgrimage to Toynbee Hall and then founded East Side House in New York (1891). Among the Mugwumps who contributed to the movement, Felix Adler, the founder and leading figure in the Society for Ethical Culture, had a considerable influence on some of the early New York settlement reformers.[29] Henry W. Maxwell was a Brooklyn Mugwump who endowed a settlement, Maxwell House, in that city. One of New Haven's settlements, originally called Lowell House, was renamed Farnam Neighborhood House in recognition of Henry W. Farnam's central role in the institution's history.[30]

More Mugwumps participated in the University Settlement Society of New York—as Coit's Neighborhood Guild was called when reconstituted in 1891—than in any other single settlement. Felix Adler, R. R. Bowker, Henry Holt, Seth Low, William S. Opdycke, Stephen H. Olin, and Carl Schurz were Mugwumps among the founders of the society. Bowker, Holt, Olin, Low, Richard Watson Gilder, Lewis L. Delafield, and Dr. Richard H. Derby served during the 1890s on the settlement's council, an executive body that concerned itself chiefly with building, financial, and personnel problems. Seth Low was president of the settlement from 1891 to 1901 and Stephen H. Olin from 1902 to 1905. R. R. Bowker, with Henry Holt one of the most active Mugwump council members, was instrumental in bringing the dynamic James B. Reynolds to the settlement as head resident. Reynolds subsequently became a close advisor to Seth Low on social reform legislation during the latter's tenure as mayor of New York. William Potts, a Mugwump civil service reformer, was for a time a resident at the settlement.[31]

The Mugwumps' role in the settlement house movement was one that generally kept them some distance from the day-to-day work at the settlement center. From the Farnam Neighborhood House and University Settlement Society papers, it is clear that Mugwumps were among the larger financial contributors and that they willingly accepted places on the institutions' executive councils. A few also participated in educational programs, giving a speech or two in a public affairs series at the settlement. The Mugwumps, however, were not the reformers who mixed daily with the immigrants or, with the exception of William Potts, the college-educated residents who lived among the working class in an attempt to bring together the "aristocracy of education and the lower half of democracy," as James B. Reynolds once put it.[32]

The Mugwumps, nevertheless, endorsed the main outlines of the settlement house creed. Many accepted, with Richard Watson Gilder, the educational aspect of the settlements, believing as he did that "if the individual child and child's family are influenced, there is the beginning, at least, of an influence on the district."[33] Others felt that the best hope for reducing class conflict and for drawing immigrants into responsible participation in American political life lay with the settlements. The neighborhood centers were, as Henry W. Farnam said, the ideal way "to impress them [the immigrants] with the real spirit of our institutions."[34]

Especially during the Citizens' Union campaign of 1897, Mugwumps counted heavily on settlement workers to create immigrant support for Low, and during the election period there was almost daily communication between the municipal reformers and the settlement leaders.[35] But R. R. Bowker was probably unusual in his desire to draw more of the "younger East Side men" into the work of the council at the University Settlement Society, as was Seth Low in his enthusiasm for organized labor's presence at the main residence. Henry Holt, on the other hand, was doubtless not unique among the Mugwumps in needling Reynolds about the "rainbow chasing in

the supposed behalf of the unemployed" and the "truckling"
to labor violence he thought he detected among the settlement workers.[36]

Social settlements and the other social and municipal reforms of the 1890s were the meeting ground between mugwumpery and progressivism. To be sure, the social and economic proposals of the Russell-Quincy Democrats in Massachusetts and of the civic pressure groups in New York from
1894 to 1901 were a rather rudimentary variety of progressivism, but this was appropriate to a transitional era.[37] Only
gradually did the theme of "progress" creep into the vocabulary of the Mugwump participants in these movements. Joseph
Larocque, chairman of the Committee of Seventy, emphasized
in 1894 that the group's social program was "progressive."[38]
Albert Shaw, the Republican editor and steadfast ally of the
Mugwump municipal reformers, by the mid-1890s ran a column in the *Review of Reviews*, "The Progress of the World,"
which chronicled such developments as Colonel Waring's street
cleaning campaign in New York City.[39] By the first year of
the new century, R. Fulton Cutting, chairman of Citizens'
Union, was saying that "Progress" must be substituted for
"Reform" as the organization's goal.[40]

Just what "progress" meant to the Mugwumps who spoke
of it becomes evident from other words and phrases—"fra-
ternalism," "collectivism," and "social duty"—that entered
their vocabularies about the same time.[41] Cutting, for instance, made it clear that "progress" meant a fusion of traditional values—"democracy," "duty," and "individual lib-
erty"—with social activism. One of the "principal instrumentalities for the solution of social issues" would be government
power. Thus, Cutting insisted, "authority" would be inculcated by popularizing it, enlisting the people's sympathies by

demonstrating a "solicitude for their welfare" through public programs.[42]   In much the same vein, Richard Watson Gilder wrote that the new "civic spirit" he observed under the Strong regime in New York seemed to move "in the direction of interference and paternalism," following the example of municipal socialism in Europe.[43]   To the older Mugwump goal of maintaining civic morality, therefore, the more socially-conscious Mugwumps now joined an instrumentalist credo. Legislation, they declared, should be used to mitigate conditions that estranged workingmen and slum residents from conventional values.

Just how closely the politics of reform were intertwined with the Mugwumps' social and cultural concerns in the 1890s becomes evident from a few examples. Stephen H. Olin, a founder of University Settlement Society and chairman of its council from 1896 to 1901, also served on the Committee of Seventy. As a member of its five-man subcommittee on education, he helped draw up the so-called School Bill of 1896. Although the bill's announced purpose was a social one, improving education in slum districts, it also had immediate political ramifications. Under the reformers' program control of the city's schools was taken out of the hands of locally elected trustees (who tended to be Tammany sympathizers) and given to a board of distinguished citizens appointed by the mayor from the city at large.[44] Similarly, the efforts of R. Fulton Cutting and Seth Low to build an effective uptown-downtown coalition within Citizens' Union were the logical political corollaries of their concern, as Social Gospel Episcopalians, with reducing conflict between social classes.[45]   Richard Watson Gilder's conviction that environment was a crucial influence on the development of character manifested itself both in his role as president of the Free Kindergarten Association

from 1891 to 1894 and in his plunge into municipal politics
as chairman of the tenement house investigation of 1894.[46]

Why this shift from anti-bossism to social progress came in
reform circles when it did and whether it was experienced by
most Mugwumps as a rejection of their old reform ideas is difficult to ascertain. Among the Mugwumps, a crucial influence
was their residence in the Northeast's largest cities. In the
1890s in New York, for example, the growing perception
among the Mugwumps and their relatively well-to-do Yankee
neighbors that the city below Fourteenth Street was a world
apart certainly shaped their political thinking. Social Gospel
Christianity, urban school reform, the settlement house movement, and tenement house reform all grew out of this con-
frontation with the city.[47] Among the Mugwumps, however,
the adoption of these new causes was generally not accompanied by an abandonment of older concerns—civil service, tariff
reform, and sound money. While influenced, therefore, by
the emerging awareness of urban conditions, the Mugwump
social reformers continued to approach public life from a
familiar cultural standpoint, one that had as its hallmarks an
attachment to cosmopolitanism, metropolitanism, and professionalism.

Professionalism was the touchstone of the Mugwump drive
for educational and sanitary reform every bit as much as it
had shaped their civil service reform convictions. Deeply committed to the late nineteenth-century professional association
movement, the Mugwumps sought to restore deference to
professional standards in municipal affairs. Their particular
targets were those public functions like education and sanitation that since the 1840s had been placed in the hands of local
electorates, though the Mugwumps and their allies felt they
rightfully should be administered by professionals and experts.

This is not to say that the professional impulse was free of political considerations, for the two forces—professionalism and the politics of municipal and social reform—actually went hand in hand. In the Metropolitan Health Bill campaign, the reformers explicitly aimed at supplanting the influence of elective officials with control by doctors and public health experts. Similarly, in the battle over New York's schools, the Mugwump educators (Felix Adler, Stephen H. Olin, and Seth Low) bent every effort to replace the school board system based on trustees elected from local wards with an appointive board which would place "power and responsibility" in the hands of "professional schoolmen."[48]

The Mugwumps also manifested a marked preference for a metropolitan perspective in municipal affairs. The analogous characteristic among the Mugwump professionals was an interest in nationalizing their professions by establishing a multitude of "American" or national professional societies. Again, the Mugwumps' cultural perspective and their role in the community's life coincided with their politics. It was metropolitan park boards that Charles Francis Adams, Jr. and Sylvester Baxter in Boston and the energetic Francis Goodwin in Hartford found so productive and meaningful.[49] Seth Low was the chairman of the commission that drew up the Greater New York Charter and was a spokesman in its ranks against any tendencies to decentralize the new municipal government.[50] Much earlier the Mugwump public health experts had supported the move for a Metropolitan Health Board on the grounds that New York's public health problems were too involved to be dealt with by each municipality separately. Significantly, in health, school, and tenement house reform, Mugwumps depended on state legislation rather than local political constituencies to achieve their ends.

Indeed, on the whole, the Mugwumps did not have deep
roots in communities and neighborhoods and derived their
reform ideas more from cosmopolitan than local sources.[51]
British precedent shaped the Mugwump approach to housing
reform, factory laws, social settlements, corrupt practices and
secret ballot legislation, and civil service reform. By contrast,
the Mugwumps' rivals (characteristically described as "partisans" or "the interests") were more likely to take their political signals from the immediate needs of the local community.
The Mugwumps feared that such partisan and locally based
programs might not serve the "general interest," whereas their
opponents found the cosmopolitan viewpoint a bit too ab-
stract—rather more a matter of the head than the heart. How
else could the laboring men in Colonel Waring's department
take his statement that he would like to spend less on wages
because only "a few hundred men benefit" from high wages
in the department, while "thousands" of taxpayers, including
the workingmen, would benefit from the tax savings?[52] Then
there was Simeon E. Baldwin's poignant observation that although few "interests" would benefit directly from lower tariff duties on their products, he regretted that the benefits of
tariff reduction were going unrecognized by "the community
at large."[53]

At the turn of the century there were signs that the long-
standing preeminence of localistic influences in American
society was receding somewhat. Cosmopolitan forces prevailed within the new urban-industrial environment—a national market economy based on large-scale corporate organizations and dependent on specialists and experts. A new
middle class of managers, professionals, and white-collar
workers was emerging within this setting, and its political
needs, especially as expressed at the federal level, would

differ considerably from those of a pre-urban, pre-industrial America.

Although the Mugwumps were a segment within this new middle class, they were scarcely in a position—given their recent political experience—to dictate the direction of events in the new century. In Massachusetts and Connecticut, the electorate had repudiated the leadership of the Cleveland Democrats in the mid-1890s, leaving the old Mugwump-Democratic coalitions in those states divided and ineffectual. Even in New York City, where the Mugwumps and their allies had won some notable victories in the 1890s, it seemed that their hybrid type of genteel progressivism was now likely to be superseded by progressivism of a full-blown sort. Just as the old Liberal Republicans of the 1860s and 1870s had been shouldered aside by the young Mugwumps of 1884 during the Cleveland Democracy's heyday, so too by 1901 one Mugwump noticed that the "present crowd" of reformers—long on "executive ability" but new to the politics of reform—was displacing the "old war horses."[54] The new "crowd" of young recruits could look forward to the twentieth century with brash self-confidence. For the Mugwump veterans, encumbered by their connection with lost causes (Clevelandism and anti-imperialism) and scarred by many battles fought and only a few won, the future was less certain.

Chapter 7

Deming

Mugwumpery & Progressivism

Any discussion of mugwumpery's relation to progressivism
must take into consideration the limitations inherent in the
traditional label for the twentieth century's first decades. A
"progressive era" it may have been for some, but not for all.
Blacks, for instance, certainly did not experience the period
as one of general progress. If, on the other hand, progressivism
is made applicable to a narrow group only, there is a risk of
being challenged by those who wish to nominate another group
as the "real" progressives of the era. Finally, some historians
have recently rejected any talk of a single, coherent progressive movement as misleading, an argument founded on the
fact that almost no ethnic group, region, or interest group
went totally untouched by the progressive spirit.[1]

There were, nevertheless, people in the period who used the

term "progressive" with some confidence. For most, it seems
to have referred less to a movement than to a viewpoint characterized by a concern with "progress." The problem of progress, as Richard Abrams has written, was how to "enjoy the
fruits of material progress without the accompanying . . .
erosion of conventional values and moral assumptions on
which the social order appeared to rest."[2] To be sure, there
was a conservative quality underlying this concern for "conventional values" and "social order," but there was also a de-
cidedly liberal element in the progressives' commitment to
correcting social injustices and to protecting "human dignity"
in the new industrial-urban society.[3] Even for the self-defined
progressives, of course, progressivism had many shades of meaning, and to make matters yet more complex the mainstream
progressives often augmented their strength by cooperating
with other groups—socialists, farmers, workingmen, urban
ethnics, and even political bosses—in temporary coalitions for
particular reforms.[4]

As for mugwumpery, the Mugwumps and their reform concerns were scarcely visible in the new age of reform. Civil
service reform and anti-imperialism were not major aspects of
the progressive thrust. The tariff was still the subject of heat-
ed debates, but midwestern Republican insurgents, not eastern Mugwumps, now led the way in the battle for tariff revision. Moreover, the foremost progressives were younger and
more widely distributed geographically than the now aging
eastern Mugwumps. (For a comparison of the surviving Mugwumps' socioeconomic profile with that of the progressives,
see Appendix B.) By 1903 the Mugwump organizations—the
Massachusetts Reform Club, the National Civil Service Reform
League, the New York Reform Club, and the New York City
Club—had seen their best days. Mugwumpery seemed only a

memory from another century, the "politics of nostalgia."
"By 1900," it seemed, "the genteel reformers had effectively withdrawn from modern America. . . . Repelled by
the developments transforming America—industrialization,
urbanization, and especially immigration—they seemed to
cling all the more firmly to a vanishing age."[5]

The apparent discontinuity between mugwumpery and
progressivism was sharpened by the disappearance of Mugwump reform as a movement after 1900. With the decline
of the anti-imperialist crusade, the Mugwumps for the most
part went their separate ways. Many remained loyal to the
old causes and corresponded with old friends, but these
ties no longer added up to a recognizable movement within
American reform. The death of the Mugwump bolt's older
leaders—George William Curtis in 1892, E. L. Godkin in
1902, and Carl Schurz in 1906—contributed to mugwumpery's declining visibility. The dispersal of the old reformers
was further manifested in the organizations that arose to
promote progressive causes—the National Civic Federation
in 1900, the New York Child Labor Committee in 1902,
and the American Association for Labor Legislation in 1909.
Individual Mugwumps joined these associations, but the
groups could not be accurately described as Mugwump in
either membership or philosophy.

Although the trail of the Mugwump becomes fainter in
the twentieth century, that does not mean there is no trail
to follow. It is true that if the progressive's own testimony
were accepted at face value, the impression that the new
liberalism owed little to the past would remain unchallenged.
Progressives liked to characterize their ideas as "new"—
whether they referred to the "New Freedom," the "New
Nationalism," the "New History," or the "New Economics."

Yet even the surface facts about progressivism conflict with this supposed discontinuity.

Many of the political reforms advocated in the progressive era were logical extensions of Mugwump proposals. The city manager plan, short ballot, and bureaus of municipal research were not all that far a cry from Mugwump causes—civil service reform, the secret ballot, and corrupt practices acts. Even direct democracy, fought for as a dramatic innovation in the struggle against bossism in Oregon, Wisconsin, and elsewhere, had largely unacknowledged precedents in the Mugwump states of Massachusetts and Connecticut where initiative and referendum were long-established practices. Little wonder, then, that a Mugwump group, the National Municipal League, so readily adopted and advocated these supposedly "progressive" reforms.[6]

Advanced social progressives rightly claimed that their demands for social welfare and regulatory legislation were departures from the genteel liberals' program. But in their strictures against laissez-faire liberalism and the supposed moralism, amateurism, and elitism of the Mugwumps, these progressives were frequently attacking viewpoints that they had recently held themselves. As George Mowry has pointed out, many a progressive "had been, at least until 1900, a conservative Republican satisfied with William McKinley and his Republican predecessors," and to this point Richard Abrams adds that many of the outstanding progressives—Jane Addams, Robert LaFollette, Lincoln Steffens, George Norris, and Louis D. Brandeis—had been extremely unsympathetic to populism in the 1890s.[7] The new liberalism, in other words, was not readily apparent before 1900 among the future progressives. Indeed, the social tensions of the 1890s led many future progressives to react to immigration and urbanization in a no less conservative way than the anti-progressive members of the Mugwump group.

The relation of the old to the new liberalism might better be measured by what the Mugwumps did than by what the progressives said. Those Mugwumps who survived until the peak of progressivism in 1910 and afterward offer the historian an excellent way of gauging the Mugwumps' response to the progressive era. (For a list of these men, see Appendix C.) Admittedly, those old bolters who lived until the second decade of the new century represent only a remnant, and a somewhat younger segment, of the 1884 bolt's membership. It is, of course, impossible to say from the survivors' behavior in the progressive era how those who did not survive would have reacted to the period. Nevertheless, the survivors provide an invaluable resource for testing whether the dismay and defeatism so frequently attributed to the Mugwumps from the 1890s onward was, in fact, characteristic of their careers in the 1900s.

One statement may be made immediately: progressive reform organizations offered the Mugwumps a second chance for civic leadership, even though fresh faces tended to dominate the groups. Seth Low, for example, very likely achieved more for reform as president of the National Civic Federation from 1908 to 1916 than he had as mayor of New York City earlier. Henry W. Farnam was an organizer and early president of the American Association for Labor Legislation, a leading agency of social progressivism. Felix Adler was one of the most active members of the New York Child Labor Committee and an early chairman of the national child labor association's executive committee. Moorfield Storey was a founder and president of the National Association for the Advancement of Colored People (NAACP), as well as being one of its most forceful representatives in legal battles during the 1910s and 1920s.

The National Municipal League advocated municipal progressivism under a succession of Mugwump presidents—James C. Carter from 1894 to 1903, Charles J. Bonaparte from 1903 to 1910, and William Dudley Foulke from 1910 to 1915.

The Mugwump response to the new era was by no means always a "progressive" one, and even the progressively inclined survivors differed among themselves. The varieties of reform ranged from the demands of good government advocates for municipal efficiency to the conviction of social progressives that social justice was the major goal to be sought. Mugwumps who wanted to regulate business or institute direct democracy measures held something of a middle position in the progressive spectrum. There were also many Mugwump survivors who rejected progressivism in all its varieties.

No surviving Mugwump was more cross-grained and Tory than Barrett Wendell, though the Harvard professor of comparative literature had a few rivals in extreme anti-progressivism. Wendell, another Mugwump, wrote, "had no sympathy with what we call modern ideas—especially of social justice. . . . He clung to rule of the best."[8]   Already in 1893 Wendell had been gloomy about the decline of his America, feeling that "Yankees are as much things of the past as any race can be. America has swept from our grasp. The future is beyond us." By 1916 he dejectedly concluded, "I am like a Federalist in Jefferson's time, a sound Whig in Jackson's, or an honest Southerner in Lincoln's."[9]   Like Henry Adams, who shared his penchant for hyperbole, Wendell felt too much deference was given the masses and majorities in American politics. The progressives, he believed, exacerbated the worst qualities of majoritarian government with their talk of direct democracy and social justice. He found both Roosevelt and Wilson honest and well meaning, but he felt that except in wartime their energies were not directed toward what he thought of as the crucial national goal of social regeneration.

All the unreconstructed Mugwumps among the surviving bolters shared Wendell's distaste for the new era to some degree, even those who remained active on behalf of genteel reform. The older Mugwump reform organizations—the City Club, Citizens' Union, and the New York Reform Club—continued their work, albeit at a reduced tempo. Generally these groups avoided social reform issues and advocated efficient, honest municipal government. The New York Reform Club, once primarily concerned with national issues, gradually became an anti-Tammany Democratic association, focusing largely on New York City politics. This brought it into competition with the City Club.[10] Both were elite groups that no longer aspired to organizing municipal reform parties and that limited their reform efforts mainly to conducting investigations and publishing critical evaluations of municipal departments, budgets, and appointments. The Citizens' Union continued to endorse some municipal candidates, occasionally with success, but the troubles Seth Low's administration had experienced and the disappointment of Low's defeat in 1903 demoralized many who had followed the fusion banner.[11]

For some of the survivors, though probably a minority, it seemed that the Mugwump goal of nonpartisan political independence had been either illusory or self-defeating. John B. Leavitt, a New York lawyer, reported that he had "quit" seeking nonpartisan purity when he found during the Low years that the "Citizens' Union leaders often did the very things, for which they denounced Tammany, made political bargains equally vicious, and knew they had to do it, or go out of business."[12] Judge Robert Grant's retrospective belief was that far from gaining influence the bolters of 1884 had lost it, while

Theodore Roosevelt and Henry Cabot Lodge, the Republican independents who had stayed in the party, had prospered politically. For those Mugwumps like Charles J. Bonaparte who returned to the Republican party, the enduring mugwumpery of a Carl Schurz seemed wrong-headed conduct that dissipated the old liberal's former influence. And Barrett Wendell, in one of his frequent fits of despondency, wondered whether the "decencies of comfortable corruption" were not preferable to the horrors of Bryanism, which he deemed "the fruit of reform."[13]

Many of the Mugwump tariff reformers, usually men with Democratic leanings—R. R. Bowker, Josiah Quincy, Charles Francis Adams, Jr., and Louis Windmuller—resolutely kept the fight for revisionism going. At times it seemed to go slowly, however. Graham McAdam, campaigning in 1912 for Wilson and a lower tariff, had trouble financing his efforts; Louis Windmuller was the lone Mugwump left on the New York Reform Club's Tariff Reform Committee in the same year; and Erving Winslow, a Boston merchant and anti-imperialist, at times during the early 1900s was holding the American Free Trade League together almost single-handedly.[14] When George Haven Putnam came to his aid and instigated a reorganization of the league in 1916, he found the ranks of the revisionists greatly depleted and some of the veteran reformers hesitant to resume battle. Even Putnam, as president, seemed to worry more about the possibility that the league would be captured from within by pacificists and single-taxers than he did about defeating the protectionists outside the organization.[15]

The ranks of the National Civil Service Reform League (NCSRL) continued to include many Mugwumps before World War I. Some of them—William Dudley Foulke and Charles J.

Bonaparte were good examples of this—moved into progressive reform causes also. Others like Nelson S. Spencer, a New York City lawyer who was president of the City Club for a decade after 1916, exemplified the opposite tendency. Spencer actively backed all the old Mugwump causes—municipal purity, civil service, and tariff reform—yet did not join the newer progressive reform associations.[16] Similarly, Richard Henry Dana III, a Cambridge lawyer and an officer in the NCSRL throughout the period, was never happy with progressivism. Except for civil service reform activities, Dana essentially withdrew from political affairs in the twentieth century. When he did vote, he occasionally manifested a mugwumpish preference for political stalemate. As another unreconstructed Mugwump put it: "I am never perfectly pleased with *sweeping* victories in politics as they are sure to have bad effects."[17]

Of all the Mugwump reform associations, none made the transition to the progressive era more smoothly than the National Municipal League. As an organization, the league was lukewarm on social justice legislation, but it adopted and promoted nearly every progressive political reform. Horace E. Deming was representative of the Mugwumps in the NML who greeted enthusiastically proposals for direct democracy measures. In his book, *The Government of American Cities* (1909), he contended that the failure of municipal government in the United States was "due not to the defects of democratic principles . . . , but to an utter failure to apply them."[18] Deming had been the chief architect of the league's "First Municipal Program" (1898), a model city charter that emphasized a strong mayor system, the elimination of partisanship from municipal affairs, and a short ballot plan. By the time his book was published, he had also become an admirer of the

commission system of city government and of proposals for
applying initiative, referendum, and recall techniques.[19]

In 1916 the league, under the direction of William Dudley
Foulke, published a revised version of its model city charter
of 1898. The Mugwump suspicion of party control in city
government was still very much in evidence. The party primary and party ballot were to be eliminated. Civil service
reform was strongly endorsed. In order to undermine the
strength of partisan ward bosses, the league urged that city
councils be elected at large rather than from smaller districts.

The newest element of the model charter was the backing
it gave to a city manager system of governance. Referendum,
recall, and initiative were favored by a majority of the committee that drew up the league platform. A firm stand on
municipal ownership of utilities was avoided; however, the
city's right to control its streets and public services was asserted and the conclusion drawn that there should be no "obstacles to municipal ownership and operation of public utilities."[20] Although consistent with earlier Mugwump convictions regarding municipal efficiency and nonpartisan rule,
the 1916 edition of the league's program, especially in its
widely adopted proposal for a city manager system, indicated
that the Mugwump creed was being updated to fit the twentieth century.

On a smaller scale, the New York Bureau of Municipal Research exemplified a largely Mugwump-sponsored innovation
that was fully in the progressive spirit. Initially sponsored by
the Citizens' Union under the name "Bureau of City Better-
ment," the bureau eventually provided the city with "a professional research staff attuned to the principles of scientific
management."[21] Its sponsors were convinced that thorough
budget hearings and careful accounting practices could foster

more effective city administration regardless of which party was in power. R. Fulton Cutting proved himself as sensitive to the progressive's love of statistics and desire to substitute "knowledge for indignation" as he had earlier been to the new era's demands for social justice.[22] He personally donated the funds to get the bureau under way and served as one of its original directors. In 1907 it was reorganized as the Bureau of Municipal Research—a name that another Mugwump director, Richard Watson Gilder, suggested would more sharply identify it as "dispassionate, scientific, and removed from partisan intentions."[23] A logical outgrowth of the earlier Mugwump professional impulse, the bureau quickly caught on and became a showcase for the application of expert knowledge in municipal administration.

Other civic reform groups used public exposure and the dissemination of information for more directly political ends than the bureau's technicians did. Just after the turn of the century a Committee of Fifteen in New York City, with three Mugwumps—Felix Adler, Austen G. Fox, and George Haven Putnam—among its members, conducted an investigation of vice and police corruption that helped dislodge Richard Croker from control of Tammany Hall and elect Seth Low mayor.[24] In 1903 Boston Mugwumps contributed to organizing a Good Government Association (GGA) to check the city Democratic machine's power. The GGA's first major victory came in 1909 with the establishment of a permanent city Finance Commission, which for the next decade conducted "hard-boiled" investigations of municipal departments. Under the leadership of another Boston Mugwump, Louis D. Brandeis, the Public Franchise League fought from 1900 to 1905 to make Massachusetts public utilities more responsive to the public's welfare.[25]

The fruits of these citizen campaigns were mixed. At times the Good Government Association, in the name of saving tax dollars, seemed bent on defending the status quo rather than modernizing the city's services. In retrospect, George Haven Putnam concluded that the long-range gains from the Committee of Fifteen's investigation of vice in New York City were at best small ones. Yet Brandeis's league scored a "phenomenal" victory in 1905, forcing the Boston Consolidated Gas Company to agree to reduce its gas rates if it increased its dividend.[26] An early director of the Bureau of Municipal Research spoke for many participants in these public interest campaigns when he said that their goal was not "penny-pinching" or obstructionism but the essentially democratic and progressive goal of reestablishing citizen participation in municipal affairs. Attention to the mechanics and mixed results of these ventures, he argued, should not obscure the fact that for a time they "set fire to conviction, aspiration, and imagination."[27]

At the other end of the political spectrum from most of the good government reformers were the social progressives. The surviving Mugwumps did not join the social justice organizations in such large numbers as they did the National Municipal League, the City Club, or the National Civil Service Reform League. Perhaps only 5 percent of the active members of the New York Child Labor Committee, the American Association for Labor Legislation, and the National Association for the Advancement of Colored People were old bolters; yet they were often active members, especially in the early history of these groups.[28]

The New York Child Labor Committee, formed in 1902, was an instant success. In 1903 four major labor reform acts passed the New York Legislature, leading one historian to conclude that the committee was "largely responsible for the high

standards of child labor legislation achieved in New York."[29]
Beginning in 1904 the reformers shifted their attention to the
problem of enforcing the new laws. In the following two
years they broadened the scope of their campaign by supporting the establishment of a National Child Labor Committee
(NCLC) and its work for federal legislation in the field. The
eminent pediatrician, Abraham Jacobi, a veteran advocate of
higher health care standards for children, and Ansley Wilcox,
an upstate lawyer and close friend of Theodore Roosevelt,
were two New York Mugwumps who backed their state committee's early efforts. In addition, the drive for regulating
child labor conditions received strong endorsements from
other Mugwump survivors—most prominently R. Fulton
Cutting, Richard Watson Gilder, R. R. Bowker, Charles W.
Eliot, and Henry W. Farnam.[30]

Of all the Mugwumps, Felix Adler made the greatest contribution to the child labor reform movement. An original
member of the New York committee, he was one of its mainstays in testifying before legislative committees. When the
national committee was organized, he became chairman of its
executive committee. The founder of the Ethical Culture
Society of New York in 1876 and for many years a professor
of political and social ethics at Columbia University, Adler
wholeheartedly endorsed a wide range of social progressive
causes—civil rights for blacks, rural credits for farmers, tenement house reform for slum dwellers, and protective legislation for workers.[31]

At the heart of Adler's thinking was a great sympathy for
weaker and exploited groups in society. For Adler the end
of reform always remained an individual one, the moral development of individual citizens. But he believed that the
economic interdependence of men in an industrial society

made it impossible to protect the "rights of the individual" without first offering legislative protection to disadvantaged groups such as child laborers. In swinging sharply away from economic individualism, Adler also rejected what he saw as the lockstep authoritarianism of socialism. He liked to call his middle way between laissez-faire capitalism and socialism by the name "functionalism" because through it he tried to recognize a functional balance between individual rights and social needs.[32]

One of the most advanced social progressive societies, the American Association for Labor Legislation (AALL), was founded in 1906. From the first it sought a diverse membership that included labor leaders (Samuel Gompers and John Mitchell), leading academicians (Richard T. Ely and Henry W. Farnam), and representative reformers (Jane Addams, Lincoln Steffens, and Florence Kelley). The AALL never supported specifically "union" demands—closed shop, higher wages, and anti-injunction laws. Initially it took a fairly academic approach, emphasizing the need to collect information regarding labor conditions. Rather quickly, however, the AALL developed a "comprehensive program of labor reform": health insurance, anti-child labor laws, regulation of women's hours and working conditions, workingmen's compensation, factory health laws, and minimum wage standards—all of which were in the group's program before 1917.[33]

Henry W. Farnam was a founder and the second president (from 1908 to 1911) of the AALL. He inherited a competent staff from Richard T. Ely, who had based its operations in Madison, Wisconsin. Farnam, therefore, acted as a liaison with eastern sympathizers, providing invaluable assistance in drumming up memberships and financial support among eastern academicians and reformers. Among Farnam's former

Mugwump associates, John Frankenheimer, John B. Leavitt, Seth Low, and Charles Richardson were early members of the AALL, and Henry Holt, Stuart Wood, Felix Adler, and Louis D. Brandeis lent financial or moral support at critical moments.[34] Just how far a departure this was from the old Mugwump creed is readily evident in Farnam himself. A student of William Graham Sumner's in a period when "Sumner was strongly under the influence, as we all were, of evolution, especially as interpreted by Herbert Spencer," Farnam now led an organization whose program for legislative intervention in economic matters placed it in the vanguard of social progressivism.[35]

Those Mugwumps who became early members of the NAACP were also well in advance of their era's position on social justice. During the Gilded Age many antislavery liberals had abandoned their attempts to legislate black civil and political rights in the South. Discouraged or disgusted with the results of Reconstruction, they came to hope that the generosity of Southern whites and a gradual improvement of the blacks' economic standing through self-help plans would solve the race issue. But by the progressive years, the condition of the blacks in America had reached its nadir.

The blatant affront of Jim Crow laws passed around the turn of the century and a major race riot in Springfield, Illinois, in 1908 awakened the old antislavery men to the failure of racial policies that relied on the good will of whites for their success.[36] A national conference on racism was proposed, and of the sixty names on "The Call" for the meeting, four were Mugwumps—Samuel Bowles of the *Springfield Republican*, William Hayes Ward of *The Independent*, William Lloyd Garrison, and Horace White.[37] After a preliminary conference in 1909, the NAACP was established in 1910. Moorfield Storey, a resourceful champion of black civil rights, was selected as the NAACP's first president. Throughout the group's early years Storey lent his legal talents freely to the organization, winning a particularly dramatic victory in the Supreme Court decision against the grandfather clause (*Guinn v. the United States*, 1915).[38] William Hayes Ward kept the columns of *The Independent* open to W. E. B. Du Bois, by 1910 the only major white magazine to which the black leader had access. Another Mugwump, Felix Adler, was almost from the first in the forefront of the NAACP counterattack on racism. Thus, the bolters of 1884 were among those whose careers constituted a thread, albeit one that was "frayed and almost broken in places," of continuity between antebellum abolitionism and twentieth-century civil rights movements.[39]

Not all the surviving Mugwumps accepted the NAACP position on the race issue. Charles W. Eliot, the president of Harvard, for a time contended that segregation was acceptable if the separate facilities were equal. Charles Francis Adams, Jr. argued that blacks had had an opportunity for social and economic advancement during Reconstruction but had failed to take full advantage of it. What reason was there to think, Adams asked, that any better results would come from a second period of civil rights agitation?   Poultney Bigelow was even more hostile to the civil rights movement, repeatedly affirming his conviction that Anglo-Saxons were superior to any "African, Hebrew, or Hibernian." Charles C. Jackson wanted Harvard's dormitories segregated, and the Reverend George R. VandeWater went through tortured maneuvers to keep his New York City Episcopalian congregation lily-white, though it was on the edge of Harlem's growing black community. Even the formerly radical abolitionist, Thomas Wentworth Higginson, while sympathetic to blacks, was nevertheless slow to catch the spirit of the new civil rights movement.[40]

For all that some Mugwumps acted illiberally toward blacks in the progressive era, it would be inaccurate to characterize the Bigelow, Jackson, and VandeWater position as "the" Mugwump point of view. If anything, the surviving Mugwumps were more likely than most men of their class and time to take a liberal stand on the race issue. Storey, Adler, and the four Mugwump signers of "The Call" are outstanding examples of this, of course, but even among the surviving bolters in no way associated with the NAACP's early days, there were men who earnestly supported racial justice. Charles J. Bonaparte wrote a scathing retort to a civil service reformer who thought blacks should be excluded from federal positions in the South. There was no democratic basis for doing so, Bonaparte replied. To say that the people of the South did not want blacks in office was to show a callous disregard for the feelings of black southerners.[41] George S. Merriam, a Mugwump author from Springfield, Massachusetts, stated flatly in his book *The Negro and the Nation* (1906) that "race prejudice, deep-rooted and stubborn," not black inadequacy, was the greatest obstacle to black advancement. Merriam, along with Moorfield Storey and Charles J. Bonaparte, called for federal aid to education as a first step toward aiding black Americans.[42]

Another issue of the period, though not one on which a single "progressive" position can be defined, was the debate over federal immigration policy. On the whole, surprisingly little attention was given to the subject by the surviving bolters. As late as 1910, one socially progressive Mugwump could write that he had not given the matter of immigration restriction much thought.[43] Most Mugwumps who did arrive at a position on the question before World War I felt, with Oscar S. Straus and Seth Low, that limited exclusions of certain undesirable classes (the insane, criminals, and the like) was appropriate, but that such exclusionist devices as the literacy test or national quotas were inadvisable.[44]   Charles W. Eliot and William James were outspoken foes of immigration restriction, condemning the movement for its "Anglo-Saxon cant" and its undemocratic rejection of ethnic variety. Thomas Wentworth Higginson was an advocate of ethnic pluralism and a critic of nativism. A marked sympathy for immigrants already in the United States was displayed by R. R. Bowker and R. Fulton Cutting, even though their role in combating the drive for restriction was not a major one. Many Mugwumps condemned West Coast discrimination against Orientals, though the problem was a remote one for all but a few surviving bolters.[45]

The opponents of open immigration were more vociferous and better organized than its defenders. Some Boston Mugwumps, particularly Thomas Bailey Aldrich and Barrett Wendell, constantly fulminated against the new immigrants as un-American intruders.[46]   Other Bay State Mugwumps, more in sorrow than in anger, noted with Gamaliel Bradford, Jr. the passing of "our old Boston, the Boston that we loved and that seems to be forever departed."[47] Thus, although the term is used broadly, "Mugwumps," along with free traders and old Cleveland Democrats, comprised the core group of the early Immigration Restriction League in Boston. Henry Lee Higginson, Robert Treat Paine, Henry Lee, and George S. Hale among the Bostonians, Henry Holt and Charles S. Davison in New York, and Franklin MacVeagh in Chicago supported the league's campaign for restricting immigration through use of a literacy test.[48]

On the immigration question, as on most progressive era issues, the striking thing about the Mugwump response was its diversity, but this does not obviate the need to attempt some generalizations about the overall relationship of mugwumpery to progressivism. Three very rough groupings provide a starting point for analyzing the responses of those surviving Mugwumps whose views are known:[49] 1) "Non-progressives," a category combining the outspokenly anti-progressive Mugwumps with the unreconstructed Mugwumps who did not, insofar as can be found, identify with any of the new causes of the progressive era; 2) "One-issue progressives," that is, those survivors who adopted at least one element of progressivism—conservation, federal regulation of public health, or direct democracy measures—while otherwise apparently not departing from Mugwump causes; 3) the broadly progressive survivors who advocated a wide range of progressive causes, including those who openly identified themselves as progressives and those who were advanced social progressives.

As shown by Table 7.1 below, the largest number of Mugwumps were found in the first group (anti-progressives and old-line Mugwumps), though they comprised only 40 percent of the total sample. Group two (the "one-issue progressives") was the smallest, only 27 percent of the sample. The remaining 33 percent of the survivors fell into group three, the broadly progressive Mugwumps. Taken together, the progressively inclined Mugwump survivors (groups two and three) outnumbered the "non-progressives" (group one) by a ratio of three to two.[50]

No major differences in socioeconomic traits or party preferences separated the progressively inclined Mugwumps from the non-progressives. The median birthdate (that date at which half the group had been born) differed only slightly, the progressively inclined group's median date being 1850 and that of the non-progressives 1847, making the latter just a bit older on the whole in 1910 (sixty-three years of age as opposed

Table 7.1
*Political Views of Eighty-Two Mugwumps
in the Progressive Era*

Group Designation	Individuals	Percent	
1. Non-pro-gressives	33	40	
2. One-issue progressives	22	27 ⎫	These progressively in-clined groups total 49
3. Broadly pro-gressive men	27	33 ⎭	individuals or 60 percent of the sample.

to sixty). Occupational distribution within the two groups was essentially identical—lawyers, publicists (including authors and editors), businessmen, and educators being the order of priority for both groups. In no occupational category was the percentage difference between the progressively inclined and the non-progressive group greater than 3 percent, a negligible variation given the size of the sample. Also, the survivors' party affiliation does not seem to have had a determining influence on their adoption or rejection of progressive ideas. The proportion of Republicans and Democrats among the progressively inclined (54 percent Republican to 46 percent Democrat) and the non-progressives (58 percent Republican to 42 percent Democrat) were very similar, and both were close to the percentages for the survivor group as a whole (56 percent Republican to 44 percent Democrat). As far as the Mugwumps were concerned, therefore, neither party could claim it had a monopoly on progressive feeling.[51]

One place where a clear distinction did appear between the progressively inclined Mugwumps and the non-progressives was in the area of office-holding. Generally speaking, the more

progressive group held offices of greater importance—three
cabinet posts (Charles J. Bonaparte, Franklin MacVeagh, and
Oscar S. Straus); a governorship (Simeon E. Baldwin); and a
Supreme Court justiceship (Louis D. Brandeis). Most of the
posts held by the anti-progressives and the undiluted Mugwumps were judgeships (appropriately enough in an age of
judicial conservatism) or (consistent with their continuing
devotion to the merit system) membership on civil service
commissions.[52] By contrast, the appointive posts held by
men who to a degree adjusted their thinking to progressive
ideas had a wider range of specialization—William R. Dudley
(California Park Commissioner); David Starr Jordan (California Fish and Game Commissioner); Talcott H. Russell (Connecticut Workmen's Compensation Board); and Horace White
(New York Commission on Speculation and Commodities).

It was not necessary to endorse progressivism in order to
find a niche in public affairs, of course, even though the early
1900s go under the "progressive era" label. Anti-progressives
like Barrett Wendell and Henry Lee Higginson, for instance,
carried on private wars against progressive tendencies by pen-
ning letters and articles. Higginson's views still carried weight
in financial circles, as did the opinions of Charles Francis
Adams, Jr. on a variety of economic issues. Although Moorfield Storey was not progressive on most questions of federal
legislation, he continued his outstanding career in civil rights
agitation through the progressive era. Richard Henry Dana
III and Frederic J. Stimson, two Bay State Mugwumps who
had little love for progressivism, nevertheless remained active
in civic life—Dana within civil service circles and Stimson from
within the Massachusetts Democratic organization. Especially
for the unreconstructed Mugwumps among the survivors,
the old causes—civil service and tariff reform—were no less

relevant to the new era than the old, and they continued to pursue these convictions of long standing.

The 60 percent or so of the survivors who adopted some element of progressivism, whether of the one-issue or the broad variety, came to it in diverse ways.[53] Municipal reform campaigns, both political and social, were a crucible within which many Mugwumps gradually changed their views of what was necessary to protect civic order and conventional values. In economic matters, the rapid consolidation of giant trusts in the 1890s and the labor violence that accompanied that development prompted some Mugwumps, particularly the nationalists like Seth Low, Oscar S. Straus, and Franklin MacVeagh, to accept the government as a third force in labor-capital relations.

Henry W. Farnam exemplified yet another Mugwump type, the intellectuals for whom exposure to newer currents of thought led them to abandon the laissez-faire creed of the 1880s. Even such mainstays in the laissez-faire liberals' ranks as William Graham Sumner and Horace White modified their former views in the light of twentieth-century conditions, though Sumner, in particular, could scarcely be called a progressive even of the one-issue type.[54] But departures from the older liberalism's more restrictive provisos were aided by a cosmopolitan exchange with British thinkers on a host of subjects—social settlements, municipal socialism, labor legislation—just as earlier trans-Atlantic influences had strengthened the Mugwump intellectuals' devotion to Manchester liberalism and to Herbert Spencer's Social Darwinism.

The way in which the surviving Mugwumps' careers often served as direct, personal links between mugwumpery and progressivism should not be allowed to diminish the integrity of each reform impulse in its time. To mugwumpery's emphasis

on the need for the best men to guard civic morality, progressivism added a stress on the government's role as the major
agent for maintaining social order by ameliorating economic
injustices. The ethical dimension remained strong in progressivism, but among progressives it was often ethics hardened
by events into a more pragmatic outlook. Many progressives
were not so ready as the purist Mugwumps had been to dismiss political parties as useful agencies of reform. Indeed,
progressives frequently moved from condemning bad individuals—whether unionist, capitalist, or slum dweller—to advocating legislation that would meet legitimate demands made by
these groups.

The consequences of the progressive perspective were evident in an older Mugwump organization, the National Municipal League. Gradually the NML shifted its goal from one of
creating municipal efficiency by throwing out the rascals to
creating efficient administration by working with whomever
was in.[55] As less emphasis was put on individual moral responsibility and more on the malfunctioning of the system,
the tone of municipal reform changed. It was a change of
style that even the progressively inclined Mugwumps found
quite jarring.[56]

Mugwumpery and progressivism were not identical, therefore, nor was Mugwump reform the major source of progressivism. Some sense of the proportional influence of Mugwumps within progressive circles may be gained from realizing
that in Otis L. Graham, Jr.'s sample of 400 leading progressives only 12 (3 percent) were clearly identifiable as Mugwumps.[57] (See Appendix B for a comparison of the Mugwump socioeconomic profile with three samples of progressives.) The proportion of old bolters found in Graham's sample
is consistent with available evidence regarding Mugwump

participation in the new progressive reform organizations. It should serve as a reminder that mugwumpery was regional in scope whereas progressivism was national, that progressives were generally much younger than the surviving Mugwumps, and that new civic-action organizations superseded those dominated by the old bolters during the new reform age.

From the somewhat narrower perspective of what happened to the Mugwumps in the twentieth century, however, these conclusions might be phrased in another way. Despite political defeats in the 1890s, the divisions within their ranks, and the challenge of a greatly changed political environment in the early 1900s, many of the Mugwumps, non-progressive and progressively inclined alike, remained active in public life. For the surviving bolters, mugwumpery had not been a dead end, and for a majority it had become a path to progressivism.

Chapter 8

Straus

Mugwumps & National Politics after 1900

Among the surviving Mugwumps the progressive era was sometimes the most prosperous and productive period of their public careers.[1] Although too few in number to have a decisive
impact on the era's politics, individual Mugwumps were frequently beneficiaries of a political environment in which
parties accepted the word "reform" as respectable again.
Moreover, from the Mugwump viewpoint, the era's presidential politics produced more presentable candidates, Bryan
excepted, than any time since Cleveland's advent on the scene.
The former bolters differed greatly in their opinions of Theodore Roosevelt and Woodrow Wilson, but nearly all of them
felt a greater affinity for the Harvard-educated Square Dealer
and the former president of Princeton than they had for the
likes of Harrison, Blaine, McKinley, and Bryan.

When Roosevelt became president in 1901, it opened the
avenue of political preferment to his Mugwump admirers.
Oscar S. Straus was exceptional among this group in having
been an anti-Bryan Democrat before becoming secretary of
labor and commerce from 1906 to 1909 under Roosevelt.
Roosevelt's other Mugwump appointees were bolters who had
returned to the Republican party before 1900. Charles J.
Bonaparte was Roosevelt's choice for a succession of major
posts—member of the United States Board of Indian Commissioners from 1902 to 1904; secretary of the navy from
1905 to 1906; and attorney general from 1906 to 1909. Seth
Low received the Republican party's backing for his 1901
fusion campaign in large part because of the president's intervention on his behalf. Roosevelt selected William C. Sanger,
a close friend of Elihu Root, as assistant secretary of war from
1901 to 1903. Joseph B. Bishop and William Dudley Foulke
were other Mugwump members of Roosevelt's inner circle
who received federal appointments, while numerous other
old bolters, such as Ansley Wilcox and Richard Welling—most
of them from patrician and Harvard backgro·nds like Roosevelt's—basked happily in the reflected light of their friend's
power and influence.

Friendship with the Rough Rider in the White House created an intense partisanship for his cause. William Dudley
Foulke, the Indiana lawyer, was something of a purist on
civil service matters, but he found little fault with Roosevelt's
patronage policies. "I was a warm friend of Mr. Roosevelt
and I believed in him absolutely," Foulke wrote later. Even
in the months before the 1908 Republican convention when
appointive positions were clearly going to the president's
allies, Foulke allowed his fears for the purity of the public
service to be allayed by strong letters from the president and

Secretary Bonaparte, himself a Mugwump with a long record
in civil service battles. Although Foulke was seldom so ingenu-
ous in his assessment of other political leaders, his defense of
Roosevelt was almost unqualified—"daring frankness," "utter
fearlessness," an "accurate sense of justice," and "immense
human sympathy" being just a few of the positive qualities he
ascribed to his hero.[2]

Affection for Roosevelt drew Mugwumps from varied backgrounds into the Rough Rider's circle. James B. Bishop had
been a reporter for the *New York Evening Post* before accept-
ing an appointment to the Panama Canal Commission. Roosevelt detested the free trade, anti-imperialist "goo-goo" reformism of the *Post* and saved some of his choicest epithets for the
"falsehoods" purveyed by that "dishonest" sheet. Yet Roosevelt shared Bishop's inveterate optimism just as much as he
was repelled by the pessimistic temperament of Bishop's long-
time chief, E. L. Godkin, an old Roosevelt-baiter. Bishop
thus not only received an appointment under the Roosevelt
administration but became its court historian, writing Roosevelt's authorized biography and an admiring book on Charles
J. Bonaparte's public career.[3] Bonaparte, the grand nephew
of Napoleon I, was an upper-class Baltimore Catholic much of
whose career was devoted to struggling against the Democratic
machine in Maryland. Oscar S. Straus, by contrast, was a
German-born Jew who made his fortune in a New York City
mercantile business and had turned Democratic after 1884,
serving as Cleveland's minister to Turkey.[4]

Philosophically, Roosevelt's Mugwump allies were mostly
nationalists. In foreign affairs they believed national power
and prestige required an expansion of America's role in world
affairs. Many, however, did not believe expansionism necessi-
tated an overseas empire. In domestic affairs they broke with

the economic policies of McKinley Republicanism and advocated government supervision of business. Modernists, they accepted organized labor and large corporations as logical counterparts in a stable industrial society. Thus Attorney General Bonaparte, for instance, followed his chief's lead in regulatory matters. He brought several trusts under suits by the Department of Justice and condemned irresponsible wealth. "Our big, strong, greedy over-prosperous trusts are animals of the like [pig] order," he said in 1906, but he did not condemn wealth or bigness as such. The Square Deal, he made it clear, was "not to make rich men poor . . . but to make rich men law abiding."[5]   Good corporations and law-abiding men of wealth would be left alone, just as law-abiding unions would be treated as a legitimate and progressive force for social stability.

Desirous of bringing business under federal supervision, the Rooseveltian Mugwumps did not initially emphasize direct democracy measures or social justice legislation in their program. Oscar S. Straus was an early president of the Direct Primary League, and a few Roosevelt men like Ansley Wilcox and Seth Low advocated child labor laws and labor legislation early in the progressive years.[6]   But most of Roosevelt's Mugwump allies felt that a stable economic order would bring democracy and social justice. It was simply necessary to establish a proper relationship between three forces—business, organized labor, and the federal government, with the latter representing the "third force" of the public interest.

Of all the progressive organizations in which Mugwumps were active the National Civic Federation (NCF) best embodied the Rooseveltians' ideal of countervailing forces. Organized in 1900 at the end of a decade marked by industrial strife, the group tried to bring together a triparte division of members.

Prominent businessmen joined along with union leaders (notably John Mitchell and Samuel Gompers) and representatives of the public sector—college teachers, publicists, and government officials—in an effort to bring economic harmony.

Frequently characterized as "conservative" because of the role Mark Hanna, August Belmont, and other well-known capitalists played in its early work, the NCF in actuality diverged sharply from the anti-union business conservatism of the nineteenth-century sort.[7] During the period from 1901 to 1907, the federation concentrated on mediation and arbitration, repeatedly finding its efforts obstructed by recalcitrant businessmen of the National Association of Manufacturers variety. Thus, although NCF labor and business members alike condemned labor violence, they also criticized anti-union business as disruptive to public order. "I think the day has gone by," Seth Low lectured one such corporate official, "when the great corporations can decline to confer with the representatives of unions. . . ."[8]

As the Roosevelt administrations progressed, the NCF and its Mugwump members became more pronounced in their support of federal regulation of the economy, including protective legislation for labor. Initially, the federation had depended upon the private influence of its prominent members to encourage the resolution of differences between capital and labor through arbitration or mediation. Trade agreements reached in this way, however, came increasingly under attack. Anti-union interests went to court to have such agreements struck down as constituting restraints of trade. It was also clear that corporations did not have to accept the federation's good offices in resolving labor disputes. They could simply ignore the NCF's definition of beneficial business practices. The federation's voluntaristic approach, in other words, was proving insufficient to check what Oscar S. Straus called the "social war" of strikes, lockouts, and injunctions.[9]

By 1907, therefore, Straus, Foulke, and other Mugwumps in the federation concluded that the federal government was the "only power" that was "fully capable" of regulating the trusts and protecting labor from corporate abuses.[10] One of Seth Low's first duties as NCF president in 1908 was to campaign for a federation-drafted revision of the Sherman Anti-Trust Act, the so-called Hepburn-Warner Bill. The bill provided for "a system of examination, inspection, and supervision" of corporations and organized labor. Companies and unions could register merger plans or trade agreements with the Bureau of Corporations (or the Interstate Commerce Commission in the case of railroads). This information would be subject to review for possible violations of federal law and corrective action. Even more crucial for the NCF's union members was a provision in the Hepburn-Warner Bill exempting labor from prosecution under antitrust laws for organizing and striking.[11]

Despite a close alignment with Roosevelt's views, the federation achieved only partial success in its legislative efforts. The president endorsed the Hepburn-Warner Bill, but it died in committee. More successful were later campaigns led by Seth Low for a revised national railroad arbitration law, the Newlands Act of 1913, which Low called the NCF's "most spectacular victory" during his term as its president. An improved workmen's compensation act passed in New York state in 1913 with an important boost from the NCF.[12] The Wilson administration's Clayton Act and Federal Trade Commission Act were consistent with the federation's New Nationalist philosophy, but the NCF had only a minor role in their passage. On the whole, however, the federation's endorsement of a national incorporation law, its persistent defense of

labor's right to bargain collectively, and its support for exempting unions from antitrust prosecution firmly established its
credentials as a progressive force. It also represented a dramatic break with the older Mugwump view that large corporations and labor unions, especially the latter, constituted dan-
gerously anti-individualistic departures from a laissez-faire
economic system.

Just how far New Nationalism took the old bolters away
from the genteel reformer's creed is evident in the dismay
with which other Mugwumps in Roosevelt's circle viewed the
evolution of his thought. Henry Adams was pleased when his
friends Roosevelt, Henry Cabot Lodge, and John Hay (Roosevelt's secretary of state from 1901 to 1905) came to power.
Adams continued to complain about twentieth-century life
and to contend that he was living a posthumous existence
in the new era, but he was obviously delighted to have his
Washington, D.C. residence humming with discussions among
administration insiders. In a short time, however, Adams was
grumbling about the president's antitrust policy and com-
plaining that "Theodore's vanity, ambition, dogmatic temper,
and cephalopodic brain [are] all united on hitting everybody,
friend or enemy, who happens to be near."[13]

Another of Roosevelt's patrician friends, Henry Lee Higginson, the Massachusetts banker and philanthropist, similarly
resisted the administration's shift from McKinleyism to the
Square Deal. Higginson repeatedly called for self-regulation
by business rather than government intervention. Having more
faith in the business community than Adams did, Higginson
nevertheless followed a parallel path in evincing a negative
attitude toward both progressive economic ideas and the rising force of organized labor. As Roosevelt's New Nationalist
predilections became more evident, Higginson's "ineradicable

distrust of legislation" naturally led him to oppose the Rough Rider's political ambitions.[14]

Not all the Mugwumps' opposition to Roosevelt stemmed from a dislike of his more progressive side. The president was also suspect because of his expansionist views. In 1904, for example, many Republican and independent Mugwumps voted for Alton B. Parker—among them Carl Schurz, Thomas Wentworth Higginson, Horace White, and Charles S. Davison—largely because they saw little hope for early Philippine independence so long as the Rough Rider was in the White House. Democratic Mugwumps shared this hostility to Roosevelt's bellicose nationalism, even though they favored Parker on other grounds as well, finding his candidacy a welcome respite from the Bryanites' control of the party. In 1908 many Mugwump anti-imperialists swallowed hard and backed Bryan rather than vote for William Howard Taft, a supporter of Roosevelt's Philippine policy. Among the Mugwump survivors as a whole, however, antipathy to Bryan remained very strong, with the result that Taft received a higher percentage of the Mugwump vote than any presidential candidate since Cleveland in 1892.[15]

Taft soon lost most of his Mugwump admirers. In 1908 Henry Adams had declared that Taft was "the only thoroughly satisfactory candidate I ever had." But Taft's antitrust policy and political ineptness soon had Adams grumbling that the corpulent chief executive was acting as though he were "feeble-minded."[16] By the end of Taft's term only a few Mugwumps remained his supporters. Some believed, with Barrett Wendell and Thomas R. Lounsbury (a Yale professor of literature), that he was closest to their conservative views; others like Henry W. Farnam and Franklin MacVeagh voted for Taft because they felt his administration had produced

many "solid achievements."[17] MacVeagh, who had served as
Taft's secretary of the treasury, was the only Mugwump to
campaign actively for the president, arguing that Taft's record
was more solidly progressive than Roosevelt's. Given the fact
that MacVeagh had at times been dismayed by his chief's political obtuseness and resistance to progressive ideas, MacVeagh's
public endorsement, though completely admiring, was likely
made with some private reservations.[18]

Among Roosevelt's Mugwump allies midterm doubts about
Taft soon turned into hostility. They were soon convinced
that the Rough Rider's personally designated successor was
abandoning his mentor's policies, especially in conservation
and tariff reform. Indignantly they rose to the former president's defense. William Dudley Foulke, after a period of trying to advise Taft, joined the opposition. By 1912 Foulke
was bitterly denouncing the president's patronage policies and
filling his letters to Roosevelt with invective about the "pre-
posterous" views of the "inbeciles" (*sic*) in the Taft administration.[19]

When their efforts to win the Republican nomination for
Roosevelt failed, Roosevelt's old Mugwump friends around the
country supported his plunge into Progressive insurgency—
Foulke and Lucius B. Swift in Indiana, Bonaparte in Maryland, and Straus in New York. Straus accepted the Bull
Moose gubernatorial nomination in New York, and Charles
Sumner Bird did likewise in Massachusetts. The two Mugwumps
ran energetic campaigns for progressive reform, though both
men were very recent converts to Roosevelt's full-fledged New
Nationalism. For Straus, in fact, the campaign was mainly a
labor of love, undertaken to advance the cause, as he put it,
of "our Inspired Leader." Bird, for all that he headed the
Bull Moose ticket in Massachusetts, was in some ways a

patrician reformer closer to the moderate reformism of Roosevelt's Square Deal than to the program of advanced social reform the Progressive party now proposed.[20]

Very few Mugwumps had supported the Bryan-led Democracy in 1908, but four years later more Mugwumps voted for Wilson than for Taft and Roosevelt combined. Unfortunately, confirmed votes are known for only 10 percent of the survivors; yet in this small group, 54 percent voted for Wilson and 46 percent for Taft and Roosevelt together. This almost exactly reversed the survivors' normal party preferences in the 1900s (56 percent Republican, 44 percent Democrat) and made it the only presidential election from 1896 to 1916 in which a majority of the Mugwumps voted Democratic.[21]

The Mugwumps' antipathy to Roosevelt ran deep, and some of it rubbed off on his former protégé, Taft, causing them to distrust him as well. The anti-imperialists, for instance, saw the 1912 election as a chance to defeat both their old opponents in a single stroke. While Taft was regarded by most Mugwumps as an inept leader, Roosevelt was seen as a positive danger. To Henry Lee Higginson, it was Roosevelt's "nonsense" about the trusts that led him to vote for Wilson, and, to Barrett Wendell, Roosevelt was advocating doctrines of social change that were "dangerous" in the "radical extreme." According to Moorfield Storey, Roosevelt was the most "dangerous" man in the United States because his predilection for a militant foreign policy would produce a concommitant centralization of domestic affairs. Often, however, the surviving Mugwumps were simply troubled by the former president's flamboyant temperament. These men mistrusted "Mr. Reckless Roosevelt," as one old bolter called him, because of his "love of risky adventure" and his seeming incapacity for "quiet reflection."[22]

Woodrow Wilson's brand of progressivism, announced as the New Freedom, was not sharply defined during the campaign, but the very ambiguity of the New Freedom program allowed Mugwumps of widely differing views to see it as the ideal antidote to Republican rule. At one end of the political spectrum were state's rights Democrats—Simeon E. Baldwin, Frederic Bancroft, and Gamaliel Bradford, Jr.—who heard in the New Freedom slogan the revival of a nineteenth-century party battlecry. State interests, they hoped, would be protected against the encroachments of a centralized federal bureaucracy. For the Democratic tariff reformers, "freedom" meant a reversal of the trend toward greater protectionism. R. R. Bowker, Graham McAdam, Josiah Quincy, and James L. Cowles, therefore, were just a few of the veteran tariff revisionists who rallied to the New Freedom banner.[23] "Freedom" also could seem to imply independence for the Philippines (as it did to the Anti-Imperialist League executive committee, which endorsed Wilson) and a new freedom for blacks (as it did to many men, black and white, in the NAACP).[24] And to the chief architect of the New Freedom philosophy, Louis D. Brandeis (the only Mugwump who was drawn into Wilson's inner circle), the concept embodied a broad range of regulatory and social justice legislation.

Diverse though the Democratic Mugwumps were in their political views, they had at least one experience in common. All had shared in the Democratic party's long Diaspora following the electoral disasters of 1894 and 1896. In Massachusetts the surviving Mugwumps often had led the party but in years when there was no place to lead it. Pro- and anti-Bryan wings of the state party, with George Fred Williams in Bryan's camp and Josiah Quincy and Frederic J. Stimson championing the opposition, squabbled constantly over control of the Massachusetts Democracy. But although each side had its day, the campaigns were futile ones against sure Republican winners. Only the energetic Brandeis achieved a clearly positive record in these years, becoming a central participant in the reform drive between 1905 and 1908 that gave Massachusetts "a record of progressive legislation probably unmatched anywhere in the country."[25]

Democratic fortunes began to revive in 1910, as the career of Simeon E. Baldwin illustrates. Out of politics from 1893 to 1910, first as an associate justice and then as chief justice of Connecticut's Supreme Court of Errors, Baldwin reached the mandatory retirement age of seventy in 1910. Later in the year he was nominated for governor by the victory-hungry Democrats. Party managers counted on Baldwin to draw both Democratic and independent Republican support, something which did indeed happen. Baldwin's fellow bolters of 1884—among them George D. Miller, Roger Foster, and Walter Learned—joined forces with Democratic regulars to give him a narrow victory statewide, even though the legislature remained under Republican control.[26]

As a traditionalist, Baldwin was suspicious of progressivism's tendency to enhance federal power at the expense of a small state such as his own. During his campaign he dwelled on the old tariff reform issue, and once in office he defended the New Haven Railroad against federal antitrust actions, a position that offended more progressive Connecticut Democrats. He was not trying to revive the past, however. During his two terms (from 1911 to 1914) he pressed a moderately progressive program through the legislature—an updated corrupt practices act; a workmen's compensation act (drafted by another Mugwump, Talcott H. Russell); a state civil service law; a public utilities commission bill; and ratification of the

seventeenth amendment providing for the direct election of
senators.[27]   When Baldwin ran for the United States Senate
in 1914, he lost partly because he failed to attract progressive
voters. Nevertheless Baldwin's willingness to support reform
measures while governor showed that by the Wilson era his thinking had evolved well beyond the Mugwump mind of the 1880s.

  The Wilson years gave many Democratic Mugwumps an active role in national affairs much in the same way that the
Roosevelt administrations had earlier resuscitated the political
fortunes of Roosevelt's Mugwump allies. For Louis D. Brandeis "the years 1910 to 1915 were the fullest of [his] public
life."[28] His part in shaping Wilson's thought during the 1912
campaign and the early years of the new administration is
well known, and Wilson's choice of Brandeis for a Supreme
Court justiceship was a fitting capstone to the latter's political service. Simeon E. Baldwin was also at the peak of his political career, albeit state rather than national affairs was its focus.
Three of the surviving Mugwumps were awarded diplomatic
posts by the Wilson administration—Robert U. Johnson,
Frederic J. Stimson, and George Fred Williams—while Charles
W. Eliot reportedly turned down the chance to be American
ambassador to Great Britain.[29] Other old bolters held elective
or appointive office at the state or local level. For some Mugwumps, then, progressivism was "an encore for reform" just
as the New Deal would be for some progressives.[30]

  Before the outbreak of World War I in August 1914, the
lines established in the Mugwump camp by the 1912 election
remained essentially unchanged. The Rooseveltian Mugwumps
remained cool toward Wilson without being reconciled with
the regular Republicans. The president's followers, meanwhile,
were almost uniformly admiring of his early application of
New Freedom ideas. The Underwood Tariff and the Federal

Reserve Act won their approval, and the establishment of the
Federal Trade Commission aroused no great opposition in
the ranks of Wilsonian Mugwumps.[31] The only negative responses to Wilson's first two years in office came from anti-
imperialists who regretted his inaction on the Philippine question, advocates of black civil rights like Storey who deplored
the administration's racial policies, and men of the Simeon E.
Baldwin and Henry Lee Higginson sort who were critical of
Wilson's few antitrust actions.[32] The net effect of the New
Freedom program, therefore, was negligible in winning or
losing Mugwump support.

Judging from the Mugwump survivors' reaction to Wilson's
policies in 1915 and 1916, historians have been correct in believing that these were the critical years for his administration
and for the history of progressivism nationally. The 1914 fall
elections had revealed that without an active Bull Moose insurgency to split the Republican vote, the Democrats were in
trouble. As the minority party, they would be likely to lose
the presidential election. Furthermore, the war in Europe and
border tensions with Mexico raised a whole set of new issues.
Foreign policy would obviously be more crucial in 1916 than
it had been four years earlier.

World War I accelerated the rapprochement between the
Republican factions, a most ominous development from the
Democratic viewpoint. Most Rooseveltian Mugwumps con-
verted to preparedness, and as they did so their ardor for
domestic progressivism dwindled. Within six months after
the war's outbreak, many old Bull Moose leaders were convinced that not progressivism but the need to be "sufficiently
armed" was the "paramount" national issue.[33] Charles J.
Bonaparte invoked ghosts of ancient party conflicts in condemning Wilson's neutrality policy as flabby and reminding

his audience that Jefferson and Madison were past Democratic
failures in foreign affairs. Even so earnest a peace advocate as
Oscar S. Straus fell prey to this spirit and soon advocated
"reasonable preparedness," saying that the war was a "rude
awakening" to him. Anti-progressive Republicans—among
them Thomas Lounsbury, Barrett Wendell, and Poultney
Bigelow—welcomed the war, seeing it as a means to social
regeneration through the reassertion of their class's leadership.[34] Ironically, the New Nationalist urge to expand federal action for progressive ends had so recently split the Republican party. Now nationalism, with its emotional emphasis on America's power and reputation in world affairs, was
serving as a rallying point for the anti-Wilson forces.

Wilson moved decisively to build a new Democratic coalition, seeking to attach the social progressive segment of the
Bull Moose movement to his cause. Early in 1916, the president suddenly reversed himself and advocated passage of several progressive measures that had been bottled up in Congress
mostly for want of his endorsement. In swift succession,
Wilson nominated Louis D. Brandeis for the Supreme Court
and pressed for enactment of a rural credits bill, a national
workmen's compensation law, federal child labor legislation,
and also what became the Adamson Act, establishing the
eight-hour day as standard for the nation's railway workers.
The result, Arthur Link reports, was that "practically the entire
leadership of the advanced wing of the progressive movement"
swung to Wilson in 1916.[35] Notably this did not include the
Rooseveltian Mugwumps, none of whom had been in the vanguard of the Progressive party's social justice element.

Wilson's bold reorientation from New Freedom to social
progressivism disturbed some of the Democratic Mugwumps.
In particular, the Adamson Act reawakened their fears of

special interest legislation and of knuckling under to labor.
George Haven Putnam wrote a Democratic friend that "Wilson's action in regard to the labor issue has, in my opinion,
placed him outside the pale. . . . He has deliberately, and
for political purposes, created precedents that will do great
harm to the country."[36]   Frederic Bancroft and Gamaliel
Bradford, Jr., two unreconstructed Mugwumps, also abandoned the Wilson banner on the grounds that the president's domestic policies were unsatisfactory. Henry Lee Higginson, a
Republican who had voted Democratic in 1912, was annoyed
by Wilson's handling of the labor and preparedness questions
and switched to Charles Evans Hughes, the GOP standard-
bearer. Moorfield Storey, an independent who had frequently
backed Democratic presidential candidates, turned against
Wilson because of the Brandeis appointment, to which he had
been inalterably opposed, as well as the Adamson Act and the
race issue.[37]

Other Mugwump survivors who might have voted for Hughes,
had the election been held in August just after the Adamson
Act's passage, supported Wilson in November. By that time
the shock of Congress having imposed a pro-union solution
in a labor dispute had worn off, and many were more disturbed by the Republican nominee's uninspiring performance during the campaign.[38]   On the whole those Mugwumps who did
finally abandon Wilson for Hughes were peripheral figures in
the Wilson camp—either independents or particularly conservative Democrats. Approval of Wilson's middle course on peace
and preparedness led most Democratic Mugwumps to vote for
Wilson. Disapproval of the President's first administration
took its toll, however, and the attrition was sufficient to drop
Mugwump support for the Democrats below the 50 percent
level again.

A handful of the old bolters defended Wilson's record virtually without qualification, frequently contrasting his moderate course in foreign affairs with the belligerent tone of the Republican campaign in 1916. Felix Adler declared that the tendency among Republicans was toward a military or quasimilitary ideal. This attitude, he felt, led to government centralization domestically and to exploitation of weaker peoples in international affairs. By contrast, Wilson, in Adler's opinion, had fought for the rights of individuals in his domestic policy (the Adamson Act was an unfortunate exception) and had shown respect for the "independence and self-determination" of other nations by not going to war with Mexico.[39]

Charles W. Eliot, now retired from the presidency of Harvard, wrote an admiring endorsement of Wilson for the *Atlantic Monthly*. He praised every aspect of Wilson's domestic policy from the Underwood Tariff to the federal income tax law, the Rural Credits Act, and federal child labor legislation.[40] In foreign affairs Eliot was no less approving of Wilson's course, contending that the president had kept the nation out of war with Mexico and extracted concessions from Germany on American neutral rights. Far from driving all the Mugwumps away, therefore, the dynamic evolution of Wilson's policies in 1915 and 1916 had solidified the support of at least a few Mugwump survivors for his administration.[41]

The Wilsonian Mugwumps' support for the president's foreign policy represented a shift from their pre-1900 ways of thinking that was almost as dramatic as that demanded by his more progressive domestic decisions. At the time of the Spanish-American War, most of the old bolters had been deeply disturbed by United States military intervention in Spain's handling of the Cuban situation. The shock of American aggression led some Mugwumps to seek new ways of substitut-

ing the rule of law for the rule of force in international disputes. These men supported the First Hague Conference (1899)
and its establishment of a Permanent Court of International
Arbitration.[42] But World Court arbitration was a voluntary
process, and much as uncooperative corporate officials forced
the National Civic Federation to abandon its dependence on
voluntary arbitration of labor-capital disputes, the outbreak
of World War I brought home the failure of non-compulsory
arbitration of international disputes. By early 1915, therefore, many Mugwumps had come around to feeling that the
best means of preserving world peace was American participation in a world parliament of nations.

The League to Enforce Peace, formed in June 1915, became
the chief agency through which proponents of the world parliament promoted their cause. Notably, it was at the organization's May 1916 meeting that Wilson first announced his support for the League of Nations idea.[43] Notably, too, the
League to Enforce Peace was neither isolationist nor pacifist.
It accepted the need for American involvement in world affairs, and—as its name implied—most of its members believed
that the League of Nations must be prepared to enforce peace
through economic and military sanctions, if necessary.

While always a minority within the League to Enforce Peace,
numerous Mugwumps were involved in the organization's
formative period. Four of the old liberals signed the pro-
visional call for the league—Oscar S. Straus, David Starr Jordan, R. Fulton Cutting, and William Dudley Foulke. Charles
S. Davison of New York and Solomon B. Griffin of the *Springfield Republican* served on committees in the national organization, while Henry W. Farnam, Frederick P. Fish, Moorfield
Storey, and Charles W. Eliot were particularly active in their
state branches of the league.[44] As with the social progressive

associations, however, Mugwump membership in the league was not in excess of 5 percent, and the group's national leadership—William Howard Taft, A. Lawrence Lowell, Hamilton Holt, and Irving Fisher—was not Mugwump in character.

The league idea split the surviving Mugwumps along familiar lines. Although membership in the League to Enforce Peace and advocacy of preparedness were not thought mutually exclusive, those Bull Moose progressives who followed the league banner found that their views created some friction with their old chief, Theodore Roosevelt, who adamantly opposed the world parliament idea as unwise and unrealistic.[45] Consistent with their long-standing nationalism, men like Charles J. Bonaparte and Franklin MacVeagh opposed the League of Nations scheme as potentially contrary to America's national self-interest; at the opposite extreme, Moorfield Storey and David Starr Jordan, both inveterate idealists and activists in the League to Enforce Peace, expressed doubt that force could ever secure peace or democracy.[46]

Old free traders—R. R. Bowker, James L. Cowles, Nelson S. Spencer, and Arthur W. Milbury—rallied to the cause practically without reservation. They were attracted less by the mutual security aspect of the proposed League of Nations program than by its promise of a rule of law through a world court and an international parliament. These institutions would promote international peace by eliminating barriers between nations much as free trade would do. "Peace on earth, good will among nations," one tariff reformer wrote in support of the League of Nations, "is to be secured through a covenant between nations like our constitution between states and by free trade and other freedoms equally without and within our own borders."[47]

Despite their desire for peace, many old bolters felt ambivalent about United States neutrality, especially if American nonparticipation meant Allied defeat. Most would have shared the feelings of Robert U. Johnson, former editor of *Century Magazine*, who wrote, "believer in peace and arbitration as I am . . . I feel almost like writing a song against peace—that is, till the prestige of the German military autocracy is destroyed."[48] Given this deep hostility to the German leadership and fear for the well-being of the Allies, most Mugwumps readily accepted American entrance into the war, especially when couched in Wilsonian idealism. This was no war to conquer weaker peoples, they believed, but a struggle to save democracy. Only a few lone souls among the surviving bolters dissented, believing that the price in civil liberties was too great to pay or that "all war is in itself a confession of failure," especially in a democracy. For, as David Starr Jordan explained this view, "war making is no fit work for democracy. The two cannot permanently exist together."[49]

Those Mugwumps who were physically able to do so supported the war effort. Almost to a man the surviving Mugwump members of Harvard's classes reported that they were doing some sort of war-related work—George D. Ayers and William A. Purrington served on the Army Registration boards in their respective cities; Francis B. Tiffany made "Four Minute" talks to movie audiences in Minnesota and "did work in aid of the suppression of disloyalty"; William C. Lawton worked as a postal censor specializing in "uncommon languages"; and William C. Sanger and Arthur E. Walradt along with many others were involved in American Red Cross programs.[50] Robert Grant and other authors joined in war writers groups to build a patriotic national spirit. Albert Strauss, a wealthy New York banker, went to Washington, D.C., as a "dollar-a-year man" of the Bernard Baruch sort,

donating his skills as an expert on international finance to
the government. Samuel A. Eliot organized a chaplain's
training camp, and J. Franklin Jameson joined with other
leading historians in supplying historical data for the Committee on Public Information's campaign to solidify war feeling.[51]

What the progressive crusade had done to revive viable reform careers for many Mugwumps, the war did to derail them
from liberal causes. Henry W. Farnam observed that he and
other members of the National Civil Service Reform League's
executive committee were so involved in Red Cross work or
other war-related activities that they hardly had time to attend
to civil service problems. Thus, when William Dudley Foulke
complained that wartime government bureaus were operating
practically without scrutiny from civil service reformers, he
had to acknowledge that even his closest friend in reform
circles was so absorbed in the war effort that he had practically withdrawn from the civil service movement.[52]   Meanwhile other reform groups—the Free Trade League, the
National Civic Federation, the American Association for
Labor Legislation, and the National Child Labor Committee—
found that expanded federal control over wartime business
conditions, laboring men's rights, and virtually every aspect
of the economy made their particular programs seem narrow
or irrelevant by comparison.

Although it was scarcely noticeable at the time, the deflec-
tion from reform to other concerns had actually begun before
American entrance into the war. One study of social progressivism in New York notes that the movement reached
its peak there in 1914.[53]   Nationally, many of the advanced
progressives' cherished programs were passed late in Wilson's
first administration—the AALL's workmen's compensation

act and the NCLC's federal child labor bill both winning congressional approval in 1916. With the adoption of these proposals by the national parties and the administration, the initiative for their management shifted from the independent reform agencies to the party leaders and government officials, and the necessity for the reform group's existence was reduced.

Among the Mugwump survivors, death and age conspired along with events to slow the momentum of their reform drive. When Seth Low died in 1916, his dynamic influence was lost to the National Civic Federation's leadership. William Dudley Foulke left the presidency of the National Municipal League in 1915, and his successor was the first non-Mugwump president in the organization's history. Henry W. Farnam, while still active in the affairs of the American Association of Labor Legislation into the 1920s, relinquished some of his control over the group's policies when he retired as its president in 1911. After 1912 the Rooseveltian Mugwumps found their effectiveness in national affairs greatly diminished by having joined their leader in temporarily isolating themselves from the Republican party.

Since there was no Mugwump movement after 1900, it is difficult to pinpoint a single date at which the momentum that the Mugwump spirit had regained in the progressive era was lost. Of course, at almost any point from 1884 onward individual bolters advanced the view that the day of the Mugwump was past. Yet even in the hostile climate of national politics during the 1890s and the still more hostile setting of the 1920s, other individuals remained optimistic and sallied forth for reform. But evidence of real vigor in these sallies was slight after 1918. The Anti-Imperialist League adjourned itself in 1920 after several years of virtual inactivity. The National Civic Federation had ceased to be a significant

factor in its field by the 1920s. The American Free Trade
League and the old tariff reformers in R. R. Bowker's circle
continued to send manifestoes to political leaders, but the
number of signatures was growing few as the ranks of the
survivors thinned.[54]   One-half the Mugwumps who were alive
in 1910 died before the election of 1924; two-thirds did not
survive until the 1930s.

During the postwar years only a few men among the survivors figured prominently in public affairs. Oscar S. Straus
accompanied Wilson's delegation to Versailles as the representative of the League to Enforce Peace. George Fred Williams made a stirring plea for the rights of the Greeks at the
conference. Charles MacVeagh was appointed ambassador
to Japan by Coolidge. But the bitter tone of the years immediately after the war rubbed off on other survivors. Frederick P. Fish, a former president of AT&T, sounded a note
out of the nineteenth century in 1919, declaring at a national
conference on labor that "the right to strike does not exist."
Robert P. Clapp, a delegate to the Massachusetts Constitutional
Convention of 1917 to 1919, reported that he did what he
could "to help stem the tide of irrational 'progressivism'" in
the convention. Charles S. Davison decried the dangers of
radicalism in America, writing tracts to warn his fellow citizens about the "Party of Destruction."[55]   Happily other survivors like R. R. Bowker and Henry W. Farnam retained their
sturdy liberalism and concluded that for all the difficulties
of their political efforts over the years, the years were not
ill-spent or wasted ones.[56]

It would be too dramatic to say that the Mugwumps' reform instincts died. The Mugwump spirit simply faded away
as the opportunity for its expression in a receptive climate
lessened. Before World War I, however, many of the surviving

Mugwumps were vigorous participants in progressive era political life, some endorsing progressivism's tendencies, others resisting. But whether they endorsed or resisted "progress," their on-going commitment to political activism belied the statement that the Mugwumps withdrew from public life after 1900. The early twentieth century was not the age of the Mugwump, of course, and the surviving bolters knew it. But the majority, whatever their reservations about progressivism's tone and method, were encouraged by its affirmation of traditional values. Moreover, that affirmation provided an opening in the years before World War I for the Mugwumps to make a final attempt at a fusion of politics and morals in public life. Though they largely failed to achieve that goal, their very pursuit of it extended yet further the already very remarkable longevity of their commitment to civic activism.

Conclusion

Two major perspectives have dominated the historical debate about the meaning of Mugwump reform. One, which I call the "realist" school, focuses on the inadequacies of Mugwump orthodoxy—"orthodoxy" here referring to the bolters' defense of classical economic theories, their genteel moral and literary standards, and their patrician ideal of public conduct (that is, their conviction that it was the duty of an educated elite to guide public affairs). Another, or "idealist," school places primary emphasis on the reformist and liberal aspects of mugwumpery. In my opinion, however, the Mugwump impulse is best understood as a blend of tradition and innovation. To be sure, not all Mugwumps displayed these qualities in equal proportion. Also, different events caused one or the other side of the Mugwump credo to surface with greater prominence, but both orthodoxy and innovation were essential ingredients of mugwumpery. An accurate rendering of the Mugwump profile, therefore, must combine, as the Mugwump movement itself did, these two faces of reform into one.

Attention mainly to the orthodox side of mugwumpery produces a negative picture of the movement's history. The Mugwump bolt, so this argument goes, originated in opposition. It was anti-Blaine first, and only later pro-Cleveland. During the period from 1884 to the mid-1890s, the Mugwumps' commitment to Cleveland grew, but their program and practice remained exceedingly narrow. Operating from a very restricted power base geographically and numerically, the Mugwumps repeatedly manifested their social and political myopia—opposing even the constructive aspects of tariff protection, setting up a clamor about "sound money" in order to defeat currency reform, and steadfastly resisting new reform ideas raised by such dissenting groups as the Populists. The events of the second Cleveland administration, a time of economic depression and social tumult, exposed the program of the Bourbon Democrats and their Mugwump allies as the politics of futility, offering nothing helpful to a nation in crisis.

But this, some would argue, is viewing the glass half empty, when it was also half full. The reformist predilections of the Mugwumps were authentic and appropriate to the late 1880s and early 1890s. From a perspective rooted in cosmopolitan social and economic commitments, the Mugwumps demanded that public life in the United States be professionalized. They tried to bring greater order and efficiency to American politics through the civil service system and the secret ballot movement. They also applied standards of professionalism in an innovative way to their occupations, taking leading roles in reshaping American professional life. These innovations reflected, albeit in a rudimentary way, an emerging bureaucratic order and a renewed deference to experts and professionals in American society. Thus, the innovative side of mugwumpery was apparent in the energy with which Mugwumps entered into a working coalition with Yankee Democrats in the Northeast and promoted the new professionalism in both public life and the learned professions.

The decade of the 1890s is crucial to an understanding of the Mugwumps' distinctive blend of orthodoxy and reform. On the national level, mugwumpery was dealt a series of blows —the depression-year election of 1894, Bryan's triumph within the Democratic party in 1896, and the failure of anti-imperialism in the last years of the century. Nevertheless, the Mugwumps found new avenues for their civic activism during these same years. To some degree in Massachusetts and Connecticut, but particularly in New York City, they pursued

old concerns—model tenement programs, municipal politics,
and sanitation reform—with fresh vigor, and adopted new
causes as well—park and playground development and settlement house reform. They played a major role in establishing
a variety of organizations—University Settlement Society, the
City Club of New York, the Good Government Association of
Boston, the National Municipal League, and Citizens' Union.
Although these ideas and associations still operated within
the traditional Mugwump framework of cosmopolitanism and
professionalism, they were evolutionary, not static, in character. And unless one insists that the Mugwumps' national credo,
Clevelandism, represents the sum and substance of mugwumpery, the bolters' contribution to these local, state, and social
reforms in the 1890s must be described as an authentic expression of the Mugwump impulse.

There was a point, however, beyond which mugwumpery,
as such, could not go. It had been sustained by a number of
special conditions that proved short-lived: the close balance
of party strength nationally in the late 1880s and early 1890s,
and the support a larger public had given its heroes—first
Grover Cleveland, then William E. Russell and William Strong,
and finally, at the turn of the century, Seth Low. As a decisive Republican national majority replaced the old equilibrium, and new Democratic regimes emerged in Boston and
New York City, the basis for the politics of mugwumpery,
always fragile, was destroyed. The Mugwump movement came
apart at the seams.

So, too, did the Mugwumps' synthesis of orthodoxy and
innovation. In the 1900s, individual bolters went their separate ways, taking up a broad spectrum of positions between
the poles of their old credo. One group of surviving bolters
gravitated toward the orthodox pole of mugwumpery. Many

of these Mugwumps continued, of course, to fight the familiar nineteenth-century reform battles for civil service and tariff revision, but they sensed the irrelevance of these causes to the reformers of the new age. All the unreconstructed Mugwumps, therefore, experienced in some degree the displacement that prompted Barrett Wendell's lament that he was like a Federalist in the age of Jefferson or a sound Whig in Jackson's heyday.

Among a slightly larger number of the surviving Mugwumps the liberal or reformist element of mugwumpery prevailed, producing in them a more positive response to progressivism. These individuals joined such new reform organizations as the American Association for Labor Legislation and the National Child Labor Committee, often taking positions of leadership in them. A few surviving Mugwumps were even appointed to high public office. Progressively inclined Mugwumps approved of the new reform generation's determination to reinvigorate traditional American values. But the Mugwump men could never totally share the enthusiasm of progressivism's young advocates for all the new allies, methods, and programs the progressive spirit seemed to force on its adherents. With characteristic Mugwump independence, the old bolters suspected that the losses that would accompany the triumph of whole hog progressivism would probably exceed the gains.

Mugwump participation in progressive causes, nevertheless, could serve to illustrate the traditional side of progressivism or to highlight the progressive side of mugwumpery. Certainly it indicates that there were continuities as well as discontinuities between the two ages of reform. But to dwell on this point would produce a distorted perspective on Mugwump reform, for mugwumpery was a nineteenth-century phenomenon and, in the final analysis, must be understood within its own setting.

Although less than a hundred years ago chronologically, the 1880s had a physical and mental climate vastly different from that experienced by most Americans living today. Back then America was not yet urban, and its economy was still predominantly agricultural. Streets that were crowded were crowded with horse-drawn conveyances. State and local governments bulked larger in the average citizen's life than the federal government. Yet the hallmarks of modernity were coming irresistibly into evidence—large-scale corporate organizations, rapid transportation and communication, and the rise of non-Anglo-Saxon ethnic groups. It was in this milieu, during the last years of the old order, that the Mugwumps had their day.

The Mugwumps contributed to the transformation taking place in late nineteenth-century America by attempting to revitalize orthodoxy. There was, to be sure, a conservative dimension to this goal. But the drive to revitalize orthodoxy also arose from impatience with the old order's growing disfunctionality, an impatience that altered traditional political and social configurations through such innovations as the civil service system and the movement to reorganize American professional life. The Mugwumps' orthodoxy was inhibiting and their innovations rudimentary, but both were very much of their time. Indeed, the Mugwumps' achievement was that, in the relatively receptive environment of the late 1880s and the early 1890s, they managed to fuse the polar elements of their reform impulse—orthodoxy and innovation. It was the interplay of these two themes that, for a time, gave vitality and meaning to Mugwump reform.

Appendix A

Mugwumps & Republicans: A Composite Biography

About the Sample

Since my article appeared on "The New York Mugwumps of 1884: A Profile" (*Political Science Quarterly*, March 1963) I have refined my sample in a number of ways. For the present study I collected the names of regular Republicans to compare with the Mugwump profile. In order to have the two groups from approximately the same geographical setting, I eliminated all bolters who were not from the "New York City area." This, together with removing a half dozen names I now believe were probably not bolters, reduced my Mugwump sample by 62 or from 410 to 348.

Next, I added 112 Mugwump names from lists I came across since 1963. These additions include the full list of the New York City Independent Republican Committee (an important coordinating body during the early bolt) gathered from the R. R. Bowker manuscript collection in the Library of Congress. That left a sample with roughly equal numbers of identifiable Republicans (470) and Mugwumps (429 identified out of a new total of 460).

A comparison of my 1963 New York State sample and the present New York City area profile reveals no very dramatic shifts in results. Elimination of the Ithaca contingent of twenty-three bolters reduced the present total in the "teacher" category by about half. The percentage of bolters who were in their thirties, city born, and from City College of New York and New York University increased disproportionately, largely because R. R. Bowker's influence brought men in those categories onto the Independent Republican Committee list.

A word about the sampling process. For the most part both the Mugwump and regular Republican samples were drawn from the same source, contemporary newspapers. The *New York Times* and *New York Tribune* printed extensive lists of men who attended Mugwump or Republican gatherings, marched in Blaine and Cleveland parades, and joined campaign groups. The resulting lists represent, I feel, a fair sample of nearly one thousand active Mugwumps and Republicans. The chief exception to the newspaper origin of my sample was the list from R. R. Bowker's papers. Since its use has not produced any very dramatic changes from my 1963 results, I believe its use has not distorted the comparative profiles.

One difficulty in the use of newspaper sources is that misspellings of names are commonplace and can lead to misidentification. Where possible, especially in those cases in which an address and occupation were also given, I collated these with information from city directories and identified an individual. But I did this only rarely, as it is a risky business in which the chances for apparently true but actually false identifications are great. In many more cases identification was impossible because the names were simply too common—James Johnson, Richard Smith, James Donohue, Edward Richards being just a few examples.

In order to identify individuals I used a variety of biographical sources, from the *Dictionary of American Biography* to more local sources such as the *Biographical Directory of New York* and city directories for Manhattan and Brooklyn. The latter include the occupations of "machinist," "plumber," "porter," "carpenter," and so forth as well as upper-class designations. The relatively high socioeconomic profile of both the Mugwumps and the Republicans doubtless reflects a tendency of newspapers to publish the names of the more prominent active campaigners. Differences, nevertheless, showed up between the two samples on this matter of status.

In addition to the general biographical directories I used a wide variety of sources to identify individuals. The *Social Register* and the *New York Times* obituaries (a handy index to which is now available) were invaluable. Membership lists were published by every major club— Union League, Union, Church, University, St. Nicholas, and Century Association. Alumni registers and files (I used those of Cornell, Columbia, New York University, City College of New York, Harvard, Yale, Amherst, and Brown) are uneven in quality and content, but often they provide much more than a skeletal sketch of dates. Occasionally, as in Harvard's and Yale's archives they preserve a great deal of personal data about a graduate's career.

What follows is a summary in charts of the materials I collected. Since most of my analytical remarks are in the main text, I have only occasionally added further comments here. In presenting these findings in charts I am not trying to create the impression of absolute statistical rigor or accuracy, though they do provide a broad profile of the groups under study. The results of my gleanings, however, as I have emphasized in the main text, are open to many statistical limitations and should be interpreted as representing tendencies rather than absolute proportions that would be true of Mugwump and Republican profiles everywhere in 1884.

Statistical Comparison of the Mugwump and Republican Samples

Table A.1
Residential Environment at Birth

Type of Environment	Mugwumps		Republicans	
	Number	Percent	Number	Percent
City (more than 10,000 residents)	104	60	64	38
Town (between 500 and 10,000 residents)	47	27	83	49
Rural (less than 500 residents)	22	13	22	13

Note: Two minor points: First, the distinctions above are too great to be explained simply by differences in geographical location at birth, though a slightly higher proportion of the Mugwumps were born in New York or New Jersey and more of the regulars were from New England by about the same margin (less than 10 percent difference). Roughly 10 percent of each sample was born in other regions of the United States.

Secondly, statistics about place of birth do not demonstrate that the Mugwumps (who on the whole were younger) had lived *longer* in urban environments than the regulars. Indeed, many of the Blaine men had moved to cities while still quite young. Their earliest memories and experiences of migration to cities were nevertheless likely to be different from those of the Mugwumps.

Not included above were nineteen regulars and twenty-two insurgent Republicans who were of foreign birth (nearly all of them from the British Isles or Germany).

Table A.2
Age in 1884

Age group	Mugwumps		Republicans	
	Number	Percent	Number	Percent
20-29	37	17	9	4
30-39	76	35	27	12
40-49	56	25	90	40
50-59	31	14	58	26
60-69	14	6	31	14
70-	6	3	10	4

Note: R. R. Bowker's comment that many prospective bolters were young men for whom the Civil War was mainly a childhood memory is vividly borne out by this comparative age profile. Those men who were in their forties, fifties, or sixties in 1884 had been from twenty to fifty years of age in the last years of the Civil War. Less than one-half the Mugwump sample fell into those age groups. Nearly four-fifths of the regular Republicans were in that age range.

Table A.3
Comparative Occupational Profile

Occupation*	Mugwumps		Republicans	
	Number	Percent	Number	Percent
Lawyer	111	26	95	20.0
Businessman	104	25	177	38.0
Financier	70	17	84	18.0
Physician	39	9	6	1.0
Publishing	34	8	14	3.0
White collar	31	7	57	12.0
Clergyman	12	3	21	5.0
Teacher	11	3	1	0.2
Miscellaneous	10	2	13	2.8

*For my purposes these general categories were specific enough. A more detailed breakdown of four of the categories is as follows: Mugwumps (Republicans). Businessman: merchant, 78 (121); manufacturer, 15 (10); miscellaneous, 13 (46). Financier: banker, 24 (34); broker, 32 (27); insurance, 8 (5); investor/capitalist, 6 (18). Publishing: editor, 23 (4); publisher, 5 (7); author/reporter, 6 (3): White-collar worker: clerk, 10 (19); secretary, 6 (0); agent, 8 (5); manager, 4 (6); government employee, 2 (21); superintendent, 0 (6); notary, 1 (1).

In the broader categories of business (excluding white-collar workers), there were 174 Mugwumps and 261 Republicans, and in the professions (excluding publishing), there were 173 Mugwumps and only 123 Republicans.

Table A.4 *Religious Affiliation*

Denomination	Mugwumps	Republicans
Episcopalian	47	16
Congregational	16	6
Unitarian	12	0
Presbyterian	12	22
Jewish	6	2
Methodist	5	16
Baptist	2	2
Catholic	1	3
Other	8	5

Table A.5 *The Percentage of Americans, New Yorkers, Republicans and Mugwumps in Various Religious Denominations*

Denomination	Americans	New Yorkers	Republicans	Mugwumps
Roman Catholic	30.0	53.0	4.0	1.0
Methodist	22.0	12.0	22.0	5.0
Baptist	18.0	7.0	3.0	2.0
Presbyterian	6.0	8.0	31.0	10.0
Episcopal	3.0	6.0	22.0	43.0
Congregational	2.0	2.0	8.0	15.0
Jewish	0.6	2.0	3.0	6.0
Unitarian	0.3	0.2	0.0	10.0

Note: Religious affiliation was one of the most difficult categories to determine. Information was available on only about one-quarter of the Mugwump sample and roughly one-sixth of the Republican group. Obviously the addition of a relatively small number of individuals in any given denomination would shift the totals significantly. Nevertheless, a comparison of the proportions of Americans, New Yorkers, Mugwumps, and Republicans (*see* table A.5) provides some interesting contrasts in the religious profiles of those groups, the Mugwumps generally swinging furthest from the typical pattern for Americans in the Gilded Age.

Note: In gathering educational data (*see* table A.6) I used college and university alumni records more extensively for the Mugwumps than the Republicans. The result may be that the figures for college training among the Mugwumps are slightly inflated. However, even with the elimination of thirteen Mugwump degree winners whom I identified solely from alumni registers, the number of Mugwumps with some college education remains both proportionately (77 percent to 46 percent) and absolutely (186 to 104) much higher than that of the Republicans.

Table A.6
Mugwump and Republican Educational Profile

	Mugwumps		Republicans	
	No.	%	No.	%
Biography omitted data on education	28	11	53	23
Man had less than a college education	28	11	72	31
Individuals had some college education	199	78	104	46

Note: Eighty-three Mugwumps and thirty-one Republicans received a B.A. plus an advanced degree—figures that do not include men who received M.A.'s (most of which were honorary degrees) or those who attended a professional school but definitely did not get an advanced degree.

Table A.7

*Comparison of Mugwump and Republican Veterans
for Length of Service in the Civil War*

	Republicans		Mugwumps	
	No.	%	No.	%
Duration of service unknown	13	17	4	13
Served well under 2 years	15	21	12	39
Served about 2 years	22	30	8	26
Duration 1861-1865 or longer	23	32	7	23

Note: Within my sample of New York Mugwumps and Republicans I kept a separate tabulation of those individuals who were Civil War veterans. Since these men ranged in age from thirty-seven to sixty-nine in 1884, I treated all men in that age range as potential members of the Civil War veteran group. The total number of those in this category was 197 for the Republicans and 121 for the Mugwumps. I was able to definitely identify 73 (37 percent) of the Republicans and 31 (26 percent) of the Mugwumps as veterans.

Although I drew heavily on Frederick Phisterer's compilation of the war records of New York state officers, *New York in the War of the Rebellion*, this source did not cover the many Mugwumps and Republicans who served in other states. I frequently had to depend, therefore, on less precise sources—obituaries and biographical dictionaries—which often mentioned merely that a man was a veteran without adding any further details.

Table A.8

*Comparison of Mugwump and Republican Promotion
Records During Civil War Service*

	Republicans individuals %		Mugwumps individuals %	
No information	16	22	6	19
Received no promotions	11	15	5	17
Promotion of 1 rank only	10	14	10	32
Promoted 2 or more ranks	36	49	10	32

Note: Lists of the two groups of veterans follow:

a. *Mugwumps:* C. Graham Bacon, Francis C. Barlow, Henry B. Beecher, Cornelius E. Billington, Benjamin H. Bristow, Daniel H. Chamberlain, Christian T. Christensen, George B. Coggswell, George A. Crocker, Richard Watson Gilder, Richard B. Greenwood, George S. Hastings, William H. Henriques, Friedrich Heppenheimer, Wakeman Holbertson, Crammond Kennedy, Frederick H. Lawrence, Orlando Leach, William Man, Charles N. Marcellus, Charles P. Miller, Richard Oliver, Edward R. Pelton, Edward Prime, Nathaniel Prime, George Haven Putnam, Henry E. Roehr, Carl Schurz, Henry C. Tallman, Robert F. Weir, John C. Welch.
b. *Republicans:* Ethan Allen, Lloyd Aspinwall, John Jacob Astor, Henry W. Banks, Henry A. Barnum, Harry H. Beadle, George Blagdon, George Bliss, Jonas M. Bundy, George B. Butler, Joseph B. Carr, David G. Caywood, William C. Church, Charles H. T. Collis, George W. Cregier, S. V. R. Cruger, William B. Derrick, John E. Dowley, Charles K. Dutton, Joel B. Erhardt, Samuel Fessenden, William H. French, Theodore B. Gates, Frederick S. Gibbs, Charles K. Graham, Walter Q. Gresham, Horace L. Hotchkiss, Henry E. Howland, Brayton Ives, Joseph C. Jackson, John W. Jacobus, Samuel Jacoby, Henry W. Knight, Waldimir Kryzanowski, Frank B. Lawrence, Anson G. McCook, Edwin A. Merrit, Jeremiah V. Meserole, Warner Miller, Samuel Minnes, Cornelius B. Mitchell, Edward Mitchell, Bankson T. Morgan, Gouverneur Morris Jr., John R. Nugent, James R. O'Beirne, Peter W. Ostrander, John R. Paxton, Lewis M. Peck, Henry C. Perley, Francis E. Pinto, John F. Plummer, Horace Porter, Thomas Rafferty, Frank Raymond, William C. Reddy, John H. Reed, Whitelaw Reid, George H. Sheldon, Charles Emory Smith, Howard M. Smith, John A. Smith, George C. Spencer, Raphael C. Stearns, Wager Swayne, James Tanner, Sinclair Tousey, Benjamin F. Tracy, John P. Windolph, Edward F. Winslow, Henry Clay Wood, Steward L. Woodford, Thomas Wright.

New York City Area Mugwumps: A Masterlist

Felix Adler
Henry M. Alden
George H. Allen
David Allerton
Walter S. Allerton

Royal W. Amidon
C. Amilez
H. Arends
Frederick Ashton
Edward W. Avery

John G. Bacchus
C. Graham Bacon
Gorham Bacon
R. S. Bacon
Lyman H. Bagg
Frederic Bancroft
Francis C. Barlow
Henry W. Barnes
Homer L. Bartlett
Edmund L. Baylies
Henry B. Beecher
Henry Ward Beecher
William C. Beecher
A. F. Belcher
John Bellows
Thomas Bennett
Edward D. Bettens
Poultney Bigelow
William B. Bigelow
Cornelius E. Billington
Joseph B. Bishop
Edward C. Boardman
F. C. Bonney
Clarence W. Bowen
Richard Rogers Bowker
Luther J. Briggs, Jr.
Benjamin H. Bristow
Edward B. Bronson
Edward V. Brown
F. Tilden Brown
H. Everit Brown
Charles N. Browne
Charles Bruff
William J. Bruff
Louis T. Brush
Albert H. Buck
Gurdon S. Buck

William L. Bull
Henry C. Bunner
Charles L. Burchard
John L. Burdett
Edward L. Burlingame
Lyman S. Burnham
Silas W. Burt
Robert S. Bussing
Prescott Hall Butler
Willard Parker Butler
Thomas S. Byers
Stephen H. Camp
William J. Campbell
George F. Canfield
Peter J. Carpenter
Walter Carr
James Coolidge Carter
Edward Cary
John W. Chadwick
Daniel H. Chamberlain
Edward W. Chamberlain
Elihu Chauncy
William H. Childs
William G. Choate
Christian T. Christensen
Frederick W. Christern
Horace B. Claflin
John Claflin
Albert E. Clark
H. H. Clarke
Clement Cleveland
J. Gilbert Cleveland
George C. Coffin
George B. Coggswell
Bowles Colgate
Charles Collins
Frederic F. Cook

William J. Coombs
Robert C. Cornell
William F. Corwin
John K. Creevy
George A. Crocker
Edward Cromwell
Frederick Cromwell
Eugene Crowell
Clement M. Cummings
George William Curtis
Ephraim S. Cutter
Robert Fulton Cutting
William Bayard Cutting
Charles S. Davison
W. D. Dawson
Lewis L. Delafield
Horace E. Deming
George P. Denman
Richard H. Derby
George G. DeWitt
John J. Donaldson
Charles E. Dorr
Ethan Allen Doty
Daniel S. Dougherty
Herman Dowd
Max Drey
John L. Dufais
Henry D. Dumont
Henry M. Duncan
Albert J. Dunham
Conrad V. Dykeman
Abraham L. Earle
Henry Earle
Albert R. Edey
William W. Ellsworth
Lawrence C. Embree
Robert C. Embree

J. Frank Emmons
Russell L. Engs
Issac N. Falk
Henry C. Field
George W. Folsom
John Foord
Frederick P. Forester
Alexander Forman
Roger Foster
George B. Fowler
Austen G. Fox
John Frankenheimer
John Fredericks
Meyer M. Friend
Richard Watson Gilder
William Gillfillan
Arthur Coit Gilman
Winfield S. Gilmore
Edwin Lawrence Godkin
Henry W. Goodrich
E. H. Goodwin
Joseph Gottlieb
George Walton Green
Richard B. Greenwood
Samuel W. Grierson
William L. Guillaudeu
Louis Guion
John C. Haddock
William H. Hamilton
B. L. W. Hanfield
Joseph Henry Harper
Joseph W. Harper, Jr.
Samuel C. Harriot
Ashton Harvey
George S. Hastings
Carl J. Hauck
George A. Haws

DeWitt C. Hayes
James Heard
William H. Henriques
John Hepburn
Frederick C. Heppenheimer
W. L. Hermance
Herman Hess
Henry R. Hicks
Henry B. Hill
Wakeman Holberton
John A. Holmes
Frederick L. Holmquist
Henry Holt
H. N. Hooper
William H. Horndidge
Isaac Howland
George E. Hoyt
Henry S. Hoyt, Jr.
John H. Hubbell
Chester Huntington
W. B. Ingaits
Frederick G. Ireland
Abraham Jacobi
D. A. Jacobi
Arthur R. Jarrett
J. Foster Jenkins
Leonard W. Jerome
Eastman Johnson
Robert U. Johnson
A. D. Johnston
George Jones
Lynds E. Jones
Henry T. Journeay
Edward L. Kalbfleisch
William Kampfmuller
Felix Kaufman
Sigismund Kaufman

Thomas Kearney
Crammond Kennedy
T. L. Kennedy
Henry F. Kent
Rockwell Kent
R. Nelson Kenyon
H. V. King
William H. Klenke
Percival Knauth
Henry T. Kneeland
Lawrence Kneeland
Charles B. Knevals
Charles E. Knoblauch
August Koch
F. Kosiniki
Joseph Larocque
William Lasell
A. A. Law
James T. Law
Frederick H. Lawrence
Francis Lawton
Orlando Leach
James E. Learned
John Brooks Leavitt
M. Lebaugh
Lewis Cass Ledyard
Charles A. Leighton
Angelo M. Lewison
Joseph Liebman
William A. Linn
Charles F. Livermore
Arthur A. Lockwood
LeGrand B. Lockwood
Seth Low
H. Lowenstein
Grosvenor P. Lowrey
Amos M. Lyon

Graham McAdam
Charles McBurney
E. D. McCarthy
George D. MacKay
Clarence McKim
Augustus McKinney
Charles MacVeagh
William Man
Thomas L. Manson
Charles N. Marcellus
Edward S. Marsh
William D. Martin
E. P. Mason
D. Masters
Albert Mathews
Charles E. Maxwell
Henry W. Maxwell
Paul F. Meinde
Frederick L. Mendel
George N. Messiter
Alfred Meyer
David F. Meyer
L. E. Meyer
Dederick H. Middendorff
Arthur W. Milbury
Charles E. Miller
Charles P. Miller
Charles R. Miller
Ernest Miller
George A. Miller
William F. Mills
Charles T. Minton
Alfred Mitchell
John L. Moffatt
R. Burnham Moffatt
Edward A. Morrison
Julian Morrison

L. L. Morrison
Lewis F. Mott
James Y. Murkland
D. Colden Murray
Joseph K. Murray
Russell W. Murray
William K. Murray
Charles C. Nadal
Ehrman S. Nadal
Stephan P. Nash
Thomas Nast
Emile D. Neustadt
Otto Neustadt
Ralph W. Newton
James A. Nibblock
William H. Nichols
C. A. Northrop
Frank F. Northrop
Henry A. Oakley
Charles M. Oelrichs
David B. Ogden
Francis L. Ogden
Ludlow Ogden
Stephen H. Olin
Richard Oliver
William S. Opdyke
Willard Parker, Jr.
William Parkin
Robert B. Parsons
S. W. Paul
Edward C. Pearson
William G. Peckham
Edward R. Pelton
Warren Place
Edward Erie Poor
James C. Potter
William Potts

S. W. Powell
Edward Prime
Nathaniel Prime
J. T. Prout
William A. Purrington
Alfred P. Putnam
George Haven Putnam
Kingman N. Putnam
J. B. Quimbly
William H. Rachau
Frank Rand
Walter L. Ranney
John Ray
William Rennick
Frederick W. Rhinelander
George Ricardo
James R. Richards
William W. Richards
G. F. Richardson
Henry Riedel
Frank W. Rockwell
John Rockwell
Henry E. Roehr
Henry A. Root
Ripley Ropes
Charles E. Rushmore
William T. Ryerson
William P. Saint John
Edward Salomon
Andrew H. Sands
B. Aymar Sands
William C. Sanger
Frank Saunders
Lewis A. Sayre
I. H. Scharman
Leopold Schepp
Edward L. Schlesinger

Frank Schlesinger
Oscar Schmidt
J. F. Schneck
W. H. Schnecker
Jacob Schoenhof
Arno H. Schoff
Constantine Schuber
Jackson S. Schultz
Carl Schurz
Arend Schutte
Frank D. Schuyler
Gustav H. Schwab
Charles Scribner
A. P. W. Seaman
B. R. Seaman
Henry G. Seaver
Edward C. Seguin
DeWitt J. Seligman
Maurice Seligman
Archibald L. Sessions
Thomas G. Shearman
Arthur M. Sherwood
John Sherwood
Henry T. Sloane
Thomas C. Sloane
Daniel D. Smith
D. Henry Smith
Duncan Smith
Elliott Smith
John Smith
William Smith
Francis H. Southwick
Nelson S. Spencer
Edward E. Sprague
N. P. Stanton
Henry L. Starbuck
James Stokes

William E. D. Stokes
Edward Storck
Jacob Stout
Oscar S. Straus
Albert Strauss
Frederick Strauss
James Strikeman
Charles E. Strong
John J. Studwell
Edward F. Sweet
Henry C. Tallman
Frederick D. Tappen
C. H. Taylor
Henry O. Taylor
John A. Taylor
Thomas Fenton Taylor
William S. Taylor
Frank Texido
Horace H. Thayer
William H. Thayer
Horace K. Thurber
Charles A. Tibbals
C. H. Tillinghast
T. B. Tilton
Owen Torrington
E. C. Townsend
Charles E. Tracy
William R. Travers, Jr.
J. Fowler Travis
J. J. Troy
Edward Tuck
R. Schuyler Tucker
William V. Tupper
Herbert B. Turner
J. A. Turney
Ezra A. Tuttle
Kinsley Twining

Edward Underhill
Charles M. Vail
John H. Van Amringe
James A. Van Benschoten
George R. VandeWater
Henry S. Van Duzer
George Willet Van Nest
Adrian H. Van Sinderen
Robert B. Van Vleck
William E. Ver Planck
Howard T. Walden
Henry M. Walker
Jerome Walker
Robert S. Walker
Elwyn Waller
Arthur E. Walradt
William Hayes Ward
Thomas F. Warner
James Warren
Jacob Washburn
Edwin S. Waterman
Robert F. Weir
John C. Welch
Richard W. G. Welling
J. S. C. Wells
Hugo Wesendonck
Anton Wetz
Albert H. Wheeler
Alfred T. White
Andrew W. White
Horace White
William A. White
Frederick W. Whitridge
David J. H. Willcox
Thomas Wilde
Christopher S. Williams
Philip H. Williams

Louis Windmuller
Andrew Wright
John Wygand

William I. Young
Edward L. Youmans
Andrew C. Zabriskie

New York City Area Republicans: A Masterlist

Charles E. Abbott
John N. Abbott
Conrad H. Abelman
Thomas C. Acton
Ethan Allen
Thomas Allison
Edward H. Ammidown
James R. Angel
Daviel F. Appleton
Nathaniel Appleton
Charles Arbuckle
Carson G. Archibald
D. Thomas Armitage
Herman O. Armour
Robert C. Armstrong
Benjamin G. Arnold
David S. Arnott
Lloyd Aspinwall
John Jacob Astor
David S. Babcock
Thomas Back
Henry W. Banks
Henry A. Barnum
Thomas Bartley
Arthur E. Bateman
Levi M. Bates
Harry H. Beadle
William H. Bellamy
James L. Benedict
Edward Benson

Garrett Bergen
Robert Betty
Bernard Biglin
Charles A. Binder
George W. F. Birch
Heber R. Bishop
George Blagdon
Samuel P. Blagdon
Birdseye Blakeman
Cornelius N. Bliss
George Bliss
George Bliss Jr.
Matthew C. D. Borden
Henry C. Botty
Wellesley W. Bowdish
Robert B. Boyd
John J. Brady
John E. Brodsky
William Brookfield
Charles B. Brown
Joseph H. Brown
Sylvester Brush
William Cullen Bryant
William Buck
Oliver W. Buckingham
Morris M. Budlong
Jonas M. Bundy
William Burt
Rufus T. Bush
George B. Butler

Hugh N. Camp
William A. Camp
Hermann Cantor
Abraham D. Carlock
Andrew Carnegie
Robert R. Carpenter
Joseph B. Carr
Stephen G. Carr
Herman G. Carter
Watson E. Case
George R. Cathcart
Henry B. Caverly
John A. Caverly
David G. Caywood
George Cecil
Edwin S. Chapin
Alfred C. Cheney
Simeon B. Chittenden
Joseph H. Choate
William C. Church
Michael E. Clare
A. W. Clark
Byron G. Clark
Gardner K. Clark
Henry Clews
Frederick Cobb
Gardner R. Colby
Charles H. T. Collis
Alfred R. Conkling
Stephen V. R. Cooper
George Copeland
Alonzo B. Cornell
Hampton A. Coursen
James A. Cowie
Michael Cregan
George W. Cregier
Charles Crocker

Charles G. Cronin
S. V. R. Cruger
Robert L. Cutting, Jr.
Michael J. Dady
William A. Darling
W. McKendree Darwood
James P. Davenport
Eugene Davis
Noah Davis
Henry M. Day
Martin N. Day
Joseph S. Decker
Eben Demarest
Thomas Denny
William B. Derrick
Joseph Deshay, Jr.
J. Rhinelander Dillon
Theodore D. Dimon
William B. Dinsmore
Abram J. Dittenhoefer
Louis F. Dodd
Harry E. Dodge
Frederick Dorr
George B. Douglas
William Dowd
John E. Dowley
Edward A. Drake
James H. Dunham
Harrison Durkee
John B. Dutcher
Silas B. Dutcher
Charles K. Dutton
Edward E. Eames
E. Eickert
Max F. Eller
Samuel Engel
John Ennis

Joel B. Erhardt
William M. Evarts
Pandelli A. Fachiri
Sigourney W. Fay
Henry Feldman
George B. Ferris
Samuel Fessenden
Cyrus W. Field Jr.
Henry M. Field
Frederick Finck
Isreal F. Fischer
John C. Fischer
Josiah M. Fiske
Henry M. Flagler
Joseph L. Follett
William H. French
Robert M. Gallaway
Nelson J. Gates
Theodore B. Gates
Joseph E. Gay
Frederick G. Gedney
William H. Gedney
Philip Germond
Frederick S. Gibbs
Charles E. Gilbert
Parke Godwin
Charles A. L. Goldey
Manassah L. Goldman
Jacob J. Goodman
Edward S. Goss
Jay Gould
Charles K. Graham
Joseph F. Graham
George Gramberg
Henry Grasse
Walter Q. Gresham
John H. Grimes

Stephen M. Griswold
Joseph H. Groht
John H. Gunner
William H. Gunther
Joseph C. Hacker
Robert R. Haines
Mitchell Halliday
Samuel B. Halliday
George W. Hamilton
George E. Hamlin
Parker D. Handy
Charles T. Harbeck
C. E. Harris
Robert Harris
Benjamin F. Hart
Henry S. Hart
Walter T. Hatch
Martin Haupt
James W. Hawes
Dexter A. Hawkins
Leonard Haxeltine
George A. Henshaw
J. Hobart Herrick
Alpheus W. Herriman
Jacob Hess
A. Foster Higgins
Samuel E. Higley
Edgar P. Hill
George Hilliard
Elizur B. Hinsdale
Edward H. Hobbs
Frederick Hoeninghaus
Martin L. Hollister
Artemas H. Holmes
George T. Hope
Horace L. Hotchkiss
J. B. House

Walter Howe
Henry E. Howland
Jesse Hoyt
Amos G. Hull
John L. N. Hunt
James W. Husted
Theodore I. Husted
Henry Irvinger
Brayton Ives
Joseph C. Jackson
Theodore Jacobsen
John W. Jacobus
Samuel Jacoby
Darwin R. James
Thomas L. James
John Jay
William T. Jebb
Augustus D. Juilliard
Elijah R. Kennedy
Gershon P. Kenyon
Robert J. Kimball
John D. Kimmey
James M. King
Abel W. Kingman
George Klim
Joseph F. Knapp
Henry W. Knight
Charles H. Knox
John Jay Knox
August Kohn
John Koster
Augustus Kountze
Wladimir Krzyzanski
Frederick Kuhne
Richard H. Laimbeer Jr.
Julius Landauer
Charles G. Landon

Woodbury G. Langdon
Philip H. Larney
George R. Lathan
Edward Lauterbach
Frank B. Lawrence
John D. Lawson
James B. Layng
Henry G. Leask
David Lennon
Stephen R. Lesher
Richard J. Lewis
Henry Lichtig
Daniel A. Lindley
Amos C. Littell
Robbins Little
Samuel Luckey
Richard M. Lush
David C. Lyall
John R. Lydecker
Daniel J. McAllister
Robert S. MacArthur
Anson G. McCook
Robert G. McCord
Thomas McElrath
Duncan McGregor
Alexander McKeever
Samuel McLean
Alexander McQueen
Albon P. Man
Luther R. Marsh
Joel W. Mason
William H. Maxwell
Frederick Mead
Clarence W. Meade
John Meegan
Frank Merkel
Edwin A. Merrit

Jeremiah V. Meserole
Anthony W. Miller
Franklin B. Miller
Nathan G. Miller
Warner Miller
David Milliken Jr.
Seth M. Milliken
Darius O. Mills
Samuel Minnes
Charles Minzesheimer
Cornelius B. Mitchell
E. D. Mitchell
Edward Mitchell
George Montague
Bankson T. Morgan
Gouverneur Morris Jr.
Horace J. Morse
Levi P. Morton
Alfred E. Mudge
James E. Muhling
David Mullen
Richard G. Murphy
Logan C. Murray
Alfred G. Nason
Louis E. Naumann
John H. Nesbitt
Thomas P. Neville
George L. Nichols
Nathaniel Niles
John R. Nugent
Richard H. Nugent
James R. O'Beirne
J. P. O'Flynn
Peter W. Ostrander
Franklin A. Paddock
J. Seaver Page
Jeremiah Pangburn

J. Ferris Patten
Jacob M. Patterson Jr.
John R. Paxton
Charles A. Peabody Jr.
George W. Pearce
Lewis M. Peck
Edward H. Perkins Jr.
Samuel M. Perkins
Henry C. Perley
Joseph L. Perley
James W. Perry
William Walter Phelps
W. L. Phillips
Francis E. Pinto
Frederick W. Pitcher
John F. Plummer
William L. Pomeroy
John R. Pope
Horace Porter
George H. Potts
Charles M. Pratt
Nathaniel A. Prentiss
Abram S. Quackenbush
John C. Quick
Thomas Rafferty
James S. Ramsey
Alfred Ray
Frank Raymond
William C. Reddy
George E. Reed
John H. Reed
Whitelaw Reid
James M. Requa
George C. Reynolds
Thomas Riker
John Roach
A. R. Roberts

George H. Roberts
William H. Robertson
Daniel Robinson
George H. Robinson
Henry H. Rogers
Charles Rohde
Daniel G. Rollins
Theodore Roosevelt
Elihu Root
Bernard Rourke
Thomas F. Rowland
Rudolph Rubens
Thomas J. Rush
Horace Russell
John Watts Russell
James H. Rutter
Thomas Rutter
Russell Sage
Frederick A. Schroeder
Gilbert H. Scribner
Jesse Seligman
Robert Sewell
George H. Sheldon
Henry K. Sheldon
Benjamin D. Silliman
John D. Slayback
John Sloane
William D. Sloane
Charles Emory Smith
Charles Stewart Smith
Howard M. Smith
Isaac T. Smith
James D. Smith
James N. Smith
John A. Smith
Solon B. Smith
Henry S. Snow

George M. Snyder
Samuel T. Spear
Charles S. Spencer
George C. Spencer
Henry L. Sprague
John Stanton
J. Thomas Stearns
Raphael C. Stearns
John A. Stewart
William E. Stiger
George P. Stockwell
Richard S. Storrs
James S. T. Stranahan
L. R. Streeter
Issac S. Strong
Samuel F. Strong
William L. Strong
Theron G. Strong
Wager Swayne
James T. Swift
Charles N. Taintor
James Tanner
William H. Ten Eyck
John T. Terry
Charles L. Tiffany
Ambrose W. Topping
W. H. B. Totten
Sinclair Tousey
Benjamin F. Tracy
Spencer Trask
Francis A. Trelease
J. Spencer Turner
Lucas L. Van Allen
George Van Alstyne
Cornelius Van Cott
Allen Vanderbogert
Archibald S. Van Orden

James T. Van Rensselaer
Abraham Van Santvoord
Cornelius D. Van Wagenen
Philip V. R. Van Wyck
James M. Varnum
Jacob D. Vermilye
Benjamin S. Walcott
Salem H. Wales
William H. Wanser
William S. Waterhouse
Charles Watrous
Thomas L. Watson
William H. Webb
George P. Webster
Joseph H. Weller
Louis Wendel
A. D. Wheelock
Stephen V. White
George L. Whitman
Alfred R. Whitney

Albert E. Whyland
Ezekiel C. Williams
Hamilton Williams
William H. Williams
R. Stuart Willis
John P. Windolph
Edward F. Winslow
John Winslow
Washington Winsor
Otto Witte
Henry Clay Wood
Thomas H. Wood
Steward L. Woodford
Lorenzo G. Woodhouse
Sylvester L. Woodhouse
Franklin Woodruff
Timothy L. Woodruff
James T. Wright
Thomas Wright
H. Livingston Young

Appendix B

Mugwumps & Progressives: A Socioeconomic Profile

In the 1950s and 1960s American historians became interested in using group socioeconomic profiles to describe a particular reform movement's membership and motivation more fully. Richard Hofstadter's *Age of Reform* drew heavily on this sort of literature and, largely due to its intriguing but somewhat elusive status-revolution theme, inspired an extensive debate among scholars about the nature of progressivism.[1]

A comparison of four such socioeconomic profiles of reformers in the progressive era is offered here. Two samples are restricted to Progressive party leaders—Richard B. Sherman's study of 50 Massachusetts Bull Moosers and Alfred D. Chandler, Jr.'s sample of 119 Progressives from the New England and mid-Atlantic states. Otis L. Graham, Jr.'s sample of 400 progressives is a national one including reformers from all parties. Finally, the socioeconomic profile of 302 Mugwumps who survived until 1910 is reported and contrasted with the three profiles of progressives.[2]

Not surprisingly, the Mugwump survivors were older than the average progressive. Sherman found that the Massachusetts Bull Moose leadership averaged 45.2 years of age at the end of 1912. Such an individual's year of birth would have been 1867, a date by which all the Mugwumps were born. Graham found in his sample of progressives that the median birthdate (the date by which one-half his sample was born) was 1862. The median birthdate for the surviving Mugwumps was 1850. Put another way, the "median" individual among Graham's progressives would have been 48 years of age and a comparable Mugwump 60 years of age in 1910. More than a decade, therefore, separated the typical Mugwump survivor from the median of the progressive age group.

Educationally, both Sherman's Bull Moosers and Graham's

progressive reformers had a very high degree of training. Sherman found that 63.7 percent of his Massachusetts insurgents had some post-high school training. Graham does not present educational data on his full sample of reformers, but for those who lived into the New Deal era he states that 89 percent (133 of 149 on whom information was available) had at least some college education. The educational level of the surviving Mugwumps was extremely high also—270 of the 302 having done some college work.

Graham states further that of those progressives in his sample who survived until the New Deal period, 60 percent were born in the Middle West, South, or Far West. This national breadth among the progressives contrasts starkly with the narrow regional origins of the Mugwump survivors. Ninety-four percent of the Mugwumps (251 of 275) were born in either New England or the mid-Atlantic states.

Broadly speaking, all three profiles of the progressive liberals—Chandler, Sherman, and Graham—show that professionals outnumbered businessmen among the reformers. The same was true of the Mugwump survivors. Lawyers in all four cases were the largest group of professionals. College professors and individuals whose livelihood was publishing (authors, journalists, editors, and publishers) comprised the next largest groups, as the figures in table B.1 indicate. Occupationally, the most dramatic contrast between the Chandler-Graham progressive profiles and that of the Mugwump survivors was the absence of social workers within the Mugwump group. Clearly this was a reform type, indeed an occupation, which had come of age after the Mugwump reform era.

In table B.1, I have compared "Chandler's Progressives" (the 119 New England and mid-Atlantic Progressives collected by Alfred D. Chandler, Jr.) with "Graham's Survivors" (Otis D. Graham, Jr.'s sample of 155 progressives still living in 1936) and the "Mugwump Survivors" (the 302 bolters living in 1910). In order to make the occupational categories as comparable and simple as possible, I have recategorized some of my occupational groups as well as two of Graham's. For Graham's original breakdown of his sample by occupational groups, see his book *An Encore for Reform*, p. 203.

One general point should be made about the profile of the Mugwump survivors. In several respects the socioeconomic traits of the surviving bolters were not entirely typical of the total sample's profile. Indeed,

Table B.1

Comparative Occupational Profile of Three Reform Samples

Occupation	Chandler's Progressives		Graham's Survivors		Mugwump Survivors	
	No.	%	No.	%	No.	%
Businessmen	39	33	15	10	68	23
Lawyers	28	23	31	20	123	41
Publishing	12*	-	46	30	33	12
Educators	?	-	14	9	36	11
Doctors	?	-	2	1	19	6
Clergymen	?	-	13	8	13	4
Social Workers	?	-	13	8	0	0
Others	40	34	21	14	10	3

*Does not include authors. Chandler grouped authors in the "other" category, along with college professors, social workers, doctors, clergymen, and other professionals.

if the Mugwumps as a whole are contrasted with the progressive samples, the distinctions between the two generations of reformers become greater.

The Mugwumps as a whole were older than those who lived until 1910. The median birthdate for the youngish sample of New York City bolters, for instance, was 1846; whereas the comparable date for the survivors was 1850. Furthermore, even though there is some overlapping between the total Mugwump and progressive age groups, the chronological center of gravity in the two generations was quite distinct. Half the New York City Mugwumps of 1884 were born between 1839 and 1853, while Graham reports (p. 196) that of his total sample "most were born between 1855 and 1872."

Even more striking is the sharp reduction in the number of businessmen within the Mugwump sample between the 1884 group and the surviving group. Including the business-oriented, white-collar workers from the 1884 sample, the percentage of 1884 New York City bolters in business was 48 percent and the percentage of Mugwump businessmen nationally was only slightly lower (40 percent).[3] This is a considerably higher proportion of businessmen than is found among the progressive era samples. Referring to the figures in table B.1, roughly one-third of Chandler's Progressives, about one-tenth of Graham's surviving progressives, and less than one-fourth of the Mugwump survivors were businessmen—compared with four-tenths to nearly one-half of the 1884 Mugwump samples.

Table B.2 further illustrates the decline in the percentage of businessmen within the Mugwump camp between 1884 and 1910. While bolters in professional occupations retained almost exactly their former proportional relationship between the 1884 and 1910 national profiles, the business category dropped off sharply. The three samples compared here are: 1) the profile of 422 New York City area Mugwumps in 1884, 2) a profile of 660 bolters nationally in 1884, and 3) the national sample of survivors as of 1910.

Table B.2
Three Mugwump Occupational Profiles Compared

Occupation	1) N. Y. C. Sample: 1884		2) National Sample: 1884		3) Survivors Sample: 1910	
	No.	%	No.	%	No.	%
Businessmen*	203	48	267	40	68	23
Lawyers	111	26	183	28	123	41
Educators	11	3	57	9	36	12
Publishing	34	8	54	8	33	11
Doctors	39	9	39	6	19	6
Clergymen	12	3	32	5	13	4
Other	12	3	28	4	10	3

*Businessmen here includes both merchants and manufacturers as well as the business-oriented, white-collar workers from the two 1884 samples.

From tables B.1 and B.2 it is clear that businessmen played a larger role numerically in the original Mugwump group than they did in any of the progressive era samples, including that of the surviving Mugwumps. This fact would seem to bear out Robert Wiebe's contention that as the progressive era approached, liberal reform was increasingly dominated by professionals—or members of the "new middle class" as he labels them. The surviving Mugwumps, too, were dominantly professional men—a fact that lends credence to my view that the younger Mugwumps figured in the transition from the old to the new liberalism in the eastern United States. Although this conclusion derives in part from my use of the socioeconomic profile technique, it does not prove or disprove the status revolution thesis. Indeed, having already expressed elsewhere my reservations about that interpretation of reform,[4] I am satisfied that the story of the nexus between mugwumpery and progressivism is sufficiently interesting in its own right.

Appendix C

Mugwumps Living in 1910: A Masterlist

Note: In some instances I have been unable to locate the date of an individual's death, and in these cases I have listed the last date on which the man was ascertainably living and added a ± mark to indicate that this date does not represent the death date.

Charles Francis Adams, Jr., 1835-1915

Henry Adams, 1838-1918

Felix Adler, 1851-1933

Henry M. Alden, 1836-1919

Walter S. Allerton, 1852-1930

John W. Alling, 1841-1927

James Bar Ames, 1846-1910

Royal Amidon, 1854-1938

Joseph Anderson, 1836-1916

William G. Andrews, 1835-1912

Earliss P. Arvine, 1846-1914

Edward W. Avery, 1841-1917

George D. Ayers, 1857-1933

Robert T. Babson, 1862-1946

John G. Bacchus, ?-1919

Benjamin W. Bacon, 1860-1932

Francis Bacon, 1831-1912

Gorham Bacon, 1855-1940

Thomas R. Bacon, 1850-1913

Lyman H. Bagg, 1846-1911

Simeon E. Baldwin, 1840-1927

Frederic Bancroft, 1860-1945

Henry W. Barnes, 1832-1914

Danford N. Barney, 1859-1936

Charles H. Barrows, 1853-1918

Sylvester Baxter, 1850-1927

Edward L. Baylies, 1857-1932

Pascal P. Beals, 1850-1934

William Beebe, 1851-1917

William C. Beecher, 1848-1929

Edward D. Bettens, 1848/9-1920

Poultney Bigelow, 1855-1954

John Binney, 1844-1913

Charles Sumner Bird, 1855-1927

Joseph B. Bishop, 1848-1927

Francis Blake, 1850-1913

Edward P. Bliss, 1850-1916

Charles J. Bonaparte, 1851-1921

Albert D. Bosson, 1853-1926

Henry E. Bothfeld, 1859-1937+

Charles P. Bowditch, 1842-1921

Clarence W. Bowen, 1852-1933

Richard Rogers Bowker, 1848-1933
Samuel Bowles, 1851-1915
Gamaliel Bradford, 1831-1911
Gamaliel Bradford, 1863-1932
Louis D. Brandeis, 1856-1941
Daniel T. Bromley, 1844-1921
Charles Sumner Brown, 1860-1926
Zephaniah Brown, 1844-1911
Albert H. Buck, 1842-1922
Gurdon S. Buck, ?-1934
Henry H. Buck, 1854-1910
James M. Bugbee, 1837-1913
William L. Bull, 1844-1914
Edward L. Burlingame, 1848-1922
Silas W. Burt, 1830-1912
Robert S. Bussing, 1853-1925
Edward P. Call, 1855-1919
William J. Campbell, 1859-1937
George F. Canfield, 1854-1933
William H. Carmalt, 1836-1929
Franklin Carter, 1837-1919
James R. Carter, 1849-1923
Edward Cary, 1840-1917
Thomas Cary, ?-1921
Zechariah Chafee, ?-1943
Heman W. Chaplin, 1847-1924
Elihu Chauncey, 1840-1916
William G. Choate, 1830-1920
Irving P. Church, 1851-1931
John Claflin, 1850-1938
Robert P. Clapp, 1855-1936
Clement Cleveland, 1843-1934
Charles R. Codman, 1829-1918
George C. Coffin, ?-1913
James F. Colby, 1850-1939
John H. Comstock, 1849-1931
Richard B. Comstock, 1854-1923

William J. Coombs, 1833-1922
Robert C. Cornell, 1852-1918
James L. Cowles, 1843-1922
John K. Creevy, 1841-1921
Frederick Cromwell, 1843-
1914
Ralph W. Cutler, 1853-1917
Ephraim S. Cutter, 1832-1917
Robert Fulton Cutting, 1852-
1934
William Bayard Cutting, 1850-
1912
Richard Henry Dana, III, 1851-
1931
Frederick W. Davis, 1855-1917
Charles S. Davison, 1855-1942
Lewis L. Delafield, 1863-1944
William B. De Las Casas, 1857-
1930
Clarence Deming, 1848-1913
Horace E. Deming, 1850-1925
George P. Denman, ?-1930
George G. DeWitt, 1845-1912
Franklin B. Dexter, 1842-1920
Frederick Dodge, 1847-1927
Ethan Allan Doty, 1837-1915
William R. Dudley, 1848-1911
John L. Dufais, 1855-1935
Conrad V. Dykeman, 1856-
1943
George H. Earle, 1856-1928
Amasa F. Eaton, 1841-1914
Frederick C. Eaton, 1862-1921
George S. Eddy, 1843-1920+
Charles W. Eliot, 1834-1926
Samuel Eliot, 1862-1950
Lawrence C. Embree, 1856-1912

William Endicott, 1826-1914
William Everett, 1839-1910
Henry W. Farnam, 1853-1933
John W. Farwell, 1843-1929
Frederick P. Fish, 1855-1930
Charles H. Fiske, 1840-1921
John Foord, 1844-1922
Roger Foster, 1857-1924
William Dudley Foulke, 1848-1935
Austen G. Fox, 1849-1937
George L. Fox, 1852-1931
Jabez Fox, 1850-1923
John Frankenheimer, 1853-1917
Simon H. Gage, 1851-1944
Thomas D. Goodell, 1854-1920
Henry W. Goodrich, 1860-1925
Francis Goodwin, 1839-1923
James J. Goodwin, 1835-1915
Robert Grant, 1852-1940
Richard B. Greenwood, 1842-1915
Solomon B. Griffin, 1852-1925
Charles E. Grinnell, 1841-1916
Francis B. Gummere, 1855-1919
John C. Haddock, 1850-1914
William H. Hamilton, 1859-1931
Joseph Henry Harper, 1850-1938
Samuel C. Harriot, 1863-1922
Ashton Harvey, ?-1925
James Heard, 1860-1940
John Herbert, 1849-1913+
Henry Lee Higginson, 1834-1919
Thomas Wentworth Higginson, 1823-1911
George C. Hodges, 1857-1929
Henry Holt, 1840-1926

Samuel R. Honey, 1842-1927
Archibald M. Howe, 1848-1916
Daniel R. Howe, 1851-1917
Louis Howland, 1857-1934
Woodward Hudson, 1858-1938
Freeman Hunt, 1855-1929
Chester Huntington, 1843-1929
Frederick G. Ireland, 1846-1915
Charles C. Jackson, 1843-1926
Abraham Jacobi, 1830-1919
William James, 1842-1910
John Franklin Jameson, 1859-1937
Arthur R. Jarrett, ?-1922
J. Foster Jenkins, 1861-1931
Robert U. Johnson, 1853-1937
David Starr Jordan, 1851-1931
William V. Kellen, 1852-1942
Crammond Kennedy, 1842-1918
R. Nelson Kenyon, ?-1939
Lawrence Kneeland, 1858-1920
George T. Ladd, 1842-1921
James T. Law, 1852-1917
Roswell Lawrence, 1856-1921
Francis Lawton, 1848-1922
William C. Lawton, 1853-1941
Walter Learned, 1847-1915
John B. Leavitt, 1849-1930
Lewis Cass Ledyard, 1851-1932
George V. Leverett, 1846-1917
William A. Linn, 1846-1917
William R. Lord, 1847-1916
Thomas R. Lounsbury, 1838-1915

Seth Low, 1850-1916
Francis Cabot Lowell, 1855-1911
Graham McAdam, ?-1917
Charles McBurney, 1845-1913
William W. McClench, 1854-1928
Clarence McKim, 1852/3-1916
Charles MacVeagh, 1860-1931
Franklin MacVeagh, 1837-1934
Edward S. Marsh, 1858-1939
George S. Merriam, 1843-1914
Alfred Meyer, 1854-1950
Arthur W. Milbury, 1852/3-1933+
Charles R. Miller, 1849-1922
George A. Miller, 1853-1936
George D. Miller, 1847-1932
R. Burnham Moffat, 1861-1916
John L. Moffatt, 1853-1917
Lewis F. Mott, 1863-1941
Charles C. Nadal, 1855-1931
Ehrman S. Nadal, 1843-1922
Harry P. Nichols, 1850-1940
William H. Nichols, 1852-1930
Charles P. Norton, 1858-1922
Charles M. Oelrichs, 1858/9-1932
David B. Ogden, 1849-1923
Ludlow Ogden, 1853-1929
Stephen H. Olin, 1847-1925
William S. Opdyke, 1836-1922
Francis A. Osborn, 1833-1914
Charles H. Owen, 1838-1922
George B. Packard, 1852-1927
S. Davis Page, 1840-1922
Robert Treat Paine, 1835-1910
William Parkin, 1854-1943
Charles H. Payne, 1860-1918
Edward C. Pearson, 1849-1929
Tracy Peck, 1838-1921

William G. Peckham, 1849-1924
William C. Poland, 1846-1929
Edward Prime, 1832/3-1915
William A. Purrington, 1852-1926
George Haven Putnam, 1844-1930
Henry W. Putnam, 1847-1912
Josiah Quincy, 1859-1919
Charles S. Rackemann, 1857-1933
George Ricardo, 1842-1914
C. A. L. Richards, 1830-1914
Eugene L. Richards, 1838-1912
William R. Richards, 1853-1910
William W. Richards, 1835-1924
Charles Richardson, 1841-1922
Henry Riedel, 1838-1922
John Ritchie, 1853-1939
Edward D. Robbins, 1853-1932
Charles E. Rushmore, 1856/7-1931
Talcott H. Russell, 1847-1917
B. Aymar Sands, 1853-1917
William C. Sanger, 1853-1921
Henry B. Sargent, 1851-1927
George P. Sawyer, 1851-1920
Leopold Schepp, 1841/2-1926
Gustav H. Schwab, 1851-1921
Charles Scribner, 1854-1930
Alfred P. W. Seaman, 1856-1940
DeWitt J. Seligman, 1853-1933
Arthur M. Sherwood, 1856/7-1928

Henry T. Sloane, 1845-1937
Charles C. Soule, 1842-1913
A. J. C. Sowdon, 1835-1911
Nelson S. Spencer, 1856-1934
Edward E. Sprague, 1848-1924
Harold W. Stevens, 1855-1915+
Frederic J. Stimson, 1855-1943
James Stokes, 1842-1918
William E. D. Stokes, 1853-1926
Moorfield Storey, 1845-1929
Oscar S. Straus, 1850-1926
Albert Strauss, 1864-1929
Frederick Strauss, 1865-1937
William Graham Sumner, 1840-1910
Lucius B. Swift, 1844-1929
Henry O. Taylor, 1856-1941
Thomas Fenton Taylor, 1852-1930
Horace H. Thayer, 1847-1924
Francis B. Tiffany, 1855-1936
Edward Tuck, 1842-1938
Ezra A. Tuttle, 1852-1917
John H. Van Amringe, 1835-1915
James H. Van Buren, 1850-1917
George R. VandeWater, 1854-1925
Henry S. VanDuzen, 1853-1928
George Willet Van Nest, 1852-1916
William W. Vaughan, 1848-1939
William E. Ver Planck, 1856-1928
Samuel Wagner, 1842-1937
Howard T. Walden, 1859-1957

Jerome Walker, 1844-1924
William J. Wallace, 1837-1917
Elwyn Waller, 1846-1919
Arthur E. Walradt, 1859-1936
William Hayes Ward, 1835-1916
Winslow Warren, 1838-1930
Jacob Washburn, 1856-1939
Robert F. Weir, 1838-1927
Stephen M. Weld, 1842-1920
Richard W. G. Welling, 1858-1946
Daniel H. Wells, 1845-1929
J. S. C. Wells, 1851-1931
Barrett Wendell, 1855-1921
Meigs H. Whaples, 1845-1928
Edmund Wheelwright, 1854-1912
John T. Wheelwright, 1856-1925
Alfred T. White, 1846-1921
Henry C. White, 1856-1914
Horace White, 1834-1916
Horace S. White, 1852-1934
William A. White, 1843-1927
Frederick W. Whitridge, 1852-1916
Ansley Wilcox, 1856-1930
George Fred Williams, 1852-1932
Moses Williams, 1846-1919
Louis Windmuller, 1835-1913
Erving Winslow, 1839-1922
Stuart Wood, 1853-1914
Walter Wood, 1849-1934
Andrew C. Zabriskie, 1853-1916

Notes

Chapter 1

1. Chauncey M. Depew, *My Memories of Eighty Years* (New York: Charles Scribner's Sons, 1922), 80. *See* also John Sherman, *Recollections of Thirty Years in the House, Senate, and Cabinet: An Autobiography* (New York: Werner Co., 1895); Thomas Collier Platt, *Autobiography* (New York: B. W. Dodge, Co., 1910); and Henry Cabot Lodge, ed., *Selections from the Correspondence of Theodore Roosevelt and Henry Cabot Lodge, 1884-1918* (New York: Charles Scribner's Sons, 1925), especially vol. 1. For a brief introduction to the Mugwump-politico rivalry, *see* H. Wayne Morgan, *From Hayes to McKinley: National Party Politics, 1877-1896* (Syracuse: Syracuse University Press, 1969), 27-31.

2. Thomas Wentworth Higginson, *Cheerful Yesterdays* (Boston: Houghton Mifflin Co., 1899), 336; Joseph B. Bishop, *Charles Joseph Bonaparte: His Life and Public Services* (New York: Charles Scribner's Sons, 1922); Edward Cary, *George William Curtis* (Boston: Houghton Mifflin Co., 1894); John White Chadwick, *George William Curtis* (New York: Harper & Brothers, 1893); William Dudley Foulke, *Lucius B. Swift, A Biography*, Indiana Historical Society Publications, vol. 9 (Indianapolis: By the Society, 1930); Edmund M. Wheelwright, "Memoir of John F. Andrew," *Publications of the Colonial Society of Massachusetts*, 3 (1895-1897); 351-74; Barrett Wendell, "Edmund M. Wheelwright, '76," *Harvard Graduates Magazine*, 21 (1912-1913): 56-8; and Robert Grant, "Barrett Wendell," *Massachusetts Historical Society Proceedings*, 54 (February 1921): 195-201; Charles Eliot Norton, ed., *Orations and Addresses of George William Curtis*, 3 vols. (New York: Harper & Brothers, 1894); and Frederic Bancroft, ed., *Speeches, Correspondence and Political Papers of Carl Schurz*, 6 vols. (New York: G. P. Putnam's Sons, 1913); and among the autobiographies the more important ones are cited in the Bibliography—Charles Francis Adams, Jr., Henry Adams, Poultney Bigelow, Gamaliel Bradford, Jr., William

Dudley Foulke, Robert Grant, J. Henry Harper, Henry Holt, David Starr Jordan, George Haven Putnam, Frederic J. Stimson, Oscar S. Straus, and Richard W. G. Welling.

3. James Bryce, *The American Commonwealth* (New York: Macmillan Co., 1888), 2: 344.

4. James Ford Rhodes, *History of the United States from the Compromise of 1850* (New York: Macmillan Co., 1900-1928), especially vol. 7; Bliss Perry, *Life and Letters of Henry Lee Higginson* (Boston: Atlantic Monthly Press, 1921), and *Richard Henry Dana, 1851-1931* (Boston: Houghton Mifflin Co., 1933); and Mark A. DeWolfe Howe, *Barrett Wendell and His Letters* (Boston: Atlantic Monthly Press, 1924) and *Portrait of an Independent, Moorfield Storey* (Boston: Houghton Mifflin Co., 1932).

5. Many works could be cited here, of course, but I am thinking of the viewpoint expressed in John D. Hicks's *The Populist Revolt* (Minneapolis: University of Minnesota, 1931), and in Vernon L. Parrington, *Main Currents in American Thought*, vol. 3, *The Beginnings of Critical Realism in America: 1860-1920* (New York: Harcourt, Brace & World, Harbinger Book edition, 1958), especially the essay "A Chapter in American Liberalism," 401-13.

6. Ari Hoogenboom, *Outlawing the Spoils: A History of the Civil Service Reform Movement, 1865-1883* (Urbana: University of Illinois Press, 1961), 196-7; John G. Sproat, *"The Best Men," Liberal Reformers in the Gilded Age* (New York: Oxford University Press, 1968), and the chapter on "Myopic Mugwumps," 112-41. John Tomsich, *A Genteel Endeavor: American Culture and Politics in the Gilded Age* (Stanford: Stanford University Press, 1971), adopts an interpretative view parallel to that of Hoogenboom and Sproat.

7. John M. Dobson, *Politics in the Gilded Age: A New Perspective on Reform* (New York: Praeger Publishers, 1972), 186.

8. E. McClung Fleming, *R. R. Bowker, Militant Liberal* (Norman: University of Oklahoma Press, 1952); Naomi W. Cohen, *A Dual Heritage: The Public Career of Oscar S. Straus* (Philadelphia: The Jewish Publication Society of America, 1969); and Gerald Kurland, *Seth Low: The Reformer in an Urban and Industrial Age* (New York: Twayne Publishers, 1971).

9. L. E. Fredman, *The Australian Ballot: The Story of an American*

Reform (East Lansing: Michigan State University Press, 1968), 87-8, 92-3, and also Fredman's article, "Seth Low: Theorist of Municipal Reform," *Journal of American Studies*, 6, 1 (April 1972), 19-39.

10. Richard Hofstadter, *The Age of Reform: From Bryan to F.D.R.* (New York: Alfred A. Knopf, 1955), 131, 137, and chapt. 4 (131-73) in general. *See* also Alfred D. Chandler, Jr., "The Origins of Progressive Leadership," in Elting E. Morison, ed., *The Letters of Theodore Roosevelt* (Cambridge, Mass.: Harvard University Press, 1954), vol. 8, appendix 3, 1462-5; and George E. Mowry, "The California Progressive and His Rationale: A Study in Middle-Class Politics," *Mississippi Valley Historical Review*, 36, 2 (September 1949): 239-50.

11. Robert H. Wiebe, *The Search for Order, 1877-1920* (New York: Hill & Wang, 1967), especially chapts. 5, 6, and 7.

12. Gabriel Kolko, *The Triumph of Conservatism: A Reinterpretation of American History, 1900-1916* (New York: Free Press of Glencoe, 1963); and James Weinstein, *The Corporate Ideal in the Liberal State, 1900-1918* (Boston: Beacon Press, 1968). *See* also Clarence J. Karier, "Testing for Order and Control in the Corporate Liberal State," *Educational Theory*, 22, 2 (Spring 1972): 154-80.

13. Samuel P. Hays, "The Politics of Reform in Municipal Government in the Progressive Era," *Pacific Northwest Quarterly*, 55, 4 (October 1964): 157-69. *See* also Hays's "The Social Analysis of American Political History, 1880-1920," *Political Science Quarterly*, 80, 3 (September 1965): 373-94, and "Political Parties and the Community-Society Continuum," in William N. Chambers and Walter Dean Burnham, eds., *The American Party Systems: Stages of Political Development* (New York: Oxford University Press, 1967), 152-81; and "A Systematic Social History," in George Billias and Gerald Grob, eds., *American History: Retrospect and Prospect* (New York: The Free Press, 1971), 315-66.

14. Geoffrey Blodgett, "Reform Thought and the Genteel Tradition," in H. Wayne Morgan, ed., *The Gilded Age*, rev. ed. (Syracuse: Syracuse University Press, 1970), 57.

15. As a portrait of progressivism in all its aspects, the revisionist writing to date has some limitations. There is a danger of identifying progressivism too exclusively with the cosmopolitans and with the

conservative aim of social order (rather than the goal of social change). Kolko and Weinstein, for example, scarcely mention the social progressives—settlement workers, labor reformers, and advocates of social legislation—except in connection with business thinking, or in Weinstein's case, briefly as a part of the National Civic Federation's program.

Chapter 2

1. Frederic Bancroft, ed., *Speeches, Correspondence, and Political Papers of Carl Schurz* (New York: G. P. Putnam's Sons, 1913), 4: 211.

2. John G. Sproat, *"The Best Men"* (New York: Oxford University Press, 1968), sets forth these weaknesses in great detail.

3. Ari Hoogenboom, *Outlawing the Spoils* (Urbana: University of Illinois Press, 1961), 186-90, 211-12.

4. Ari Hoogenboom, "Civil Service Reform and Public Morality," in H. Wayne Morgan, ed., *The Gilded Age*, rev. ed. (Syracuse: Syracuse University Press, 1970), 95.

5. Speech to the Brooklyn Young Republican Club, October 21, 1883, Scrapbook III, 1883 (Low papers, Columbia University). Other helpful books on Low's Brooklyn career are Harold C. Syrett, *The City of Brooklyn 1865-1898* (New York: Columbia University Press, 1944), and Gerald Kurland, *Seth Low* (New York: Twayne Publishers, 1971).

6. *New York Times*, 30 September 1884.

7. Other Massachusetts Mugwumps elected to the legislature or Congress between 1865 and 1884 were: Samuel M. Quincy, Moses Williams, Francis E. Parker, John F. Andrew, Samuel Hoar, Robert Treat Paine, and Joseph H. Walker.

8. Massachusetts Reform Club, *Report, 1888* (Boston: By the Club, 1888), 3.

9. Geoffrey Blodgett, *The Gentle Reformers: Massachusetts Democrats in the Cleveland Era* (Cambridge, Mass.: Harvard University Press, 1966), 19-20.

10. National Committee of Independents and Republicans, "Pamphlet 1," July 30, 1884.

11. *New York Times*, 26 October 1884.

12. Albert Shaw to J. Franklin Jameson, July 20, 1884, as quoted in Elizabeth Donnan and Leo F. Stock, eds., *An Historian's World: Selec-*

tions from the Correspondence of John Franklin Jameson, Memoirs of the American Philosophical Society, vol. 42 (Philadelphia: American Philosophical Society, 1956), 36.

13. Henry Nash Smith and William M. Gibson, eds., *Mark Twain-Howells Letters: The Correspondence of Samuel L. Clemens and William D. Howells, 1872-1910* (Cambridge, Mass.: Belknap Press of Harvard University Press, 1960), 2:501-8.

14. As quoted in Robert L. Beisner, *Twelve Against Empire: The Anti-Imperialists, 1898-1900* (New York: McGraw-Hill Book Co., 1968), 144. On Lodge and Roosevelt, *see* Claude M. Fuess, "Carl Schurz and Henry Cabot Lodge in 1884," *New England Quarterly*, 5, 3 (July 1932): 453-82; and James C. Malin, "Roosevelt and the Elections of 1884 and 1888," *Mississippi Valley Historical Review*, 14, 1 (June 1927): 25-38.

15. Theodore Dwight Woolsey to Simeon E. Baldwin, August 30, 1884 (Simeon E. Baldwin papers, Yale University). *See* also George Frisbee Hoar's letter of August 30, 1884, *Hartford Evening Post*, October Political Supplement.

16. *New York Times*, 23 July 1884.

17. William Dudley Foulke, *Lucius B. Swift, A Biography*, Indiana Historical Society Publications, vol. 9 (Indianapolis: By the Society, 1930), 15.

18. "Minutes," January 12, 1885, post-election meeting of the National Committee of Independents and Republicans (Richard Rogers Bowker papers, New York Public Library), 44.

19. Ibid., 36.

20. Ibid., 37.

21. Ibid., 44. On one independent paper, *see* Mark D. Hirsch, "The New York Times and the Election of 1884," *New York History*, 39, 3 (July 1948): 301-8. On the plight of Mugwumps in cities without an independent newspaper, *see* Edward D. Robbins (of Hartford) to Henry W. Farnam, July 19, 1884 (Henry W. Farnam papers, Yale University). Frank L. Mott devotes a section of his standard work on *American Journalism*, rev. ed. (New York: Macmillan Co., 1950), 411ff, to "The Rise of the Independent Press, 1872-1892," but the reasons for the emancipation of the press from party control remain unclear. Some influences mentioned were: increased availability of advertising revenue,

greater attention to human-interest news rather than political reporting, and higher educational levels among newspaper readers after the Civil War.

22. U.S. Department of the Interior, Census Office, *Compendium of the Tenth Census*, part I (Washington, D.C., 1882), figures for 1880.

23. J. Lawrence Dunham to Simeon E. Baldwin, September 12, 1884 (Baldwin papers). *See* also Francis A. Henry to Baldwin, September 25, 1884, ibid., in which this Ridgefield, Connecticut (population 1,685), bolter claimed, "I am left *quite alone* [here] to represent spontaneous Cleveland Republicanism."

24. Philip P. Chase, "The Attitude of the Protestant Clergy in Massachusetts During the Election of 1884," *Massachusetts Historical Society Proceedings*, 64 (1930-1932): 471-2, 485. James Browne Gardner to James Freeman Clarke, September 5, 1885 (James Freeman Clarke papers, Harvard University).

25. Gerald W. McFarland, "Politics, Morals, and the Mugwump Reformers" (Ph.D. diss., Columbia University, 1965), 149.

26. Even the towns from which the Mugwumps came often had industrial economies. Of nine instances in Massachusetts for which information was available, seven towns were manufacturing towns (more than 50 percent of the gainfully employed residents were working in industrial jobs). The other two communities were mainly farm communities.

27. Alfred P. Putnam to James Freeman Clarke, November 9, 1884 (Clarke papers).

28. McFarland, "Politics, Morals, and the Mugwump Reformers," 151. One hundred eighty-seven were in their twenties or thirties. Two hundred two were forty or older.

29. A Young Republican [R. R. Bowker], "An Open Letter to Mr. Curtis," *New York Evening Post*, 2 September 1879, and "No Surrender," ibid., 5 September 1879. E. McClung Fleming, *R. R. Bowker* (Norman: University of Oklahoma Press, 1952), is the standard biography. A Republican state boss wrote that the way to quiet the "grumbling and discontent" among Republicans was to emphasize the "old war and 'solid South' issue." Thomas C. Platt to Whitelaw Reid, September 18, 1879 (Whitelaw Reid papers, Library of Congress).

30. David Ames Wells to Carl Schurz, April 13, 1883 (Carl Schurz papers, Library of Congress). Earlier Horace White had written Schurz,

ibid., April 10, 1880, "I think you and I and the 1872 men generally, ought to keep away from the St. Louis Convention and leave it wholly to the new recruits. I would not have taken a leading part in the Independent movement if the young men who started it could have found any body of prominence to take hold—they could not."

31. Blodgett, *Gentle Reformers*, 23. Gordon S. Wood, "The Massachusetts Mugwumps," *New England Quarterly*, 33, 4 (December 1960): 435-51.

32. Raymond L. Bridgman, *The Independents of Massachusetts in 1884* (Boston: Cupples, Upham & Co., Publishers, 1885), 22.

33. A Young Republican [R. R. Bowker], *New York Tribune*, 5 April 1876. Later Bowker wrote the *Tribune's* editor, Whitelaw Reid, "I cannot accept the military metaphors that appeal to me not to desert my 'general.'" October 16, 1879 (Reid papers).

34. George Haven Putnam to Carl Schurz, June 13, 1884 (Schurz papers). The records of the National Committee of Independents and Republicans are in the R. R. Bowker papers, New York Public Library and Library of Congress, hereafter cited as "Bowker papers, NYPL" or "Bowker papers, LoC."

35. Nationally the proportion of professionals ran even higher. McFarland, "Politics, Morals, and the Mugwump Reformers," 152. Cities whose "best men" were more business-oriented, Hartford and Philadelphia, for example, were among the weaker locales for Mugwump protest in the East. On the Philadelphia Mugwumps, *see* Philip S. Benjamin, "Gentlemen Reformers in the Quaker City, 1870-1912," *Political Science Quarterly*, 85, 1 (March 1970): 61-79.

36. Henry W. Farnam, "Diary," June 23, 1884 (Farnam papers). For a similar incident in Massachusetts, *see* Blodgett, *Gentle Reformers*, 35-6.

37. Sidney Ratner, ed., *New Light on the History of Great American Fortunes* (New York: Augustus M. Kelley, 1953) reprints lists of American millionaires compiled by the *New York Tribune* and *New York World* in 1892 and 1902.

38. Mainly from the *Social Register, New York, 1890*, vol. 6, no. 1 (New York: Social Register Association, 1890), though some other names were gleaned from additional volumes in the late 1880s.

39. During the 1884 campaign Mugwumps sometimes excused them-

selves from political work because of pressing business commitments, as with Charles W. Holbrook to Henry W. Farnam, October 15, 1884 (Farnam papers). For other instances in which Mugwumps limited their political careers partly on financial grounds, *see* Charles R. Codman, "Notes and Reminiscences," 2:54 (Charles R. Codman papers, Massachusetts Historical Society); and Edmund M. Wheelwright to John F. Andrew, January 20, 1887 (John F. Andrew papers, Massachusetts Historical Society).

40. U.S., Department of Commerce, *Historical Statistics of the United States from Colonial Times to 1957* (Washington, D.C., 1960), 211, 214.

41. I did not count the M.A. degrees, of which the New York bolters received thirty-seven, in this total because all but a few were either honorary or awarded perfunctorily a year or so after the B.A.

42. J. Henry Harper, *I Remember* (New York: Harper & Brothers, 1934), 247. Will Irwin, *A History of the Union League Club of New York City* (New York: Dodd, Mead & Co., 1952), 125, 155. Union League of New York, *Report and List of Members* (New York: G. P. Putnam's Sons, 1887).

43. The Century Association, *The Century 1847-1947* (New York: The Century Association, 1944), 27, and University Club, *Report, 1884-1885* (New York: Henry Bessey, 1885). Henry Holt, *Garrulities of an Octogenarian Editor* (New York: Houghton Mifflin Co., 1923), 110-11, wrote that in the 1880s the Century, so small that everyone knew everyone, was "the most active center of culture in New York."

44. Contrast, for instance, the early confidence of one Mugwump source (*New Haven Morning News*, 30 June 1884) that ministers generally supported the bolt, with its post-scandal admission that religious leaders and journals were abandoning the Mugwump cause (ibid., 21, 15, and 28 August 1884). *See* also Chase, "Attitude of the Protestant Clergy," 467-98.

45. The most dramatic examples of this pattern were those Republicans who did not attend college (their highest academic education is listed here in parentheses), but "read law" and were subsequently admitted to the bar: Theodore B. Gates (Gilbertsville Academy), Elizur B. Hinsdale (public schools), Anson G. McCook (public school until fifteen years of age), Nathaniel Niles (Phillips Andover), William H. Robertson (Union Academy), and Benjamin F. Tracy (Oswego Academy).

46. These veterans are listed in appendix A, most of them identified through the New York (State), Adjutant General's Office, *New York in the War of the Rebellion*, comp. Frederick Phisterer, 3rd ed., 5 vols. and Index (Albany: J. B. Lyon Co., 1912).

47. Admittedly this statement is based on very impressionistic evidence, namely, a comparison of family backgrounds as described in brief biographical sketches in sources such as the *Dictionary of American Biography*, *Who Was Who*, and so forth.

48. Ari Hoogenboom, "An Analysis of Civil Service Reformers," *The Historian*, 23, 1 (November 1960): 54-78.

Chapter 3

1. Charles Eliot Norton, ed., *Orations and Addresses of George William Curtis* (New York: Harper & Brothers, 1894), 1: 266.

2. Rosamond Gilder, ed., *Letters of Richard Watson Gilder* (Boston: Houghton Mifflin Co., 1916), 221. *See* also E. L. Godkin to Moorfield Storey, May 23, 1891 (Edwin Lawrence Godkin papers, Harvard University).

3. Matthew Josephson, *The Politicos, 1865-1898* (New York: Harcourt, Brace & Co., 1938), 96, and Ari Hoogenboom, "Civil Service Reform and Public Morality," in H. Wayne Morgan, ed., *The Gilded Age*, rev. ed. (Syracuse: Syracuse University Press, 1970), 90-2.

4. Henry L. Stimson and McGeorge Bundy, *On Active Service in Peace and War* (New York: Harper & Brothers, 1948), 17, and also George Fred Williams to Carl Schurz, January 1, 1885 (Schurz papers).

5. Charles Francis Adams, Jr., *Charles Francis Adams, 1835-1915: An Autobiography* (Boston: Houghton Mifflin Co., 1916), 190; Moorfield Storey, *Politics as a Duty and as a Career* (New York: G. P. Putnam's Sons, 1889), 29; and Charles Eliot Norton to E. L. Godkin, March 13, 1867 (Godkin papers).

6. This account is drawn mainly from Daniel H. Calhoun, *Professional Lives in America: Structure and Aspiration, 1750-1850* (Cambridge, Mass.: Harvard University Press, 1965).

7. Ibid., 192.

8. Merle Curti, *The Growth of American Thought* (New York:

Harper & Brothers, 1943), 581. Professional esteem, it was hoped, would also promote "social esteem." Richard T. Ely, *Ground Under Our Feet* (New York: Macmillan Co., 1938), 122-3.

9. Curti, *Growth of American Thought*, 587.

10. *Constitution, Address, and List of Members of the American Association for the Promotion of Social Science* (Boston: Wright & Potter, Printers, 1866), 3. An interesting, brief analysis of the ASSA is Irwin Unger, *The Greenback Era: A Social and Political History of American Finance, 1865-1879* (Princeton: Princeton University Press, 1964), 136-9.

11. Curti, *Growth of American Thought*, 587.

12. Dorman B. Eaton to Whitelaw Reid, January 18, 1870 (Reid papers).

13. Association of the Bar of the City of New York, *Yearbook 1870* (New York: Douglas Taylor's Commercial Printing House, 1870), 6.

14. Everett P. Wheeler, *Sixty Years of American Life* (New York: E. P. Dutton & Co., 1917), 127.

15. Association of the Bar of the City of New York, *Yearbook 1870*, 5.

16. Robert H. Wiebe, *The Search for Order, 1877-1920* (New York: Hill & Wang, 1967), 116-17.

17. The American Bar Association, *Call for a Conference; Proceedings of Conference; First Meeting of the Association; Officers, Members, etc.* (Philadelphia: Jackson Brothers, Printers, 1878), 16.

18. Stephen Smith, "The History of Public Health, 1871-1921," in Mazÿck P. Ravenel, ed., *A Half Century of Public Health: Jubilee Historical Volume of the American Public Health Association* (New York: American Public Health Association, 1921), 10-11.

19. Ibid., 14. *Public Health: Reports and Papers of the American Public Health Association*, vol. 1, 1873 (New York: Hurd & Houghton, 1875), xii.

20. Calhoun, *Professional Lives in America*, 3, 187.

21. *Public Health* (1873), x. Also Gert H. Brieger, "Sanitary Reform in New York City: Stephen Smith and the Passage of the Metropolitan Health Bill," *Bulletin of the History of Medicine*, 40, 5 (September-October, 1966): 424; and Gerald W. McFarland, "Partisan of Nonpartisanship: Dorman B. Eaton and the Genteel Reform Tradition,"

Journal of American History, 54, 4 (March 1968): 809. Wiebe, *Search for Order*, 116, reports that by the twentieth century even Tammany Hall boss Charlie Murphy said public health was above politics.

22. R. R. Bowker, "The Work of the Nineteenth-Century Librarian for the Librarian of the Twentieth," in *Papers and Proceedings of the Sixth General Meeting of the American Library Association, held at Buffalo, August 14 to 17, 1883* (Boston: Rockwell & Church, 1883), 85-6.

23. Richard Hofstadter and C. DeWitt Hardy, *The Development and Scope of Higher Education in the United States* (New York: Columbia University Press, 1952), 64-5.

24. *Hartford Evening Post*, 1 July 1884.

25. J. Franklin Jameson to John Jameson, November 2, 1884, in Elizabeth Donnan and Leo F. Stock, eds., *An Historian's World, Memoirs of the American Philosophical Society*, vol. 42 (Philadelphia: American Philosophical Society, 1956), 37. Walter Scaife (another Johns Hopkins man) made much the same observation to Albert Shaw, December 1, 1884 (Albert Shaw papers, New York Public Library). On Cornell, *see New York Times*, 16 and 31 October 1884. David Starr Jordan, *The Days of a Man: Being Memories of a Naturalist, Teacher, and Minor Prophet of Democracy* (Yonkers, N.Y.: World Book Co., 1922), 1: 317.

26. *Journal of the American Chemical Society*, vol. 1 (1879); and "American Historical Association," file for October 1885-April 1886 (Baldwin papers).

27. *Proceedings of the First Annual Session of the American Philological Association, held at Poughkeepsie, New York, July, 1869* (New York: S. W. Green, Printer, 1870), 5.

28. *Proceedings of the American Psychological Association, 1892-3* (New York: Macmillan Co., 1893). Other presidencies held in professional groups by Mugwumps were: American Economic Association, Henry W. Farnam (1910-1911); American Historical Association, Simeon E. Baldwin (1905); American Medical Association, Lewis A. Sayre (1880) and Abraham Jacobi (1912); American Philological Association, Thomas R. Lounsbury (assistant secretary, 1871), Tracy Peck (president, 1885-1886), and Thomas D. Goodell (vice president, 1909-1911 and president, 1911-1912); Modern Language Association, Francis

B. Gummere (1905) and Lewis F. Mott (1911); American Surgical
Association, Robert F. Weir (1900) and William H. Carmalt (1907);
American Oriental Society, William D. Whitney (1884-1890); American
Dialect Society, Lewis F. Mott (treasurer, 1892-1898, president 1899-
1900). American Opthalmological Society, Samuel B. St. John (secre-
tary 1888-1904, president 1904).

29. Kurland, *Seth Low* (New York: Twayne Publishers, 1971), 37-47.

30. Robert U. Johnson, *Remembered Yesterdays* (Boston: Little,
Brown & Co., 1923), 241-60. The piracy theme is found on pages 246
and 257. *See* also Gilder, ed., *Letters of Richard Watson Gilder*, 190-
204, and E. McClung Fleming, *R. R. Bowker* (Norman: University of
Oklahoma Press, 1952), 185-7.

31. Wiebe, *Search for Order*, 127-31 and 160-1.

32. For the campaign and biographical information on the candidates,
see Allan Nevins, *Grover Cleveland: A Study in Courage* (New York:
Dodd, Mead & Co., 1948); and David S. Muzzey, *James G. Blaine, A
Political Idol of Other Days* (New York: Dodd, Mead & Co., 1934).

33. Lee Benson, "Research Problems in American Political Historiog-
raphy," in Mirra Komarovsky, ed., *Common Frontiers of the Social
Sciences* (Glencoe, Ill.: The Free Press, 1957), 124-68, and Robert T.
Bower, "Opinion Research and Historical Interpretation of Elections,"
Public Opinion Quarterly, 12, 2 (Fall 1948): 455-64.

34. Robert D. Marcus, *Grand Old Party: Political Structure in the
Gilded Age, 1880-1896* (New York: Oxford University Press, 1971),
5-7.

Chapter 4

1. Horace E. Deming to Henry W. Farnam, November 15, 1884;
George Fred Williams to Farnam, November 18, 24 (A.M. and P.M.);
and Simeon E. Baldwin to Farnam, December 1, 1884 (Farnam papers),
and Carl Schurz to George Fred Williams, November 23, 1884, in
Frederic Bancroft, ed., *Speeches, Correspondence, and Political Papers
of Carl Schurz* (New York: G. P. Putnam's Sons, 1913), 4: 293-4.

2. Grover Cleveland to George William Curtis, December 25, 1884,
in Allan Nevins, ed., *The Letters of Grover Cleveland* (Boston:

Houghton Mifflin Co., 1933), 52-3, and George Fred Williams to Carl Schurz, January 1, 1885 (Schurz papers).

3. Carl Schurz to Grover Cleveland, November 15, and December 10, 1884, in Bancroft, ed., *Speeches . . . Carl Schurz*, 4: 288-90 and 297-305. Cleveland to Schurz, December 6, 1884, and Horace White to Schurz, January 24, 1885 (Schurz papers). Horace White to Cleveland, November 24, 1884 and February 2, 1885, and to Francis L. Stetson, December 15, 1884; George Jones to Cleveland, January 4, 1885; and George William Curtis to Cleveland, February 10, 1885 (Grover Cleveland papers, Library of Congress).

4. Horace White to Cleveland, February 25, 1885; John Foord to Cleveland, February 26, 1885, and E. L. Godkin to Cleveland, February 26, 1885 (Cleveland papers). Horace White to Carl Schurz, January 24, 30, and February 1, 1885 (Schurz papers); and Schurz to L. Q. C. Lamar, March 2, 1885, in Bancroft, ed., *Speeches . . . Carl Schurz*, 4: 355-6. *New York Evening Post*, 6 March 1885. A. J. C. Sowdon to Charles S. Fairchild, March 9, 1885, and William Potts to Fairchild, March 12, 1885 (Charles S. Fairchild papers, New York Historical Society).

5. Winslow Warren to William Everett, September 27, 1886 (William Everett papers, Massachusetts Historical Society). Warren to Carl Schurz, October 9, 1886, and George Fred Williams to Schurz, same date (Schurz papers). *See* also the Mugwump letters to Andrew: A. J. C. Sowdon, October 1, 1886; Benjamin Kimball, October 1, 1886; Robert Grant, September 30, 1886; Henry L. Higginson, October 5, 1886; and James Freeman Clarke, October 6, 1886 (Andrew papers).

6. Cleveland to Silas W. Burt, November 8, 1885, and to John T. Graves, July 30, 1887, in Nevins, ed., *Letters of Grover Cleveland*, 92-3, 146-7. For a sample of the purists' style, *see* Schurz to Cleveland, September 24, 1885; Silas W. Burt to Daniel Lamont, November 5, 6, 14, and 24, 1885, and to Cleveland, November 5, 9, and 17, 1885; and E. L. Godkin to Cleveland, November 10, 1885 (Cleveland papers). Also, George William Curtis to Silas W. Burt, November 1, 1885 (Silas W. Burt papers, New York Historical Society).

7. George Fred Williams to William C. Endicott, March 16, and April 5, 1886 (William C. Endicott papers, Massachusetts Historical Society). Winslow Warren to William Everett, March 23, 1885, and

Charles R. Codman to Everett, April 28, 1886 (Everett papers). Carl
Schurz to George Fred Williams, March 18, 1886, in Bancroft, ed.,
Speeches . . . Carl Schurz, 4: 419-31.

8. Alton B. Parker to Cleveland, October 5, 1885; Austin C. Chapin to
Cleveland, October 3, 1885; Dennis O'Brien to Cleveland, same date;
John Anketell to Daniel Lamont, October 6, 1885; Mark M. Pomeroy
to Lamont, October 9, 1885; J. S. Thompson to Cleveland, October 17,
1885; and David B. Hill to Cleveland, October 31, 1885 (Cleveland
papers).

9. Gerald W. McFarland, "The Breakdown of Deadlock: The Cleveland Democracy in Connecticut, 1884-1894," *The Historian*, 31, 1
(May 1969): 388-90. *New Haven Morning News*, 15 October 1885.
Henry W. Farnam to Simeon E. Baldwin, October 1, 1885 (Baldwin
papers). A. W. Thomas to Farnam, October 16, 1885, and to the members of the Tariff Reform League, October 2, 1886 (Farnam papers).

10. Gordon S. Wood, "The Massachusetts Mugwumps," *New England
Quarterly*, 33, 4 (December 1960): 445-6.

11. Charles R. Codman, "Notes and Reminiscences," 2: 61-3 (Codman papers). Horace White to David Ames Wells, January 11, 1887
(David Ames Wells papers, Library of Congress). George William Curtis
to Silas W. Burt, August 11, 1887 (Burt papers). William Dudley Foulke
to Carl Schurz, February 15, 1888 (William Dudley Foulke papers,
Library of Congress). Charles J. Bonaparte to William Potts, June 6,
1887, and to Francis L. Stetson, June 6 and 9, 1887 (Charles J. Bonaparte papers, Library of Congress).

12. In addition to those mentioned later in the paragraph, some of
the leading Mugwump manufacturers included: Henry T. and Thomas
C. Sloane and Edward P. Bliss (carpets); Robert Bleakie and Spencer
Borden (woolens); Felix Kaufman (leather goods); James Means and
William B. Rice (shoes); and Gorham D. Williams (hardware).

13. Everett P. Wheeler, *Sixty Years of American Life* (New York:
E. P. Dutton & Co., 1917), 178-9.

14. *National Conference of Free Traders and Revenue Reformers . . .
Chicago, November 11 & 12, 1885* (New York: New York Free Trade
Club, 1885), 100ff.; and Roland Hazard to Carl Schurz, January 7,
April 30, and June 14, 1876 (Schurz papers).

15. *National Conference of Free Traders and Revenue Reformers,*

91; and Joseph B. Sargent, *Protection a Burden* (Boston: Massachusetts Tariff Reform League, 1885).

16. *See*, for instance, William Graham Sumner's *Protection and Revenue in 1877* (New York: G. P. Putnam's Sons, 1878), and "Protectionism, the Ism Which Teaches That Waste Makes Wealth," in Albert G. Keller and Maurice R. Davie, eds., *Essays of William Graham Sumner* (New Haven: Yale University Press, 1934), 2: 365-467.

17. David Ames Wells, *Free Trade Essential to Future National Prosperity* (New York: William C. Martin's Steam Printing House, 1882), 29, and *A Primer of Tariff Reform* (New York: State Revenue Reform League, 1884), 36. *See* also Tom E. Terrill, "David A. Wells, the Democracy, and Tariff Reduction, 1877-1894," *Journal of American History*, 55, 3 (December 1969): 540-55; and Bruce Curtis, "William Graham Sumner 'On the Concentration of Wealth,'" *Journal of American History*, 60, 4 (March 1969): 823-32.

18. *New Haven Morning News*, 12 September 1888.

19. *National Conference of Free Traders and Revenue Reformers*, 12, and *The People's Cause*, 1 (January 1889): 2. Bowker's mentor in tariff reform, Abraham L. Earle, wrote that protection was "legislation controlled by capital" similar to "the granting of enormous subsidies in lands to railroads, and the conferring of special privileges and immunities upon banking institutions, manufacturing institutions, and other forms of monopoly." *Our Revenue System and the Civil Service* (New York: G. P. Putnam's Sons, 1878), 12, and Earle to Bowker, November 18, 1880 (Bowker papers, NYPL).

20. Farnam, "Autobiography," section taken from diary entry for September 23, 1883 (Farnam papers).

21. Thomas G. Shearman, "The Owners of the United States," *The Forum*, 8, 3 (November 1889): 262-73, and "The Coming Billionaire," ibid., 10, 5 (January 1891): 546-57; and Shearman to Henry George, March 28, 1881 (Henry George papers, New York Public Library). Abraham L. Earle, George A. Miller, Henry G. Seaver, George St. John Leavens, and Lawrence Dunham were other Mugwump single-taxers. Miller to Henry George, June 28, 1881 (George papers), and Seaver to Carl Schurz, March 5, 1899 (Schurz papers).

22. Thomas Wentworth Higginson, George D. Ayers, Sylvester Baxter, and Joseph Sargent were the Mugwump Bellamyites. Higginson, "Step

by Step," *The Nationalist*, 1 (September 1889): 146; Ayers, "National-ism—True Conservatism," ibid. (November 1889), 230-5; Baxter, "Bellamy's New Book of the New Democracy," *Review of Reviews*, 16, 1 (July 1897), 62-7; and Sargent to L. S. Hull, October 23, 1896, "Letter Book, 1890-1899" (Sargent Family papers, Yale University). James L. Cowles, Charles Holbrook, and George Fred Williams were also sympathetic to the Nationalist program: "Scrapbook of Clippings Relating to Joseph B. Sargent" (Yale University Library stacks), and Sylvester Baxter to Williams, December 26, 1891, April 13, 22, and May 24, 1892 (George Fred Williams papers, Massachusetts Historical Society).

23. Young Men's Democratic Club, *List of Members, 1889* (William E. Russell papers, Massachusetts Historical Society). Henry W. Swift wrote John F. Andrew (November 7, 1888) regarding the latter's successful congressional campaign in 1888, "[Patrick] Maguire was the man who did most of all" to promote Andrew's victory. (Andrew papers).

24. Among the Mugwump YMDC members who received political recognition were: Sherman Hoar, John F. Andrew, and George Fred Williams (elected to Congress); Josiah Quincy (member of the Massachusetts Legislature, assistant secretary of state under Cleveland, and twice Mayor of Boston); John T. Wheelwright (Massachusetts gas and light commissioner and assistant corporation counsel of Boston); Freeman Hunt (Democratic state senator, 1890); Spencer Borden (Governor William E. Russell's staff); Robert Grant (Boston water commissioner); William De Las Casas and Sylvester Baxter (metropolitan park commissioners); and Robert P. Clapp (Democratic nominee for the State Senate, 1890).

25. For a record of one debate, *see Protection vs. Free Trade* (Boston: Home Market Club, 1888). A typical monthly meeting address was "The Place of the Independent in Politics" (April 13, 1888), in James Russell Lowell, *Literary and Political Addresses*, vol. 7 *The Complete Writings of James Russell Lowell* (Boston: Houghton Mifflin Co., Elmwood edition, 1904), 233-68.

26. A Reform Club circular, dated February 1, 1888, described the organization's "immediate purpose" as securing tariff reform. (Bowker papers, NYPL). Mugwump members of the first board of trustees included R. R. Bowker, Daniel H. Chamberlain, Horace E. Deming, E. J. Donnell, and George Haven Putnam.

27. *New Haven Morning News*, 31 May and 2 June 1888. *See* also R. R. Bowker to Henry W. Farnam, May 11, 1887, and the *Constitution of the Reform Club of New Haven* (Farnam papers).

28. Baldwin to E. A. Joachinson, August 1, 1888 (Baldwin papers).

29. Winslow Warren to William Everett, November 24, 1888 (Everett papers). George William Curtis to William Dudley Foulke, March 25 and June 28, 1888 (Foulke papers); William Potts to Charles J. Bonaparte, November 21, 1888, and February 13, 1889 (Bonaparte papers); George William Curtis to Silas W. Burt, February 24, April 10, and June 28, and November 9, 1888 (Burt papers); and Horace White to Carl Schurz, September 16, 1888, and R. R. Bowker to Schurz, July 9 and September 20 1888 (Schurz papers).

30. Winslow Warren to William Everett, April 8, 1889 (Everett papers).

31. George William Curtis to Carl Schurz, March 27, 1889 (Schurz papers); Curtis to Silas W. Burt, March 20 and 29, and April 7, 1889 (Burt papers); and William Potts to Charles J. Bonaparte, February 13, 1889 (Bonaparte papers). Lucius B. Swift, "Civil Service Reform: A Review of Two Administrations," *The Forum*, 14, 1 (October 1892): 201-5, calls for Harrison's defeat.

32. Samuel T. McSeveney, *The Politics of Depression: Political Behavior in the Northeast, 1893-1896* (New York: Oxford University Press, 1972), 3-31; McFarland, "Breakdown of Deadlock," 391-2; Michael E. Hennessy, *Twenty-five Years of Massachusetts Politics, 1890-1915* (Boston: Practical Politics, 1917), 2; and Blodgett, *The Gentle Reformers*, 98, 157.

33. *The Connecticut Register for 1880* (Hartford, 1881); and the *Connecticut Register and Manual for 1886* (Hartford, 1886).

34. McFarland, "Breakdown of Deadlock," 392; and Hennessy, *Twenty-five Years of Massachusetts Politics*, 2.

35. *New Haven Morning News*, 6 October 1889, and Norris G. Osborn, *A Glance Backward* (New Haven: Tuttle, Morehous & Taylor, 1905), 88-90.

36. Joseph B. Sargent to L. S. Hull, October 23, 1896, Joseph B. Sargent letterbook (Sargent Family papers); and the *New Haven Morning News*, 12 February 1886.

37. Richard Henry Dana III, "Journal," 2: 597 (Richard Henry Dana papers, Massachusetts Historical Society); Eldon Cobb Evans, *A History*

of the Australian Ballot System in the United States (Chicago: University of Chicago Press, 1917), 18-19; and Dana, "Practical Working of the Australian System of Voting in Massachusetts," *Annals of the American Academy of Political and Social Science*, 2, 6 (May 1892): 733-50.

38. Commonwealth Club file, 1886-1893 (Bowker papers, NYPL), and New York Ballot Reform League file, Box 1 (Everett P. Wheeler papers, New York Public Library).

39. Herbert J. Bass, "The Politics of Ballot Reform in New York State, 1888-1890," *New York History*, 42, 3 (July 1961): 253-71.

40. A fully secret ballot was adopted five years later. New York Ballot Reform League file, Box 1 (Wheeler papers).

41. "Connecticut," *Appleton's Annual Cyclopaedia*, 1888 and 1889.

42. Stephen D. Albright, *The American Ballot* (Washington, D.C.: American Council on Public Affairs, 1942), 28-9.

43. Simeon E. Baldwin to W. D. Warren, February 18, 1890, and to Wayne MacVeagh, October 6, 1892 (Baldwin papers).

44. *New Haven Morning News*, February 14, 1890. Besides Baldwin, former Mugwumps on the club's committees were: James L. Cowles, Charles G. Root, and Talcott H. Russell. "Connecticut Democratic Club," file for 1890 and 1891 (Baldwin papers).

45. Roland Hazard to William Everett, October 26, 1888 (Everett papers).

46. Grover Cleveland to E. Ellery Anderson, February 10, 1891, in Nevins, ed., *Letters of Grover Cleveland*, 245-6.

47. Many Mugwumps acclaimed George Fred Williams as the leader of the anti-silver forces: Henry Lee Higginson to Williams, February 16, 1892; C. C. Jackson to Williams, April 11 and 22, 1892; and Charles Sumner Bird to Williams, February 26, 1892 (Williams papers).

48. William L. Wilson to Charles S. Fairchild, March 15, 1892; Benjamin Ide Wheeler to Fairchild, April 18, 1892; and Edward M. Shepard to Fairchild, May 25, 1892 (Fairchild papers).

49. Cleveland's Warwick, William C. Whitney, received reports from Samuel R. Honey of Rhode Island, March 3 and 23, 1892; John E. Russell of Massachusetts, March 11, 27, and 31, 1892; and David Ames Wells of Connecticut, March 16, 1892 (William C. Whitney papers, Library of Congress).

50. James Means to William Everett, November 25, 1891 (Everett papers).

51. R. R. Bowker to Charles S. Fairchild, December 5, 1894 (Bowker papers, NYPL).

52. Joseph Huthmacher, "Urban Liberalism and the Age of Reform," *Mississippi Valley Historical Review*, 64, 2 (September 1962): 233, questions how progressivism "in places like New York and Massachusetts —states that were heavily populated with non-Protestant, non-Anglo-Saxon immigrants and sons of immigrants"—can be explained by a thesis that progressivism was the work of middle-class WASP reformers. Yet the Cleveland Democracy provides an interesting model of a WASP reform group that achieved its goals through a coalition with ethnics in Massachusetts.

53. McSeveney, *Politics of Depression*, 87-133.

54. Ibid., 108-15, 118-20, 133, 190-200.

55. Richard Henry Dana III, "Journal," 2: 670-2 (Dana papers). Carl Schurz to Silas W. Burt, August 22, 1893; and Burt to Schurz, August 17 and November 29, 1893 (Schurz papers).

56. Theodore Roosevelt to William Dudley Foulke, October 19, 1893 (Foulke papers).

57. Richard Henry Dana III, "Journal," 2: 674 (Dana papers). *See* also two scrapbooks on Winslow Warren's career as collector of the Port of Boston (Winslow Warren collection, Massachusetts Historical Society).

58. Gilder to William E. Russell, March 14 and August 9, 1894 (Russell papers); and Richard Henry Dana III, "Journal," 2: 697 (Dana papers).

59. Richard Henry Dana III, "Journal," 2: 677; and Charles R. Codman, "Notes, Letters, and Essays," 234-76 (Codman papers). *See* also Winslow Warren to William Everett, January 15, 1894 (Everett papers), and Silas W. Burt to Carl Schurz, November 29, 1893 (Schurz papers).

60. William Everett to Henry Jackson, February 10, 1894; and Winslow Warren to Everett, May 15, 1894 (Everett papers).

61. George Walton Green, "Mr. Cleveland's Second Administration," *The Forum*, 21, 5 (July 1896): 548.

62. Ibid., 548. Winslow Warren to William Everett, May 15 and 23, 1894; Richard Henry Dana III to Everett, May 24, 1894; and George Walton Green to Everett, June 1, 1894 (Everett papers).

63. *See* Samuel T. McSeveney's description of this mood among

Cleveland Democrats in *Politics of Depression*, 192.

64. Green, "Mr. Cleveland's Second Administration," 557.

65. My actual count runs sixty-seven Cleveland voters to five for Harrison, with probable Cleveland and Harrison votes running in much the same ratio.

66. Charles S. Hamlin, "Diary," July 6, 1896 (Charles S. Hamlin papers, Library of Congress).

67. Clinton A. Cilley to William Everett, August 21, 1896 (Everett papers).

68. The distribution was twenty-nine McKinley, sixteen Palmer, five Bryan, and fifteen more definitely anti-Bryan, though their final choice between McKinley and Palmer is not ascertainable.

69. The Mugwumps' party preference ratio in the twentieth century was 56 percent Republican to 44 percent Democrat, based on 103 of the 302 Mugwumps who were living in 1910.

70. Naomi W. Cohen, *A Dual Heritage* (Philadelphia: The Jewish Publication Society of America, 1969), 39; and Henry W. Farnam to the chairman, Democratic State Committee of Connecticut, November 3, 1916 (Farnam papers).

71. Codman to J. W. Clapp, September 25, 1896 (Codman papers); and Codman to Carl Schurz, September 13, 1896 (Schurz papers).

72. George Haven Putnam, *Memories of a Publisher, 1865-1915* (New York: G. P. Putnam's Sons, 1915), 72.

73. Spencer Borden to George Fred Williams, September 18, 1896 (Williams papers).

74. Beisner's *Twelve Against Empire* (New York: McGraw-Hill Book Co., 1968) is the best introduction to the anti-imperialist movement. Extensive materials on the movement are in Mugwump manuscript collections, particularly those of Henry W. Farnam (Yale University), Carl Schurz (Library of Congress), Edward Atkinson (Massachusetts Historical Society), and Charles Eliot Norton (Harvard University).

75. Edward Atkinson, *Taxation and Work* (New York: G. P. Putnam's Sons, 1892), especially chapt. 17, "Protection Promotes War." *See* also R. R. Bowker, *Free Trade the Best Protection to American Industry* (New York: G. P. Putnam's Sons, 1883), 10; and David Ames Wells, "The Creed of Free Trade," *Atlantic Monthly*, 36, 214 (August 1875), 204-20.

76. The issue of racism and anti-imperialism is discussed in Beisner, *Twelve Against Empire*, 219, 232-5; and in Christopher Lasch, "The Anti-Imperialists, the Philippines, and the Inequality of Man," *Journal of Southern History*, 24, 3 (August 1958): 319-31.

77. Richard E. Welch, Jr., "Motives and Objectives of Anti-Imperialists, 1898," *Mid-America*, 51, 2 (April 1969): 119-29, specifically mentions David Starr Jordan, E. L. Godkin, Carl Schurz, and Charles Francis Adams, Jr., as anti-imperialists (Mugwumps) exhibiting a racist orientation but lists other old bolters—Moorfield Storey, Edward Atkinson, Winslow Warren, William James, and Thomas Wentworth Higginson— among the anti-imperialists to whom the term "racist," he believes, scarcely applies.

78. Robert L. Beisner, "1898 and 1968: The Anti-Imperialists and the Doves," *Political Science Quarterly*, 85, 2 (June 1970): 187-216. Among the anti-imperialist arguments against their opponents, Beisner lists racial fears fourth in importance behind the view that imperialism was morally wrong, that democracy and empire would not mix, and that imperialism was a denial of America's mission to establish a free and just society.

79. E. Berkeley Tompkins, *Anti-Imperialism in the United States: The Great Debate, 1890-1920* Philadelphia: University of Pennsylvania Press, 1970), 217ff. Edwin Burritt Smith to Carl Schurz, March 17, 1900; and Moorfield Storey to Schurz, August 2, 1900 (Schurz papers).

80. The actual count in my anti-imperialist sample was seventeen for Bryan and four for McKinley, with four others who either were ineligible or did not vote.

81. Charles Francis Adams, Jr. to Carl Schurz, November 3, 1899; Horace White to Schurz, March 23, 1900; R. R. Bowker to Schurz, November 17, 1900; and Charles Eliot Norton to Schurz, October 4, 1900 (Schurz papers).

82. Carl Schurz as quoted in Tompkins, *Anti-Imperialism in the United States*, 235. *See* also Carl Schurz to Herbert Welch, October 5, 1900, and Edwin Burritt Smith to Schurz, October 15, 1900 (Schurz papers). The *Springfield Republican*, 22 October 1900, listed the anti-imperialists who intended to vote for Bryan and urged the public to do likewise.

83. Gerald Kurland, *Seth Low* (New York: Twayne Publishers,

1971), 213.

84. Richard Welling, "Diary," October 2, 1898 and January 26, 1901 (Richard W. G. Welling papers, New York Public Library); and Charles J. Bonaparte to W. L. Chaffin, October 25, 1904 (Bonaparte papers).

Chapter 5

1. Many books could be cited here, but two of the more forceful are: Gabriel Kolko, *The Triumph of Conservatism* (New York: Free Press of Glencoe, 1963); and James Weinstein, *The Corporate Ideal and the Liberal State, 1900-1918* (Boston: Beacon Press, 1968).

2. Richard M. Abrams, "A Paradox of Progressivism: Massachusetts on the Eve of Insurgency," *Political Science Quarterly*, 75, 3 (September 1960): 379-80.

3. The quotation is from Geoffrey Blodgett, *The Gentle Reformers* (Cambridge, Mass.: Harvard University Press, 1966), 281. An overview of the state's progressive legislation during the 1890s is also found in Richard M. Abrams, *Conservatism in a Progressive Era: Massachusetts Politics, 1900-1912* (Cambridge, Mass.: Harvard University Press, 1964), 1-24.

4. Blodgett, *Gentle Reformers*, 109-113 and 225. George Fred Williams, "Diary Notes," September 3-11, 1895; and Sylvester Baxter to Williams, May 24, 1892 (Williams papers); Winslow Warren to Williams, June 12 and July 3, 1890; and Solomon B. Griffin to Williams, June 14, 1892 (Russell papers).

5. Josiah Quincy, "The Working of the Massachusetts Corrupt Practices Law," *The Forum*, 15, 2 (April 1893): 142-7.

6. Blodgett, *Gentle Reformers*, 100-15, and Michael E. Hennessy, *Twenty-Five Years of Massachusetts Politics, 1890-1915* (Boston: Practical Politics, 1917), 35-6. The strong executive idea was well known in Mugwump circles: Seth Low, "The Government of Cities in the United States," *The Century Magazine*, 42, 5 (September 1891): 730-36; and Gamaliel Bradford, Sr., "Government by Commission," *New England Magazine*, 10, 4 (June 1894): 453-60.

7. Hennessy, *Twenty-five Years of Massachusetts Politics*, 14, Sherman Hoar to William E. Russell, March 12, 1892 (Russell papers).

8. See Thomas Wentworth Higginson, "Step by Step," *The Nationalist*, 1 (September 1899): 147-8; Sylvester Baxter, *Berlin, A Study of Municipal Government* (Boston: A. J. Philpott & Co., 1890); and Baxter to William E. Russell, January 2, June 14, and July 1, 1892 (Russell papers).

9. Blodgett, *Gentle Reformers*, 128-37.

10. Geoffrey T. Blodgett, "Josiah Quincy, Brahmin Democrat," *New England Quarterly*, 38, 4 (December 1965): 435-53; George E. Hooker, "Mayor Quincy of Boston," *Review of Reviews*, 19, 112 (May 1899): 575-8; and George Fred Williams, "Diary Notes," (Williams papers).

11. Blodgett, *Gentle Reformers*, 249-52; Arthur Mann, *Yankee Reformers in the Urban Age* (Cambridge, Mass.: Harvard University Press, 1954), 248; and Allen F. Davis, *Spearheads for Reform: The Social Settlements and the Progressive Movement, 1890-1914* (New York: Oxford University Press, 1967), 148-50.

12. Charles Francis Adams, Jr., *Charles Francis Adams, 1835-1915* (Boston: Houghton Mifflin Co., 1916), 185; and Edward Chase Kirkland, *Charles Francis Adams, Jr., 1835-1915: The Patrician at Bay* (Cambridge, Mass.: Harvard University Press, 1965), 187-9.

13. Abrams, *Conservatism in a Progressive Era*, 58-62.

14. Richard Hofstadter, *The Age of Reform* (New York: Alfred A. Knopf, 1955), 164-5. *See* also William H. Tolman, *Municipal Reform Movements in the United States* (New York: Fleming H. Revell Co., 1895).

15. Comparing the New York City Mugwump and Republican samples with City Club and Citizens' Union membership lists (Bowker papers, NYPL), the City Club list (March 1, 1892) contained twenty-four Mugwumps and twelve Republicans. The Citizens' Union Committee on Organization (1897) included twenty-six Mugwumps and only nine Republicans.

16. Alexander B. Callow, *The Tweed Ring* (New York: Oxford University Press, 1966), 253-78.

17. An excellent description of the machine's role in New York is provided by Seymour J. Mandelbaum, *Boss Tweed's New York* (New York: John Wiley, 1965), 58-75.

18. *New York World*, 15 April 1883. *See* also the City Reform Club Minutes, 1882-1887 (City Club papers, New York Public Library);

Richard W. G. Welling, *As the Twig is Bent* (New York: G. P. Putnam's, 1942); and Robert Muccigrosso, "The City Reform Club: A Study in Late Nineteenth-Century Reform," *New York Historical Society Quarterly*, 52, 3 (July 1968): 235-54.

19. City Reform Club Minutes, April 27, 1889 and September 24, 1890 (City Club papers).

20. Ibid., November 8, 1888, November 7, 1889, and October 2, 1892. *See* also Welling, *As the Twig is Bent*, 41.

21. Welling, "Diary" (Welling papers), especially entries for January 18 and 29, February 12, and March 11, 1896. Edwin Lawrence Godkin, ed., *The Triumph of Reform* (New York: Souvenier Publishing Co., 1895), 9 and biographical sketches in the back of the book, listing W. Harris Roome, Lewis L. Delafield, Albert Stickney, and Abram C. Bernheim as CRC men serving on the Committee of Seventy in 1894.

22. Welling, *As the Twig is Bent*, 48.

23. People's Municipal League folder (Fairchild papers). For contemporary Mugwump writings, *see* James C. Carter, *How Can Municipal Government Be Divorced from National Party Lines?* (New York: Nineteenth Century Club, 1895); and Seth Low, "Obstacles to Good City Government," *The Forum*, 5, 2 (May 1888): 260-6.

24. Albert Shaw, "Municipal Problems of New York and London," *Review of Reviews*, 5, 27 (April 1892): 282-308.

25. Tolman, *Municipal Reform Movements*, 123; Welling, *As the Twig is Bent*, 48; and Frank Mann Stewart, *A Half Century of Municipal Reform: The History of the National Municipal League* (Berkeley: University of California Press, 1950), 16-20.

26. William B. Munro, *The Government of American Cities* (New York: Macmillan Co., 1920), 111.

27. Horace E. Deming to Albert Shaw, January 17, 1901 (Shaw papers); Horace E. Deming, *The Government of American Cities* (New York: G. P. Putnam's Sons, 1909), 97; and Welling, *As the Twig is Bent*, 48.

28. Charles Garrett, *The La Guardia Years: Machine and Reform Politics in New York City* (New Brunswick: Rutgers University Press, 1961), 18.

29. Gustavus Myers, *The History of Tammany Hall* (New York: Boni & Liverwright, 1917), 271-5.

30. Joseph B. Bishop, *A Chronicle of One Hundred and Fifty Years: The Chamber of Commerce of the State of New York, 1768-1918* (New York: Charles Scribner's Sons, 1918), 93.

31. Tolman, *Municipal Reform Movements*, 86.

32. Godkin, ed., *Triumph of Reform*, lists the seventy, page 9. Godkin's role in the urban reform campaigns is described in Diana Klebanow, "E. L. Godkin, the City, and Civic Responsibility," *New York Historical Society Quarterly*, 55, 1 (January 1971): 52-75.

33. The conflict between cosmopolitan reformers and ward-based ethnic politicians persisted into the progressive era. *See* Samuel P. Hays, "The Politics of Reform in Municipal Government in the Progressive Era," *Pacific Northwest Quarterly*, 55, 4 (October 1964), 157-69.

34. Godkin, ed., *Triumph of Reform*, 14-19.

35. Robert J. Finley, "The Cartoon in Politics: The Story of the New York Campaign in Outline," *Review of Reviews*, 12, 6 (December 1895): 671-3.

36. City Club of New York, *Report* (New York, 1893), 10.

37. Ibid., 7.

38. Munro, *Government of American Cities*, 375-6.

39. Putnam, *Memories of a Publisher, 1865-1915* (New York: G. P. Putnam's Sons, 1915), 334; Godkin, ed., *Triumph of Reform*, 259; and the City Club papers.

40. Kelly and some younger City Club men—Richard Welling, James Pryor, and John Jay Chapman—felt the leadership of James C. Carter and the Cuttings was too conservative. Welling, "Diary," May 4, 1896 (Welling papers).

41. City Club of New York, *Minutes of Meeting, December 16, 1892* (New York: Evening Post Printer, 1893), 11.

42. Godkin, ed., *Triumph of Reform*, 150.

43. Ibid., 149, and Myers, *History of Tammany Hall*, 279.

44. The reformers were well aware that Tammany's organization gave it great staying power. *See* Edward Cary, "Tammany Past and Present," *The Forum*, 26, 2 (October 1898): 200-10.

45. Samuel T. McSeveney, *The Politics of Depression* (New York: Oxford University Press, 1972), 113.

46. Henry F. Pringle, *Theodore Roosevelt* (New York: Harcourt,

Brace, & Co., Harvest Book edition, 1956), 93-106.

47. Mugwumps tended to be moderate on the prohibition issue, as noted earlier in my discussion of Connecticut state politics. In New York City the drive for Sunday closing was spearheaded by Protestant evangelical ministers (from denominations to which few Mugwumps belonged) and Republican leaders like Warner Miller. *See* McSeveney, *Politics of Depression*, 145-6. The high church Episcopal and intellectual or upper-class Mugwumps whose views are known—Felix Adler, Austen G. Fox, Henry Holt, Seth Low, and Carl Schurz—were either hostile to or very skeptical of the prohibitionist mentality. Gerald Kurland, *Seth Low* (New York: Twayne Publishers, 1971), 149-51, and Henry Holt, *Garrulities of an Octogenarian Editor* (New York: Houghton Mifflin Co., 1923), 396.

48. *New York Times*, 9 and 17 May 1895. Proposed Citizens' Union platform, 1901, Box 3 (Wheeler papers), and R. Fulton Cutting, *Address Given to Citizens' Union Dinner, January 7, 1902* (New York: privately printed, 1902), 9.

49. Albert Shaw, "Municipal Cleansing," *Review of Reviews*, 11, 3 (March 1895): 322, and *Life of Colonel George E. Waring, Jr.* (New York: The Patriotic League, 1899).

50. Albert Shaw, "Our Civic Renaissance," *Review of Reviews*, 11, 4 (April 1895): 415-27, and Frank Pavey, "Mayor Strong's Experiment in New York City," *The Forum*, 23, 5 (July 1897): 539-53.

51. *New York Times*, 17 May 1895.

52. Michael G. Kammen, "Richard Watson Gilder and the New York Tenement House Commission of 1894," *Bulletin of the New York Public Library*, 66, 6 (June 1962): 371, 376.

53. These tensions appeared in the fusion coalition very early. *See* Robert J. Finley, "The Cartoon in Politics," *Review of Reviews*, 12, 6 (December 1895): 668-77, and McSeveney, *Politics of Depression*, 146-8.

54. McSeveney, *Politics of Depression*, 151-6.

55. For the 1897 campaign, *see* Kurland, *Seth Low*, 82-106.

56. Low to Robert Fulton Cutting, December 26, 1899 (Low papers). For a sense of the debate between the fusionists and the anti-fusionists, *see* John K. Creevey to Low, September 1, 1897; and Low to Richard Watson Gilder, September 8, 1897, ibid.

57. Bowker to Low, November 6, 1897, ibid.

58. Low to Cutting, Schurz, and Larocque, June 7, 1897; and the notice of Brooklyn meeting for Low, June 30, 1897, ibid.

59. Committee on Organization (1897), Citizens' Union. (Bowker papers, NYPL).

60. Gerald Kurland, "The Amateur in Politics: The Citizens' Union and the Greater New York Mayoral Campaign of 1897," *New York Historical Society Quarterly*, 53, 4 (October 1969): 355. *See* also Richard Welling, "Diary," April 9, 1897 (Welling papers); and James B. Reynolds to Seth Low, September 8, 1897. Reel 5 (University Settlement Society papers, microfilm copy, State Historical Society of Wisconsin.

61. Horace White to Seth Low, August 25, 1897 (Low papers).

62. Kurland, *Seth Low*, 206; and Richard Welling, "Diary," November 10, 1901 (Welling papers).

63. Welling, "Diary," November 6, 1901, ibid.

64. Gustav H. Schwab to James B. Reynolds, February 15, 1897, reel 5 (University Settlement Society papers).

65. Citizens' Union, *The City for the People! Campaign Book of the Citizens' Union* (New York: privately printed, 1901), 8.

66. Ibid., 8ff.

67. Richard Welling, "Diary," October 11 and 17, 1901 (Welling papers).

68. Felix Adler to Everett P. Wheeler, April 15, 1901 (Wheeler papers); Davis, *Spearheads for Reform*, 182-3; and Francis B. Thurber to James B. Reynolds, May 10, 1897, reel 4 (University Settlement Society papers).

69. Putnam, *Memories of a Publisher*, 339; and Henry G. Seaver to Everett P. Wheeler, April 26, 1901 (Wheeler papers).

70. "Robert Fulton Cutting," Who's Who File (Citizens' Union papers, Columbia University), and Clyde C. Griffen, "Rich Laymen and Early Social Christianity," *Church History*, 34, 1 (March 1967): 3-23.

71. Cutting, *Address Given to Citizens' Union Dinner, January 7, 1902*, 7.

72. Ibid., 12.

73. Kurland, *Seth Low*, 140-68; and Steven C. Swett, "The Test of a Reformer: A Study of Seth Low, New York City Mayor, 1902-1903,"

New York Historical Society Quarterly, 44, 1 (January 1960): 20-7.

74. Kurland, *Seth Low*, 192-212; Swett, "Test of a Reformer," 35-41; and Lincoln Steffens, "New York: Good Government to the Test," in his *The Shame of the Cities* (New York: Hill & Wang, American Century Series edition, 1957), 195-214.

75. Nancy Joan Weiss, *Charles Francis Murphy, 1858-1924: Respectability and Responsibility in Tammany Politics* (Northampton, Mass.: Smith College, 1968).

76. Welling, *As the Twig is Bent*, vii.

Chapter 6

1. Gert H. Brieger, "Sanitary Reform in New York City," *Bulletin of the History of Medicine*, 40, 5 (September-October, 1966): 420-9; and Gordon Atkins, *Health, Housing, and Poverty in New York City, 1865-1898* (Ann Arbor, Michigan: Edwards, 1947), 1-26.

2. Arthur Mann, "British Social Thought and American Reformers of the Progressive Era," *Mississippi Valley Historical Review*, 42, 4 (March 1956): 683-7. On earlier Mugwump ties with British liberalism, *see* Robert L. Kelley, *The Transatlantic Persuasion: The Liberal-Democratic Mind in the Age of Gladstone* (New York: Alfred A. Knopf, 1969), 297-302, 324-8.

3. Atkins, *Health, Housing, and Poverty*, 35-7; Harold C. Syrett, *The City of Brooklyn, 1865-1898* (New York: Columbia University Press, 1944), 111; and Adolf F. Meisen, "A History of Street Cleaning in New York City," (M.A. thesis, Columbia University, 1939).

4. Buffalo Charity Organization, *Report 1884* (Buffalo: Bigelow Printing & Publishing Co., 1884).

5. Robert L. Bremner, *From the Depths: The Discovery of Poverty in the United States* (New York: New York University Press, 1956), 12.

6. New York Association for Improving the Condition of the Poor, *Report 1884* (New York: by the Association, 1884), 29-30.

7. Richard Henry Dana III, "Journal," 2: 545 (Dana papers), and William H. Tolman, *Municipal Reform Movements in the United States* (New York: Fleming H. Revell, Co., 1895), 145. Richard Henry Dana III, George S. Hale, and Robert Treat Paine were Mugwumps

among the founders of the Associated Charities of Boston. Associated
Charities of Boston, *Publications and Miscellaneous Circulars and Reports, 1879-1898* (Boston: by the Association, 1879-1898).

8. Tenement House Building Company, *The Tenement Houses of
New York City* (New York: A. B. King, 1891), 11.

9. Alfred T. White, *Sun-Lighted Tenements* (New York: National
Housing Association, 1912), 3-4. For the public attitude, *see* Atkins,
Health, Housing, and Poverty, 216-17.

10. Francis G. Peabody, *Reminiscences of Present-Day Saints* (Boston:
Houghton Mifflin Co., 1929), 140ff; Atkins, *Health, Housing, and
Poverty*, 123; and Roy Lubove, *The Progressives and the Slums: Tenement House Reform in New York City, 1890-1917* (Pittsburgh: University of Pittsburgh Press, 1962), 35-7.

11. U.S., Federal Housing Administration, *Four Decades of Housing
With a Limited Dividend Corporation* (Washington, D.C.: Division of
Economics and Statistics, 1939), 5.

12. William B. Shaw, "Alfred Tredway White," *Dictionary of American Biography* (New York: Charles Scribner's Sons, 1936), 20: 86-87.

13. Lubove, *Progressives and the Slums*, 9, 27, 33, 37.

14. Alfred T. White, *Improved Dwellings for the Laboring Classes*
(New York: Reform Club, 1877), 6.

15. Robert Treat Paine, for instance, wrote that as of 1902 model
tenement projects had but an "insignificant" effect on housing conditions in Boston and that immediate legislation was needed to eliminate
substandard buildings: "The Housing Conditions of Boston," *Annals
of the American Academy of Political and Social Science*, 20, 1 (July
1902): 121-36.

16. Atkins, *Health, Housing, and Poverty*, 223-4.

17. R. R. Bowker, "Workingmen's Homes," *Harper's Monthly*, 28,
407 (April 1884): 769-84; and Arthur W. Milbury to Bowker, August 12, 1896 (Bowker papers, NYPL).

18. Atkins, *Health, Housing, and Poverty*, 225. Two Mugwump
lawyers, A. P. W. Seaman and Richard Welling, were among the more
active supporters of the Tenement House Building Company. *See* also
Tenement House Building Company, *Tenement Houses of New York
City*, 3.

19. Richard M. Abrams, *Conservatism in a Progressive Era* (Cambridge,

Mass.: Harvard University Press, 1964), 47, 50; and F. A. Hobart and Robert Treat Paine to George Fred Williams, October 23, 1896, telegram (Russell papers).

20. *Boston Evening Transcript*, 12 August 1910. *See* also Sam B. Warner, Jr.'s evaluation in Paine, *Streetcar Suburbs: The Process of Growth in Boston, 1870-1900* (Cambridge, Mass.: Harvard University Press, 1962), 101-5.

21. Of the many books which link the Social Gospel movement and progressivism, two of the most thorough are Charles H. Hopkins, *The Rise of the Social Gospel in American Protestantism, 1865-1915*, Yale University Studies in Religious Education, vol. 14 (New Haven: Yale University Press, 1940), and Henry F. May, *Protestant Churches and Industrial America* (New York: Octagon Books, Octagon Books edition, 1963).

22. For the complete story of the investigation, *see* Michael G. Kammen, "Richard Watson Gilder and the New York Tenement House Commission of 1894," *Bulletin of the New York Public Library*, 66, 6 (June 1962): 362-82.

23. Rosamond Gilder, ed., *Letters of Richard Watson Gilder* (Boston: Houghton Mifflin Co., 1916), 263.

24. Kammen, "Gilder and the New York Tenement House Investigation," 380.

25. Gilder, ed., *Letters of Richard Watson Gilder*, 277; and E. R. L. Gould to R. R. Bowker, November 11, 1896 (Bowker papers, NYPL).

26. U.S., Federal Housing Administration, *Four Decades of Housing With a Limited Dividend Corporation* takes the company as its subject. *See* also "New York's Great Movement for Housing Reform," *Review of Reviews*, 14, 6 (December 1896): 693-701.

27. Alfred F. Davis, *Spearheads for Reform* (New York: Oxford University Press, 1967), 33.

28. R. R. Bowker, "Toynbee Hall, An Interesting Social Experiment," *Century Magazine*, 34, 1 (May 1887), 158-59.

29. Davis, *Spearheads for Reform*, 8-10.

30. Among the Mugwump contributors to Lowell House were Simeon E. Baldwin, William Beebee, William H. Carmalt, Charles S. Morehouse, Talcott H. Russell, Henry C. White, Tracy Peck, and F. S. Bradley. Lowell House file (Farnam papers).

31. Council Minutes, 1891-1929, microfilm reel 1; and Founder's File, reel 21 (University Settlement Society papers), and William Potts to R. R. Bowker, July 16, 1898 (Bowker papers, NYPL).

32. James B. Reynolds to Arthur T. Hadley, November 21, 1900, microfilm reel 5 (University Settlement Society papers).

33. Richard Watson Gilder, "The Kindergarten, An Uplifting Social Influence in the Home and the District," manuscript of an address given before the National Educational Association, July 10, 1903 (Richard Watson Gilder papers, New York Public Library).

34. Henry W. Farnam, undated address in Lowell House file (Farnam papers).

35. *See*, for example, the many letters from Mugwumps to James B. Reynolds in reels 4 and 5 of the University Settlement Society papers on microfilm: R. Fulton Cutting (June 28, 1897), William Bayard Cutting (August 5, 1897), James B. Leavitt (July 21 and September 12, 1897), Charles C. Nadal (September 1, 1897), George Haven Putnam (September 7, 1897), and John Frankenheimer (May 25, 1897).

36. R. R. Bowker to James B. Reynolds, February 16, 1900 (Bowker papers, NYPL); Low statement to *New York Times*, 1895, in Founder's File, reel 21, and Henry Holt to James B. Reynolds, May 8, and August 10, 1894, also in the Founder's File (University Settlement Society papers).

37. Richard Skolnik, "Civic Group Progressivism in New York City," *New York History*, 51, 4 (July 1970): 413, 435-9.

38. As quoted in Sol Cohen, *Progressives and Urban School Reform: The Public Education Association of New York City, 1895-1954* (New York: Teachers College, Columbia University, 1964), 23.

39. *Review of Reviews*, 12, 1 (August 1895): 144; Albert Shaw to Seth Low, June 2, 1897, and Albert Shaw to Horace E. Deming, June 2, 1899 (Shaw papers).

40. Richard Welling, "Diary," January 8, 1901 (Welling papers).

41. R. Fulton Cutting, *Address Given to Citizens' Union Dinner, January 7, 1902.* Richard Welling, "Diary," June 23, 1901 (Welling papers), and Gilder as quoted in Kammen, "Gilder and the New York Tenement House Commission," 382.

42. Cutting, *Address Given to Citizens' Union Dinner, January 7, 1902*; and *The Citizens Union, Its Origin and Purpose; Address*

Given at the Nineteenth Century Club, April 14, 1903 (New York: privately printed, 1903), especially 1 and 6. My views of the conventional values mentioned here have been based chiefly on discussions in Henry F. May, *The End of American Innocence* (New York: Alfred A. Knopf, 1959), chapts. 1-3, and Hofstadter, *The Age of Reform* (New York: Alfred A. Knopf, 1955), 131-64.

43. Gilder as quoted in Kammen, "Gilder and the New York Tenement House Commission," 382.

44. Stephen H. Olin section in the Founder's File, microfilm reel 21 (University Settlement Society papers); and Cohen, *Progressives and Urban School Reform*, 24. Other Mugwumps who served on the Citizens Committee on Public School Reform included James C. Carter, Austen G. Fox, Joseph Larocque, Abraham Jacobi, and Henry Holt, according to the *New York World*, 15 February 1896.

45. Gerald Kurland, *Seth Low* (New York: Twayne Publishers, 1971), 142-3, 166-8, 244-8; and Albert Shaw to Albert Beveridge, February 24, 1900 (Shaw papers).

46. Gilder, "Kindergarten" (Gilder papers); and Kammen, "Gilder and the New York Tenement House Commission," 365.

47. Cohen, *Progressives and Urban School Reform*, 1-15; Davis, *Spearheads for Reform*, 8-25; and Lubove, *Progressives and the Slums*, 37-67.

48. Cohen, *Progressives and Urban School Reform*, 131. The cosmopolitan reformers' victory over Tammany's ward-based power structure in the school bill fight was closely analogous to the pattern attributed to progressive era municipal reform battles by Samuel P. Hays, "The Politics of Reform in Municipal Government in the Progressive Era," *Pacific Northwest Quarterly*, 55, 4 (October 1964), 157-69.

49. Charles Francis Adams, Jr., *Charles Francis Adams, 1835-1915* (Boston: Houghton Mifflin Co., 1916), 185; and Sherrod Soule, *Francis Goodwin of Hartford* (Hartford: privately printed, 1939), 1, 30-2.

50. Kurland, *Seth Low*, 77-81.

51. Geoffrey Blodgett, "Reform Thought and the Genteel Tradition," in H. Wayne Morgan, ed., *The Gilded Age*, rev. ed. (Syracuse: Syracuse University Press, 1970), 55-76.

52. *New York Times*, 19 February 1895.

53. As quoted in Samuel T. McSeveney, *The Politics of Depression* (New York: Oxford University Press, 1972), 91.

54. Richard Welling, "Diary," October 28-29, 1901 (Welling papers).

Chapter 7

1. *See* especially Peter G. Filene, "An Obituary for 'The Progressive Movement,'" *American quarterly*, 22, 1 (Spring 1970): 20-34.

2. Richard M. Abrams, "The Failure of Progressivism," in Richard Abrams and Lawrence W. Levine, eds., *The Shaping of Twentieth-Century America*, 2nd ed. (Boston: Little, Brown & Co., 1971), 209.

3. An interpretation emphasizing the "conservative" side of progressivism is Gabriel Kolko, *The Triumph of Conservatism* (New York: Free Press of Glencoe, 1963), 1-10. Abrams, "Failure of Progressivism," 208, points to some of the more obvious omissions in the Kolko thesis, particularly its failure to account for progressives whose primary concern was with social and humanitarian reforms.

4. John D. Buenker argues that progressivism manifested itself less as a movement than through "several concurrent attempts" by diverse coalitions "to cope with the circumstances of their new environment." Buenker, "The Progressive Era: A Search for A Synthesis," *Mid-America*, 51, 3 (July 1969): 175-94.

5. "The Politics of Nostalgia" is a chapter title from John G. Sproat, *"The Best Men"* (New York: Oxford University Press, 1968). The quotation is from John Tomsich, *A Genteel Endeavor* (Stanford: Stanford University Press, 1971).

6. Frank Mann Stewart, *A Half Century of Municipal Reform* (Berkeley: University of California Press, 1950), 54-62.

7. George E. Mowry, "The California Progressive and His Rationale: A Study in Middle-Class Politics," *Mississippi Valley Historical Review*, 36, 2 (September 1949): 242; and Abrams, "Failure of Progressivism," 214, note 20.

8. Robert Grant as quoted in the *Massachusetts Historical Society Proceedings*, 54 (1920-1921): 198.

9. Wendell to Colonel Robert Thomson, December 17, 1893; and to Frederic J. Stimson, December 10, 1916, as quoted in M. A. DeWolfe Howe, *Barrett Wendell and His Letters* (Boston: Atlantic Monthly Press, 1924), 108-277.

10. R. R. Bowker to Bert Hanson, December 16, 1911, and to E. P. Wheeler, April 30, 1915 (Bowker papers, NYPL).

11. Putnam, *Memories of a Publisher, 1865-1915* (New York: G. P. Putnam's Sons, 1915), 342-4.

12. John B. Leavitt to Henry DeF. Baldwin, November 14, 1811 (Baldwin papers).

13. Wendell to his wife, summer of 1896, as quoted in Howe, *Barrett Wendell and His Letters*, 109; Robert Grant, *Fourscore: An Autobiography* (Boston: Houghton Mifflin Co., 1934), 189; and Bonaparte to Clinton R. Woodruff, October 14, 1904 (Bonaparte papers).

14. Graham McAdam to R. R. Bowker, September 21, October 1, and October 3, 1912; and George Haven Putnam to Bowker, July 26, 1916 (Bowker papers, NYPL).

15. Putnam to Bowker, August 3, 1916, and May 31, 1917, ibid.

16. Nelson S. Spencer to Henry DeF. Baldwin, September 23, 1913 (Baldwin papers), illustrates Spencer's typical reform focus.

17. Elizabeth Donnan and Leo F. Stock, eds., *An Historian's World* (Philadelphia: American Philosophical Society, 1956), 151; and Bliss Perry, *Richard Henry Dana, 1851-1931* (Boston: Houghton Mifflin Co., 1933), 195.

18. Horace E. Deming, *The Government of American Cities* (New York: G. P. Putnam's Sons, 1909), v.

19. Ibid., 97 and 105ff; and Deming as quoted in Stewart, *A Half Century of Municipal Reform*, 43.

20. Stewart, *Half Century of Municipal Reform*, 54-62.

21. Jane S. Dahlberg, *The New York Bureau of Municipal Research, Pioneer in Government Administration* (New York: New York University Press, 1966), 9-11.

22. Ibid., 25, quoting the *New York Times*, 1 June 1907.

23. Henry Bruere, "Reminiscences" (Columbia University Oral History Project), 36, and on Cutting: 18, 20, and 23. The National Municipal League made the bureau idea part of its model charter in 1916. *See* Stewart, *Half Century of Municipal Reform*, 58.

24. Putnam, *Memories of a Publisher*, 345-50; and Jeremy P. Felt, "Vice Reform as a Political Technique: The Committee of Fifteen in New York, 1900-1901," *New York History*, 54, 1 (January 1973); 24-51.

25. Lorin Peterson, *The Day of the Mugwump* (New York: Random House, 1961), 258, 260-1. A collection of scrapbooks on the Good Government Association may be consulted at the Massachusetts Historical Society. On Brandeis' League, *see* Richard M. Abrams, *Conservatism in a Progressive Era* (Cambridge, Mass.: Harvard University Press, 1964), 138-43.

26. Putnam, *Memories of a Publisher*, 349; and Abrams, *Conservatism in a Progressive Era*, 60.

27. William H. Allen, "Reminiscences" (Columbia University Oral History Project), 158-9. Richard Skolnik reaches much the same conclusion; *see* "Civic Group Progressivism in New York City," *New York History*, 51, 4 (July 1970): 437-8.

28. My estimate of 5 percent is a rough one, but it is solidly based on a study of early membership lists of three organizations: the American Association for Labor Legislation, the NAACP, and the Committee of One Hundred on the Federal Regulation of Public Health.

29. Jeremy P. Felt, *Hostages of Fortune: Child Labor Reform in New York State* (Syracuse: Syracuse University Press, 1965), 220.

30. Henry W. Farnam to Washington Gardner, December 19, 1910 (Farnam papers); and New York Child Labor Committee membership appeal sent to Seth Low, February 21, 1903 (Low papers).

31. Felix Adler, "Principles Which Should Guide the Citizen in His Choice of A President," *The Standard*, 3, 2 (November 1916): 27-33; Felt, *Hostages of Fortune*, 60; Allen F. Davis, *Spearheads for Reform* (New York: Oxford University Press, 1967), 8, 63, 129, and 131; and Charles Flint Kellogg, *NAACP: A History of the National Association for the Advancement of Colored People, 1909-1920* (Baltimore: The Johns Hopkins Press, 1967), 1: 75 and 129.

32. Felix Adler, *The World Crisis and Its Meaning* (New York: D. Appleton & Co., 1915), 190; and Horace L. Friess, "Felix Adler," *Columbia University Quarterly*, 26, 2 (June 1934): 135-49.

33. Irwin Yellowitz, *Labor and the Progressive Movement in New York State, 1897-1916* (Ithaca: Cornell University Press, 1965), 58.

34. Henry W. Farnam to Adna F. Weber, October 12 and 30, 1905; Louis D. Brandeis to John R. Commons, March 16, 1908; and Felix Adler to Commons, same date; and the AALL membership list, May 22,

1908 (John B. Andrews papers, School of Industrial and Labor Relations, Cornell University); and Ralph W. Easley to Seth Low, January 9 and February 15, 1912 (National Civic Federation papers, New York Public Library).

35. Farnam to Albert G. Keller, December 23, 1932 (Farnam papers); and Yellowitz, *Labor and the Progressive Movement*, 55, 58.

36. Kellogg, *NAACP*, 5; and Tilden G. Edelstein, *Strange Enthusiasm, A Life of Thomas Wentworth Higginson* (New Haven: Yale University Press, 1968), 388.

37. Kellogg, *NAACP*, 298-9.

38. The authoritative biography of Storey is William B. Hixson, Jr., *Moorfield Storey and the Abolitionist Tradition* (New York: Oxford University Press, 1972).

39. James M. McPherson, "The Antislavery Legacy: From Reconstruction to the NAACP," in Barton J. Bernstein, ed., *Towards a New Past: Dissenting Essays in American History* (New York: Random House, 1968), 151; Mary White Ovington, *The Walls Came Tumbling Down* (New York: Harcourt, Brace & Co., 1947), 109 and 129; and Kellogg, *NAACP*, 177 and 206.

40. Kellogg, *NAACP*, 3-4; Poultney Bigelow, *Seventy Summers* (New York: Longmans, Green & Co., 1925), 2: 226; and Edelstein, *Strange Enthusiasm*, 388-92, 400.

41. Bonaparte to Robert Catherwood, July 10, 1916 (Bonaparte papers).

42. George S. Merriam, *The Negro and the Nation* (New York: Henry Holt & Co., 1906), 393, 404-5; and Kellogg, *NAACP*, 189.

43. Henry W. Farnam to Prescott F. Hall, February 23, 1910 (Farnam papers).

44. Oscar S. Straus to Walter H. Newton, October 23, 1912 (Oscar S. Straus papers, Library of Congress); Gerald Kurland, *Seth Low* (New York: Twayne Publishers, 1971), 329; and further Mugwumps holding this view, as listed on a Friends of Russian Freedom circular, January 1915, sent to Seth Low (Low papers).

45. Barbara M. Solomon, *Ancestors and Immigrants, A Changing New England Tradition* (Cambridge, Mass.: Harvard University Press, 1956), 181 and 187; Edelstein, *Strange Enthusiasm*, 371-2; and David Starr Jordan, *The Days of a Man* (Yonkers, N.Y.: World Book Co., 1922), 2: 445-50.

46. Tomsich, *A Genteel Endeavor*, 82; and Howe, *Barrett Wendell and His Letters*, 249.

47. Bradford to Robert Grant, October 10, 1931, as quoted in Van Wyck Brooks, ed., *The Letters of Gamaliel Bradford* (Boston: Houghton Mifflin Co., 1934), 358.

48. Solomon, *Ancestors and Immigrants*, 104; and the subject file on "Immigration Restriction League" (Franklin MacVeagh papers, Library of Congress).

49. The generalizations that follow are based on a sample of 82 individuals, or 27 percent of the 302 survivors. Some information is available on the public careers of more than half the survivors, but the data is sufficient for generalization in these 82 cases only.

50. The non-progressive category is composed of 12 anti-progressives and 21 old-line Mugwumps. The broadly progressive category includes 8 advanced social progressives. My ratings for Group 2 (one-issue progressives) were rather cautious, and some of these individuals might be classified with the broadly progressive men, if more information were available on their views.

51. In the non-progressive group there were eight Democrats and eleven Republicans. In the progressively inclined group the numbers were thirteen Democrats and fifteen Republicans. By the barest of margins, certainly not a statistically significant one, the non-progressives tended to be older, business-oriented, and Republican, while the progressively inclined were more often professionals and Democrats.

52. Representative of the judges were Jabez Fox, Frederick Dodge, and William J. Wallace; of the civil service commissioners, Nelson S. Spencer and Frederick G. Ireland.

53. Marcus Cunliffe's analysis (*The Nation Takes Shape, 1789-1837*, Chicago: University of Chicago Press, 1959, 190-201) may be helpful in understanding the transformation of laissez-faire Mugwumps into progressives. How, for instance, could Jefferson be against Hamiltonianism in the 1790s and endorse it in the 1800s? Cunliffe suggests that ideological "polarities are more or less fixed [in America, but] the personnel are not. The people choose the position that matches their need or conviction of the moment and will shift to another if pressed." (199-200) In the post-Civil War era, the Mugwump elite found itself

shut off from power and consequently attempted to deny its opponents power by affirming a laissez-faire ideal of government action. By the 1900s, however, the emerging "new middle class" greatly augmented the cosmopolitan elite's numbers and potential political leverage. In this new setting government intervention—government was not so bad if one controlled it, after all—might regain its attraction for the surviving Mugwump descendents of New England Whigs and Federalists.

54. Bruce Curtis, "William Graham Sumner 'On the Concentration of Wealth,'" *Journal of American History*, 60, 4 (March 1969): 823-32; and Joseph Logsdon, *Horace White, Nineteenth Century Liberal* (Westport, Conn.: Greenwood Publishing Corp., 1971), 387-92.

55. Stewart, *Half Century of Municipal Reform*, 157.

56. Charles J. Bonaparte to William Dudley Foulke, April 22, 1918; and Richard Henry Dana to Foulke, same date (Foulke papers).

57. Otis L. Graham, Jr., *An Encore for Reform: The Old Progressives and the New Deal* (New York: Oxford University Press, 1967), 213-17.

Chapter 8

1. Alpheus T. Mason, *Brandeis: A Free Man's Life* (New York: Viking Press, 1956), 422.

2. William Dudley Foulke, *Fighting the Spoilsmen: Reminiscences of the Civil Service Reform Movement* (New York: G. P. Putnam's Sons, 1919), 145, 201, 211-12, and 257. Roosevelt to Foulke, January 19, February 3, and March 14, 1908; and Charles J. Bonaparte to Foulke, January 22, 1908 (Foulke papers).

3. *See*, for instance, Joseph B. Bishop, *Notes and Anecdotes of Many Years* (New York: Charles Scribner's Sons, 1925), 108, 124-7, and 146; and Bishop, *Charles Joseph Bonaparte, His Life and Public Services* (New York: Charles Scribner's Sons, 1922).

4. Naomi W. Cohen, *A Dual Heritage* (Philadelphia: The Jewish Publication Society of America, 1969), 38-9.

5. As quoted in Bishop, *Charles Joseph Bonaparte*, 129.

6. Cohen, *Dual Heritage*, 46; and Jeremy P. Felt, *Hostages of Fortune* (Syracuse: Syracuse University Press, 1965), 46.

7. Marguerite Green, *The National Civic Federation and the American Labor Movement, 1900-1925* (Washington, D.C.: Catholic University of America Press, 1956), 90-132.

8. Kurland, *Seth Low* (New York: Twayne Publishers, 1971), 253; and Low to Ralph W. Easley, August 27, 1907 (National Civic Federation papers).

9. Straus to William Dudley Foulke, September 13, 1916 (Foulke papers). *See* also Oscar S. Straus, *Under Four Administrations: From Cleveland to Taft* (Boston: Houghton Mifflin Co., 1922), 196-8, and Green, *National Civic Federation*, 193.

10. Kurland, *Seth Low*, 260, 280; and William Dudley Foulke to William Howard Taft, February 10, 1901 (Foulke papers).

11. Green, *National Civic Federation*, 201-5, 212-13; and Kurland, *Seth Low*, 265-70.

12. Kurland, *Seth Low*, 311-17. Ralph W. Easley to Seth Low, January 9 and February 15, 1912, are but two of the many letters on workmen's compensation between Low and Easley during the 1900-1913 period (National Civic Federation papers).

13. Adams to Elizabeth Cameron, March 2, 1902, in Worthington C. Ford, ed., *Letters of Henry Adams, 1892-1918* (Boston: Houghton Mifflin Co., 1938), 2: 376. Ernest Samuels, *Henry Adams, The Major Phase* Cambridge, Mass.: Harvard University Press, 1964), 245-52, 321.

14. Bliss Perry, *Life and Letters of Henry Lee Higginson* (Boston: Atlantic Monthly Press, 1921), 479, 425, 440-5.

15. E. V. Abbott to R. R. Bowker, October 19, 1904 (Bowker papers, NYPL); and M. A. DeWolfe Howe, *Portrait of an Independent, Moorfield Storey, 1845-1929* (Cambridge, Mass.: Houghton Mifflin Co., The Riverside Press, 1932), 281. Taft received 88 percent of the Mugwump vote, Bryan 12 percent. George Haven Putnam in *Memories of a Publisher, 1865-1915* (New York: G. P. Putnam's Sons, 1915), 358, spoke for many Democratic Mugwumps when he wrote that he was in the habit of voting Republican "whenever the Democrats nominated Bryan."

16. Adams to Charles M. Gaskell, June 18, 1908, and to Elizabeth Cameron, February 21, 1910, in Ford, ed., *Letters of Henry Adams*, 2: 511 and 535.

17. M. A. DeWolfe Howe, *Barrett Wendell and His Letters* (Boston:

The Atlantic Monthly Press, 1924), 250; William Howard Taft to Lounsbury, January 3, 1912 (Thomas R. Lounsbury papers, Yale Rare Book
Division); Farnam to Taft, June 29, 1912 (Farnam papers); and Franklin
MacVeagh, "President Taft and the Roosevelt Policies," *The Outlook*,
101 (May 18, 1912): 110-16.

18. October 21, 1909 memo; and Franklin MacVeagh to Mr. Perrin,
July 2, 1912 (MacVeagh papers).

19. Foulke to Taft, March 15, July 17, and November 10, 1909;
Foulke to Albert J. Beveridge, March 9, 1910; and Foulke to E. H.
Abbott, April 6, 1912, and to W. H. Goodwin, February 3, 1912, and
to Theodore Roosevelt, May 27, 1912 (Foulke papers).

20. On Straus, *see* Straus to Foulke, September 15, 1912 (Foulke
papers); and Cohen, *Dual Heritage*, 200. On Bird *see* Richard M.
Abrams, *Conservatism in a Progressive Era* (Cambridge, Mass.: Harvard
University Press, 1964), 284; and Richard B. Sherman, "Charles Sumner
Bird and the Progressive Party in Massachusetts," *New England Quart-
erly*, 33, 3 (September 1960): 325-40.

21. For a table of the Mugwump voting preferences, *see* p. 75.

22. E. Berkeley Tompkins, *Anti-Imperialism in the United States*
(Philadelphia: University of Pennsylvania Press, 1970), 282; Howe,
Barrett Wendell and His Letters, 242; and Perry, *Life and Letters of
Henry Lee Higginson*, 439, and *Portrait of an Independent*, 284; and
George D. Miller to Simeon E. Baldwin, October 4, 1910 (Baldwin
papers).

23. McAdam to Bowker, September 21, 1912; and Bowker to
McAdam, October 1, 1912 (Bowker papers, NYPL).

24. Tompkins, *Anti-Imperialism in the United States*, 282; and
Charles Flint Kellogg, *NAACP* (Baltimore: The Johns Hopkins Press,
1967), 167.

25. Abrams, *Conservatism in a Progressive Era*, 131-2.

26. Frederick H. Jackson, *Simeon Eben Baldwin: Lawyer, Social
Scientist, Statesman* (New York: Columbia University, King's Crown
Press, 1955), 160; Walter Learned (August 22, 1910), George D. Miller
(October 4, 1910), and Roger Foster (November 9, 1910), all written
to Baldwin (Baldwin papers).

27. Talcott H. Russell to Baldwin, August 2, 1911; and an appeal from
"The Democratic Party of Connecticut to the Independent Voters of

Connecticut" (1914) in the Baldwin papers. Jackson, *Simeon Eben Baldwin*, 172, 176, 184, and 192-5.

28. Mason, *Brandeis*, 422.

29. Henry James, *Charles W. Eliot* (Boston: Houghton Mifflin Co., 1930), 2: 229.

30. Henry E. Bothfeld (Massachusetts House of Representatives, 1910 to 1914); Charles Sumner Brown (United States Fuel Administration engineer, 1918); George L. Fox (Connecticut commissioner on arbitration and mediation, from 1917 to 1920); Talcott H. Russell (Connecticut Workmen's Compensation Board); Oscar S. Straus (New York Public Service Commission, from 1915 to 1918), and Andrew C. Zabriskie (chairman, Dutchess County Board of Supervisors, 1914).

31. Frederic J. Stimson, *My United States* (New York: Charles Scribner's Sons, 1931), 101; and Solomon B. Griffin, *People and Politics Observed by a Massachusetts Editor* (Boston: Little, Brown & Co., 1923), 459-65.

32. Tompkins, *Anti-Imperialism in the United States*, 285-6; Kellogg, *NAACP*, 167-78; Simeon E. Baldwin to James C. McReynolds, November 4, 1914 (Baldwin papers).

33. William Dudley Foulke to Theodore Roosevelt, December 7, 1914 (Foulke papers); Oscar S. Straus to Hudson Maxim, March 17, 1916 (Straus papers); and Foulke, *Lucius B. Swift*, Indiana Historical Society Publications, vol. 9 (Indianapolis: By the Society, 1930), 138.

34. Bishop, *Charles Joseph Bonaparte*, 196; Straus to Hudson Maxim, March 17, 1916 (Straus papers); Poultney Bigelow, *Seventy Summers* (New York: Longmans, Green & Co., 1925), 2: 252-3; Howe, *Barrett Wendell and His Letters*, 259; and Taft to Lounsbury, September 16, 1914 (Lounsbury papers).

35. Arthur S. Link, *Woodrow Wilson and the Progressive Era, 1910-1917* (New York: Harper & Row, Publishers, 1954), 239.

36. George Haven Putnam to Everett P. Wheeler, September 13, 1916 (Wheeler papers); and Putnam, *Memories of a Publisher*, 435-86. Many preparedness advocates, some of them former Wilson men, joined the American Rights League of which Putnam was president: Putnam to R. R. Bowker, August 23, 1919 (Bowker papers, NYPL).

37. The Mugwump attitude toward Brandeis's appointment is an interesting sidelight. Some—Storey and Austen G. Fox of New York—

fought the confirmation. Mason, *Brandeis*, 472-3, concedes nothing to Brandeis's critics. Abrams, *Conservatism in a Progressive Era*, 190ff (especially 212-16), indicates that at least in the crucial New Haven merger fight more was involved than a simple battle between reactionary Yankees and a champion of liberalism, Brandeis. Of fifty-five representative anti-Brandeis Bostonians, three were Mugwumps. *Boston Herald*, 12 February 1916.

38. R. R. Bowker to George Haven Putnam, August 8, 1916, and to Everett P. Wheeler, August 12, 1916 (Bowker papers, NYPL); and Donnan and Stock, eds., *An Historian's World* (Philadelphia: American Philosophical Society, 1956), 201. Similar feelings led Henry W. Farnam to switch from his normally Republican stance to Wilson's side; *see* Farnam to Mary C. Collins, August 24, 1916, and to Samuel C. Bushnell, November 6, 1916 (Farnam papers).

39. Felix Adler, "Principles Which Should Guide the Citizen in His Choice of A President," *The Standard*, 3, 2 (November 1916): 27-33.

40. Charles W. Eliot, "The Achievements of the Democratic Party and Its Leader Since March 4, 1913)," *The Atlantic Monthly*, 118, 4 (October 1916): 433-6, 439-40.

41. Ibid., 437-8. Arthur W. Milbury to R. R. Bowker, November 11, 1916 (Bowker papers, NYPL).

42. Oscar S. Straus, for instance, was appointed the American member of the Hague Tribunal. Cohen, *Dual Heritage*, 104-14.

43. Link, *Woodrow Wilson and the Progressive Era*, 233.

44. Plentiful examples of the League to Enforce Peace materials may be found in the Farnam, Foulke, and Straus papers. *See* also Ruhl F. Bartlett, *The League to Enforce Peace* (Chapel Hill: University of North Carolina Press, 1944).

45. William Dudley Foulke to Theodore Roosevelt, June 4, 1915; Roosevelt to Foulke, June 16, 1915; and Foulke to Roosevelt, March 19, 1917 (Foulke papers).

46. Howe, *Portrait of an Independent*, 314-15; David Starr Jordan, *The Days of a Man* (Yonkers, New York: World Book Co., 1922), 2: 671-81. Bishop, *Charles Joseph Bonaparte*, 192, 196, and 200.

47. R. R. Bowker to Lee Meriwether, July 30, 1919 (Bowker papers, NYPL). Bowker, Henry W. Farnam, Charles W. Eliot, and Moorfield Storey were some of the Mugwumps who carried the fight for the

league into the 1920s; *see* Irving Fisher to Farnam, October 18, 1920 (Farnam papers).

48. Robert U. Johnson to Simeon E. Baldwin, September 21, 1914 (Baldwin papers). For additional examples of anti-German feeling, *see* Joseph Logsden, *Horace White* (Westport, Conn.: Greenwood Publishing Corp., 1971), 388-389; Putnam, *Memories of a Publisher*, 435; Robert Grant, *Fourscore* (Boston: Houghton Mifflin Co., 1934), 335; and Erving Winslow to David Starr Jordan, August 21, 1915 (David Starr Jordan papers, Hoover Institute, Stanford University).

49. Jordan, *The Days of a Man*, 2: 734-5, 750; Jordan to Erving Winslow, February 5, 1918 (Jordan papers); and E. McClung Fleming, *R. R. Bowker* (Norman: University of Oklahoma Press, 1952), 356.

50. These facts are drawn from the fortieth anniversary alumni reports for the classes of 1877 and 1878 in the Harvard Archives.

51. Donnan and Stock, eds., *An Historian's World*, 201, 208.

52. William Dudley Foulke to Richard Henry Dana III, April 26 and 29, 1918, and Foulke to Charles J. Bonaparte, January 3, 1919 (Foulke papers).

53. Irwin Yellowitz, *Labor and the Progressive Movement in New York* (Ithaca: Cornell University Press, 1965), 76.

54. Tompkins, *Anti-Imperialism in the United States*, 282; R. R. Bowker to Horace E. Deming, February 22, 1927 (Bowker papers, NYPL); and Charles J. Bonaparte to William Dudley Foulke, April 22, 1918 (Foulke papers).

55. *New York Times*, 24 November 1942 on Davison, and Harvard class files on Fish and Clapp (Harvard Archives).

56. Fleming, *R. R. Bowker*, 359; Bowker to Horace E. Deming, September 20, 1922 (Bowker papers, NYPL); James F. Colby to Farnam, May 3, 1933, and Farnam to Colby, August 5, 1933 (Farnam papers). *See* also David Starr Jordan to J. A. H. Hopkins, May 14, 1924 (Jordan papers), and Moorfield Storey to R. R. Bowker, June 24, 1925 (Bowker papers, NYPL).

Appendix B

1. An excellent critical review of this debate is David Thelen, "Social Tensions and the Origins of Progressivism," *Journal of American History*, 56, 2 (September 1969): 323-41. *See* also my article, cited in note 4.

2. Richard B. Sherman, "The Status Revolution and Massachusetts Progressive Leadership," *Political Science Quarterly*, 78, 1 (March 1963): 59-65; Alfred D. Chandler, Jr., "The Origins of Progressive Leadership," in Elting E. Morison, ed., *The Letters of Theodore Roosevelt* (Cambridge, Mass.: Harvard University Press, 1954), vol. 8, appendix 3, 1462-5; and Otis L. Graham, Jr., *An Encore for Reform: The Old Progressives and the New Deal* (New York: Oxford University Press, 1967), 195-204.

3. Gerald W. McFarland, "Politics, Morals, and the Mugwump Reformers" (Ph.d. diss., Columbia University, 1965), 152.

4. Gerald W. McFarland, "Inside Reform: Status and Other Evil Motives," *Soundings*, 54, 2 (Summer 1971): 164-76.

Selected Bibliography

To record every source relating to the Mugwump reformers would be to encumber this bibliography unnecessarily with the obvious and the obscure. For this reason I have omitted several types of materials altogether and have selected only the most relevant source materials in every other category.

Among those omitted categories are lists of biographical dictionaries and other biographical source materials used in identifying the Mugwump and Republican samples. These range from the familiar *Who Was Who* type to club membership lists and college alumni registers. I have also refrained from repeating references to club and association publications (proceedings, etc.), many of which are cited in my footnotes.

As for Mugwump writings, I have listed only a small number, mainly those which relate specifically to an individual's political opinions. To offer even a reasonably thorough bibliography of the complete corpus of Mugwump writings—novels, tracts, autobiographies, and scholarly works—would serve little purpose except to demonstrate *ad nauseum* that the Mugwumps published prolifically.

I have not repeated individual article references from Gilded Age sources here, as the major examples of contemporary articles may be found in my footnotes. Finally, most materials that relate to Mugwump activities before 1884 are omitted, though in the early stages of my research I made a painstaking survey of these manuscript, periodical, and secondary sources. They do not bear directly on the focus of this book, however; and completely adequate listings of these materials appear elsewhere.

I. Unpublished Sources

A. *Manuscripts*

Andrew, John F. Papers. Massachusetts Historical Society.
Andrews, John B. Papers. School of Industrial and Labor Relations, Cornell University.
Atkinson, Edward. Papers. Massachusetts Historical Society.

Baldwin, Simeon Eben. Papers. Yale University.

Bancroft, Frederic. Papers. Columbia University.

Bigelow, Poultney. Miscellaneous Papers. New York Public Library.

Bonaparte, Charles J. Papers. Library of Congress.

Bowker, Richard Rogers. Papers. Library of Congress.

———. Papers. New York Public Library.

Burt, Silas W. Papers. New York Historical Society.

Citizens' Union. Papers. Columbia University.

City Club. Papers. New York Public Library.

Clarke, James Freeman. Papers. Harvard University.

Clemens, Samuel L. Papers. University of California, Berkeley.

Cleveland, Grover. Papers. Library of Congress.

Codman, Charles R. Papers. Massachusetts Historical Society.

Curtis, George William. Papers. Harvard University.

Dana, Richard Henry. Papers. Massachusetts Historical Society.

Endicott, William C. Papers. Massachusetts Historical Society.

Everett, William. Papers. Massachusetts Historical Society.

Fairchild, Charles S. Papers. New York Historical Society.

Farnam, Henry W. Papers. Yale University.

Foulke, William Dudley. Papers. Library of Congress.

George, Henry. Papers. New York Public Library.

Gilder, Richard Watson. Papers. New York Public Library.

Godkin, Edwin Lawrence. Papers. Harvard University.

Good Government Association of Boston. Papers. Massachusetts Historical Society.

Grant, Robert. Papers. Harvard University.

Hamlin, Charles S. Papers. Library of Congress.

Higginson, Thomas Wentworth. Papers. Harvard University.

Jordan, David Starr. Papers. Hoover Institute, Stanford University.

Lounsbury, Thomas R. Papers. Yale Rare Book Division.

Low, Seth. Papers. Columbia University.

MacVeagh, Franklin. Papers. Library of Congress.

National Civic Federation. Papers. New York Public Library.

Norton, Charles Eliot. Papers. Harvard University.

Reid, Whitelaw. Papers. Library of Congress.

Russell, William E. Papers. Massachusetts Historical Society.

Sargent, Joseph B. Family Papers. Yale University.

Schurz, Carl. Papers. Library of Congress.
Shaw, Albert. Papers. New York Public Library.
Stimson, Frederic J. Papers. Massachusetts Historical Society.
Straus, Oscar S. Papers. Library of Congress.
University Settlement Society. Papers. State Historical Society of
   Wisconsin.
Villard, Henry. Papers. Harvard University.
Warren, Winslow. Scrapbooks. Massachusetts Historical Society.
Welling, Richard W. G. Papers. New York Public Library.
Wells, David Ames. Papers. Library of Congress.
Wheeler, Everett P. Papers. New York Public Library.
White, Andrew D. Papers. Cornell University.
White, Horace. Papers. New York Historical Society.
Whitney, William C. Papers. Library of Congress.
Williams, George Fred. Papers. Massachusetts Historical Society.

B. Memoirs, Columbia University Oral History Project.

Allen, William H.
Bennet, William Stiles.
Bruere, Henry.
Childs, Richard S.
Kelley, Nicholas.
Schieffelin, William Jay.
Veiller, Lawrence.

II. Serial Publications.

Annals of the American Academy of Political and Social Science.
   Scattered issues.
Atlantic Monthly. Scattered issues, 1884-1900.
Boston Daily Advertiser. 1884.
Boston Evening Transcript. 1884-1887.
Boston Globe. 1884.
Boston Herald. Scattered issues.
The Century Magazine. 1884-1895.
The Forum. 1886-1898.

Harper's Monthly. 1884.
Harper's Weekly. 1884-1887.
Hartford Courant. 1884.
Hartford Evening Post. 1884.
Hartford Times. 1884.
Louisville Courier-Journal. Scattered issues.
Minneapolis Tribune. 1884.
The Nation. 1884-1886.
The Nationalist (Boston). 1889.
New England Magazine. Scattered issues.
New Haven Morning News. 1884-1896.
New Haven Weekly Register. 1884-1894.
New York Evening Post. Scattered issues.
The New York Times. 1884-1920.
New York Tribune. 1884.
New York World. Scattered issues.
North American Review. 1884-1900.
The Outlook. 1910-1916.
The People's Cause. 1889.
Philadelphia Public Ledger and Daily Transcript. 1884.
Review of Reviews. 1890-1908.
Springfield Daily Republican. 1884 and scattered issues.

III. Mugwump Writings

Adams, Charles Francis, Jr. *Charles Francis Adams, 1835-1915: An Autobiography.* Boston: Houghton Mifflin Company, 1916.
Adams, Henry. *The Education of Henry Adams.* New York: Random House, Modern Library edition, 1931.
Adler, Felix. *The World Crisis and Its Meaning.* New York: D. Appleton and Company, 1915.
Atkinson, Edward. *Taxation and Work.* New York: G. P. Putnam's Sons, 1892.
Bancroft, Frederic, ed. *Speeches, Correspondence and Political Papers of Carl Schurz.* 6 vols. New York: G. P. Putnam's Sons, 1913.
Baxter, Sylvester. *Greater Boston.* Boston: A. J. Philpott and Company, 1891
Bigelow, Poultney. *Seventy Summers.* 2 vols. New York: Longmans, Green and Company, 1925.

Bishop, Joseph B. *A Chronicle of One Hundred and Fifty Years: The Chamber of Commerce of the State of New York, 1768-1918.* New York: Charles Scribner's Sons, 1918.
———. *Notes and Anecdotes of Many Years.* New York: Charles Scribner's Sons, 1925.
———. *Charles Joseph Bonaparte, His Life and Public Services.* New York: Charles Scribner's Sons, 1922.
Bowker, Richard Rogers. *A Primer for Political Education.* New York: The Society for Political Education, 1886.
———. *Free Trade the Best Protection to American Industry.* New York: G. P. Putnam's Sons, 1883.
Bradford, Gamaliel, Jr. *Life and I.* Boston: Houghton Mifflin Company, 1928.
Bradford, Gamaliel, Sr. *The Lesson of Popular Government.* 2 vols. New York: Macmillan Company, 1899.
Bridgman, Raymond L. *The Independents of Massachusetts in 1884.* Boston: Cupples, Upham and Company, 1885.
Brooks, Van Wyck, ed. *The Letters of Gamaliel Bradford.* Boston: Houghton Mifflin Company, 1934.
Carter, James C. *How Can Municipal Government Be Divorced From National Party Lines?* New York: Nineteenth Century Club, 1895.
Cowles, James L. *A General Freight and Passenger Post.* New York: G. P. Putnam's Sons, 1898.
Cutting, Robert Fulton. *Citizens Union: Its Origin and Purpose.* New York: Winthrop Press, 1903.
Deming, Clarence. *Yale Yesterdays.* New Haven: Yale University Press, 1915.
Deming, Horace E. *The Government of American Cities.* New York: G. P. Putnam's Sons, 1909.
Donnan, Elizabeth, and Stock, Leo F., eds. *An Historian's World: Selections for the Correspondence of John Franklin Jameson.* vol. 42. *Memoirs of the American Philosophical Society.* Philadelphia: American Philosophical Society, 1956.
Ford, Worthington C., ed. *Letters of Henry Adams, 1892-1918.* 2 vols. Boston: Houghton Mifflin Company, 1938.
Foulke, William Dudley. *Fighting the Spoilsmen: Reminiscences of the Civil Service Reform Movement.* New York: G. P. Putnam's Sons, 1919.

——. *Lucius B. Swift, A Biography.* Indiana Historical Society Publications. vol. 9. Indianapolis: By the Society, 1930.

Gilder, Richard Watson. *Grover Cleveland: A Record of Friendship.* New York: The Century Company, 1910.

Gilder, Rosamond, ed. *Letters of Richard Watson Gilder.* Boston: Houghton Mifflin Company, 1916.

Godkin, Edwin Lawrence. *Problems of Modern Democracy.* New York: Charles Scribner's Sons, 1896.

——. *Reflections and Comments, 1865-1895.* New York: Charles Scribner's Sons, 1895.

——, ed. *The Triumph of Reform.* New York: Souvenier Publishing Company, 1895.

——. *Unforeseen Tendencies of Democracy.* Boston: Archibald Constable and Company, 1898.

Grant, Robert. *Fourscore: An Autobiography.* Boston: Houghton Mifflin Company, 1934.

Greene, Jacob L. *Our Currency Problems.* Hartford: Case, Lockwood and Brainard Company, 1896.

Griffin, Solomon B. *People and Politics Observed by a Massachusetts Editor.* Boston: Little, Brown and Company, 1923.

Hale, Edward Everett, ed. *James Freeman Clarke: Autobiography, Diary and Correspondence.* Boston: Houghton Mifflin Company, 1891.

Harper, J. Henry. *I Remember.* New York: Harper and Brothers, 1934.

Holt, Henry. *Garrulities of an Octogenarian Editor.* New York: Houghton Mifflin Company, 1923.

Hughes, Sarah Forbes, ed. *Letters and Recollections of John Murray Forbes.* 2 vols. Boston: Houghton Mifflin Company, 1899.

Johnson, Robert U. *Remembered Yesterdays.* Boston: Little, Brown and Company, 1923.

Jordan, David Starr. *The Days of a Man: Being Memories of a Naturalist, Teacher, and Minor Prophet of Democracy.* 2 vols. Yonkers, New York: World Book Company, 1922.

Keller, Albert G. and Davie, Maurice R., eds. *Essays of William Graham Sumner.* 2 vols. New Haven: Yale University Press, 1934.

Merriam, George S. *The Negro and the Nation.* New York: Henry Holt and Company, 1906.

Norton, Charles Eliot, ed. *Orations and Addresses of George William Curtis.* 3 vols. New York: Harper and Brothers, 1894.

Norton, Sara, and Howe, Mark A. DeWolfe, eds. *Letters of Charles Eliot Norton with Biographical Comment.* 2 vols. Boston: Houghton Mifflin Company, 1913.

Ogden, Rollo, ed. *Life and Letters of Edwin Lawrence Godkin.* 2 vols. New York: MacMillan Company, 1907.

Owen, Charles H. *Why a Consistent Republican Should Vote the Democratic Ticket.* Hartford: privately printed, 1884.

Potts, William. *Evolution and Social Reform: The Socialistic Method.* Boston: James H. West, 1890.

Putnam, George Haven. *Memories of a Publisher, 1865-1915.* New York: G. P. Putnam's Sons, 1915.

Sargent, Joseph B. *Protection a Burden.* Boston: Massachusetts Tariff Reform League, 1885.

Schoenhof, Jacob. *The Economy of High Wages.* New York: G. P. Putnam's Sons, 1893.

———. *The Industrial Situation.* New York: G. P. Putnam's Sons, 1885.

Shearman, Thomas G. *Free Trade: The Only Road to Manufacturing Prosperity and High Wages.* New York: American Free Trade League, 1883.

———. *Natural Taxation.* New York: Doubleday, Page and Company, 1915.

———. *Tariff Reform in Favor of the Poor.* New York: George S. Wilcox, 1882.

Smith, Henry Nash, and Gibson, William M., eds. *Mark Twain-Howells Letters, 1872-1910.* 2 vols. Cambridge, Massachusetts: Belknap Press of Harvard University Press, 1960.

Stimson, Frederic J. *My United States.* New York: Charles Scribner's Sons, 1931.

Storey, Moorfield. *Politics As a Duty and As a Career.* New York: G. P. Putnam's Sons, 1889.

Straus, Oscar S. *Under Four Administrations: From Cleveland to Taft.* Boston: Houghton Mifflin Company, 1922.

Sumner, William Graham. *What Social Classes Owe to Each Other.* New York: Harper and Brothers, 1883.

264 : Selected Bibliography

Welling, Richard W. G. *As the Twig is Bent.* New York: G. P. Putnam's
Sons, 1942.
White, Alfred T. *Improved Dwellings for the Laboring Classes.* New
York: Reform Club, 1877.
———. *Sun-Lighted Tenements.* New York: National Housing
Association, 1912.
White, Horace. *The Surplus and the Tariff.* Boston: Massachusetts
Tariff Reform League, 1888.
Whitridge, Frederick W. *Addresses by F. W. W.* New York: privately
printed, 1933.

IV. Secondary Sources.

A. Books

Abrams, Richard M. *Conservatism in a Progressive Era: Massachusetts
Politics, 1900-1912.* Cambridge, Massachusetts: Harvard University
Press, 1964.
Albright, Spencer D. *The American Ballot.* Washington, D.C.:
American Council on Public Affairs, 1942.
Alexander, James W. *A History of the University Club of New York,
1865-1915.* New York: Charles Scribner's Sons, 1915.
Andrews, Kenneth R. *Nook Farm, Mark Twain's Hartford Circle.*
Cambridge, Massachusetts: Harvard University Press, 1950.
Atkins, Gordon. *Health, Housing, and Poverty in New York City, 1865-
1898.* Ann Arbor, Michigan: Edwards, 1947.
Bartlett, Ruhl F. *The League to Enforce Peace.* Chapel Hill: University
of North Carolina Press, 1944.
Bass, Herbert J. *"I Am a Democrat": The Political Career of David B.
Hill.* Syracuse: Syracuse University Press, 1961.
Beisner, Robert L. *Twelve Against Empire: The Anti-Imperialists, 1898-
1900.* New York: McGraw-Hill Book Company, 1968.
Blodgett, Geoffrey. *The Gentle Reformers: Massachusetts Democrats
in the Cleveland Era.* Cambridge, Massachusetts: Harvard University
Press, 1966.
Bremner, Robert L. *From the Depths: The Discovery of Poverty in the
United States.* New York: New York University Press, 1956.

Calhoun, Daniel H. *Professional Lives in America: Structure and Aspiration, 1750-1850.* Cambridge, Massachusetts: Harvard University Press, 1965.

Callow, Alexander B. *The Tweed Ring.* New York: Oxford University Press, 1966.

Cohen, Naomi W. *A Dual Heritage: The Public Career of Oscar S. Straus.* Philadelphia: The Jewish Publication Society of America, 1969.

Cohen, Sol. *Progressives and Urban School Reform: The Public Education Association of New York City, 1895-1954.* New York: Teachers College, Columbia University, 1964.

Cooke, Jacob E. *Frederic Bancroft, Historian.* Norman: University of Oklahoma Press, 1957.

Curti, Merle. *The Growth of American Thought.* New York: Harper and Brothers, 1943.

Dahlberg, Jane S. *The New York Bureau of Municipal Research: Pioneer in Government Administration.* New York: New York University Press, 1966.

Davis, Allen F. *Spearheads for Reform: The Social Settlements and the Progressive Movement, 1890-1914.* New York: Oxford University Press, 1967.

Dobson, John M. *Politics in the Gilded Age: A New Perspective on Reform.* New York: Praeger Publishers, 1972.

Duberman, Martin. *James Russell Lowell.* Boston: Houghton Mifflin Company, 1966.

Edelstein, Tilden G. *Strange Enthusiasm, A Life of Thomas Wentworth Higginson.* New Haven: Yale University Press, 1968.

Ely, Richard T. *Ground Under Our Feet.* New York: Macmillan Company, 1938.

Evans, Eldon Cobb. *A History of the Australian Ballot System in the United States.* Chicago: University of Chicago Press, 1917.

Fairfield, Francis G. *The Clubs of New York.* New York: Henry L. Hinton, 1873.

Felt, Jeremy P. *Hostages of Fortune: Child Labor Reform in New York State.* Syracuse: Syracuse University Press, 1965.

Fleming, E. McClung. *R. R. Bowker, Militant Liberal.* Norman: University of Oklahoma Press, 1952.

Fredman, L. E. *The Australian Ballot: The Story of an American Reform.* East Lansing: Michigan State University Press, 1968.

Garrett, Charles. *The LaGuardia Years: Machine and Reform Politics in New York City.* New Brunswick: Rutgers University Press, 1961.

Graham, Otis L. Jr. *An Encore for Reform: The Old Progressives and the New Deal.* New York: Oxford University Press, 1967.

Green, Marguerite. *The National Civic Federation and the American Labor Movement, 1900-1925.* Washington, D.C.: Catholic University of America Press, 1956.

Grimes, Alan P. *The Political Liberalism of the New York "Nation," 1865-1932.* Chapel Hill: University of North Carolina Press, 1953.

Hennessy, Michael E. *Four Decades of Massachusetts Politics.* Norwood, Massachusetts: Norwood Press, 1935.

————. *Twenty-Five Years of Massachusetts Politics, 1890-1915.* Boston: Practical Politics, 1917.

Hirsch, Mark D. *William C. Whitney, Modern Warwick.* New York: Dodd, Mead and Company, 1948.

Hixson, William B. Jr. *Moorfield Storey and the Abolitionist Tradition.* New York: Oxford University Press, 1972.

Hofstadter, Richard. *The Age of Reform: From Bryan to F.D.R.* New York: Alfred A. Knopf, 1955.

————, and Hardy, C. DeWitt. *The Development and Scope of Higher Education in the United States.* New York: Columbia University Press, 1952.

Hoogenboom, Ari. *Outlawing the Spoils: A History of the Civil Service Reform Movement, 1865-1883.* Urbana: University of Illinois Press, 1961.

Hopkins, Charles H. *The Rise of the Social Gospel in American Protestantism, 1865-1915.* Yale University Studies in Religious Education. vol. 14. New Haven: Yale University Press, 1940.

Howe, Mark A. DeWolfe. *Barrett Wendell and His Letters.* Boston: Atlantic Monthly Press, 1924.

————. *Portrait of an Independent, Moorfield Storey, 1845-1929.* Boston: Houghton Mifflin Company, 1932.

Huggins, Nathan. *Protestants Against Poverty; Boston's Charities, 1870-1900.* Westport, Connecticut: Greenwood Publishing Corporation, 1971.

Irwin, Will. *A History of the Union League Club of New York City.* New York: Dodd, Mead and Company, 1952.

Jackson, Frederick H. *Simeon Eben Baldwin: Lawyer, Social Scientist, Statesman.* New York: King's Crown Press, 1955.

James, Henry. *Charles W. Eliot.* 2 vols. Boston: Houghton Mifflin Company, 1930.

Jones, Howard Mumford. *The Life of Moses Coit Tyler.* Ann Arbor: University of Michigan Press, 1933.

Josephson, Matthew. *The Politicos, 1865-1896.* New York: Harcourt, Brace and Company, 1948.

Kelley, Robert L. *The Transatlantic Persuasion: The Liberal-Democratic Mind in the Age of Gladstone.* New York: Alfred A. Knopf, 1969.

Kellogg, Charles Flint. *NAACP: A History of the National Association for the Advancement of Colored People, 1909-1920.* vol. 1. Baltimore: The Johns Hopkins Press, 1967.

Kirkland, Edward Chase. *Charles Francis Adams, Jr., 1835-1915: The Patrician at Bay.* Cambridge, Massachusetts: Harvard University Press, 1965.

Kolko, Gabriel. *The Triumph of Conservatism: A Reinterpretation of American History, 1900-1916.* New York: Free Press of Glencoe, 1963.

Kurland, Gerald. *Seth Low: The Reformer in an Urban and Industrial Age.* New York: Twayne Publishers, 1971.

Link, Arthur S. *Woodrow Wilson and the Progressive Era, 1910-1917.* New York: Harper and Row, 1954.

Logsdon, Joseph. *Horace White, Nineteenth Century Liberal.* Westport, Connecticut: Greenwood Publishing Corporation, 1971.

Lubove, Roy. *The Progressives and the Slums: Tenement House Reform in New York City, 1890-1917.* Pittsburgh: University of Pittsburgh Press, 1962.

McSeveney, Samuel. *The Politics of Depression: Political Behavior in the Northeast, 1893-1896.* New York: Oxford University Press, 1972.

Mandelbaum, Seymour J. *Boss Tweed's New York.* New York: John Wiley, 1965.

Mann, Arthur. *Yankee Reformers in the Urban Age.* Cambridge, Massachusetts: Harvard University Press, 1954.

Marcus, Robert D. *Grand Old Party: Political Structure in the Gilded Age, 1880-1896.* New York: Oxford University Press, 1971.

Mason, Alpheus T. *Brandeis: A Free Man's Life.* New York: Viking Press, 1956.

May, Henry F. *Protest Churches and Industrial America.* org. pub. 1949. New York: Octagon Books, 1963.

————. *The End of American Innocence: A Study of the First Years of Our Own Times, 1912-1917.* New York: Alfred A. Knopf, 1959.

Merrill, Horace S. *Bourbon Democracy of the Middle West, 1865-1896.* Baton Rouge: Louisiana State University Press, 1953.

————. *Bourbon Leader: Grover Cleveland and the Democratic Party.* Boston: Little, Brown and Company, 1957.

Morgan, H. Wayne. *From Hayes to McKinley: National Party Politics, 1877-1896.* Syracuse: Syracuse University Press, 1969.

————, ed. *The Gilded Age.* Revised edition. Syracuse: Syracuse University Press, 1970.

Mowry, George E. *The Era of Theodore Roosevelt and the Birth of Modern America, 1900-1912.* New York: Harper Bros., 1958.

Munro, William B. *The Government of American Cities.* New York: Macmillan Company, 1920.

Muzzey, David S. *James G. Blaine, A Political Idol of Other Days.* New York: Dodd, Mead and Company, 1934.

Myers, Gustavus. *The History of Tammany Hall.* New York: Boni and Liverwright, 1917.

Nevins, Allan. *Grover Cleveland: A Study in Courage.* New York: Dodd, Mead and Company, 1948.

————, ed. *The Letters of Grover Cleveland.* Boston: Houghton Mifflin Company, 1933.

Ovington, Mary White. *The Walls Came Tumbling Down.* New York: Harcourt, Brace and Company, 1947.

Peel, Roy V. *The Political Clubs of New York City.* New York: G. P. Putnam's Sons, 1935.

Perry, Bliss. *Richard Henry Dana, 1851-1931.* Boston: Houghton Mifflin Company, 1933.

————. *Life and Letters of Henry Lee Higginson.* Boston: Atlantic Monthly Press, 1921.

Peterson, Lorin. *The Day of the Mugwump.* New York: Random

House, 1961.

Ravenel, Mazÿck P., ed. *A Half Century of Public Health: Jubilee Historical Volume of the American Public Health Association.* New York: American Public Health Association, 1921.

Samuels, Ernest. *Henry Adams, The Major Phase.* Cambridge, Massachusetts: Harvard University Press, 1964.

Shaw, Albert. *Life of Colonel George E. Waring, Jr.* New York: The Patriotic League, 1899.

Solomon, Barbara M. *Ancestors and Immigrants: A Changing New England Tradition.* Cambridge, Massachusetts: Harvard University Press, 1956.

Sproat, John G. *"The Best Men," Liberal Reformers in the Gilded Age.* New York: Oxford University Press, 1968.

Steffens, Lincoln. *The Shame of the Cities.* New York: Hill and Wang, American Century Series edition, 1957.

Stewart, Frank Mann. *A Half Century of Municipal Reform: The History of the National Municipal League.* Berkeley: University of California Press, 1950.

Syrett, Harold C. *The City of Brooklyn, 1865-1898.* New York: Columbia University Press, 1944.

Thelen, David P. *The New Citizenship: The Origins of Progressivism in Wisconsin, 1885-1900.* Columbia: University of Missouri Press, 1972.

Tolman, William H. *Municipal Reform Movements in the United States.* New York: Fleming H. Revell Company, 1895.

Tompkins, E. Berkeley. *Anti-Imperialism in the United States: The Great Debate, 1890-1920.* Philadelphia: University of Pennsylvania Press, 1970.

Tomsich, John. *A Genteel Endeavor: American Culture and Politics in the Gilded Age.* Stanford: Stanford University Press, 1971.

Truax, Rhoda. *The Doctors Jacobi.* Boston: Little, Brown and Company, 1952.

Unger, Irwin. *The Greenback Era: A Social and Political History of American Finance, 1865-1879.* Princeton: Princeton University Press, 1964.

U.S. Federal Housing Administration. *Four Decades of Housing With a Limited Dividend Corporation.* Washington, D.C.: Division of

Economics and Statistics, 1939.

Warner, Sam B. Jr. *Streetcar Suburbs: The Process of Growth in Boston, 1870-1900.* Cambridge, Massachusetts: Harvard University Press, 1962.

Weinstein, James. *The Corporate Ideal in the Liberal State, 1900-1918.* Boston: Beacon Press, 1968.

Weiss, Nancy Joan. *Charles Francis Murphy, 1858-1924: Respectability and Responsibility in Tammany Politics.* Northampton, Massachusetts: Smith College, 1968.

Wheeler, Everett P. *Sixty Years of American Life.* New York: E. P. Dutton and Company, 1917.

Wiebe, Robert R. *The Search for Order, 1877-1920.* New York: Hill and Wang, 1967.

Williamson, Harold F. *Edward Atkinson: The Biography of an American Liberal, 1827-1905.* Boston: Old Corner Book Store, 1934.

Yellowitz, Irwin. *Labor and the Progressive Movement in New York State, 1897-1916.* Ithaca: Cornell University Press, 1965.

Young, Arthur N. *The Single Tax Movement in the United States.* Princeton: Princeton University Press, 1916.

B. Articles.

Abrams, Richard M. "A Paradox of Progressivism: Massachusetts on the Eve of Insurgency," *Political Science Quarterly.* 75, 3 (September 1960): 379-99.

———. "The Failure of Progressivism," in Richard Abrams and Lawrence W. Levine, eds. *The Shaping of Twentieth-Century America.* 2nd edition, Boston: Little, Brown and Company, 1971.

Bass, Herbert J. "The Politics of Ballot Reform in New York State, 1888-1890," *New York History.* 42, 3 (July 1961): 253-71.

Beisner, Robert L. "1898 and 1968: The Anti-Imperialists and the Doves," *Political Science Quarterly*, 85, 2 (June 1970): 187-216.

Benjamin, Philip S. "Gentlemen Reformers in the Quaker City, 1870-1912," *Political Science Quarterly.* 85, 1 (March 1970): 61-79.

Benson, Lee. "Research Problems in American Political Historiography," in Mirra Komarovsky, ed. *Common Frontiers of the Social Sciences.* Glencoe, Illinois: The Free Press, 1957.

Berkelman, Robert. "Mrs. Grundy and Richard Watson Gilder," *American Quarterly*. 4, 1 (Spring 1952): 66-72.

Blodgett, Geoffrey T. "Josiah Quincy, Brahmin Democrat," *New England Quarterly*. 38, 4 (December 1965): 435-53.

Bower, Robert T. "Opinion Research and Historical Interpretation of Elections," *Public Opinion Quarterly*. 12, 3 (Fall 1948): 455-64.

Brieger, Gert H. "Sanitary Reform in New York City: Stephen Smith and the Passage of the Metropolitan Health Bill," *Bulletin of the History of Medicine*. 40, 4 (September-October 1966): 407-29.

Buenker, John. "The Progressive Era: A Search for a Synthesis," *Mid-America*. 51, 3 (July 1969): 175-94.

Chandler, Alfred D. Jr. "The Origins of Progressive Leadership," in Elting E. Morison, ed. *The Letters of Theodore Roosevelt*. vol. 8. Cambridge, Massachusetts: Harvard University Press, 1954, appendix 3, 1462-5.

Chase, Philip P. "The Attitude of the Protestant Clergy in Massachusetts during the Election of 1884," *Massachusetts Historical Society Proceedings*. 64 (1930-1932): 467-98.

Curtis, Bruce. "William Graham Sumner 'On the Concentration of Wealth,'" *Journal of American History*. 60, 4 (March 1969): 823-32..

Felt, Jeremy P. "Vice Reform as a Political Technique: The Committee of Fifteen in New York, 1900-1901," *New York History*. 54, 1 (January 1973): 24-51.

Filene, Peter G. "An Obituary for 'The Progressive Movement,'" *American Quarterly*. 22, 1 (Spring 1970): 20-34.

Fredman, L. E. "Seth Low: Theorist of Municipal Reform," *Journal of American Studies*. 6, 1 (April 1972): 19-39.

Friess, Horace L. "Felix Adler," *Columbia University Quarterly*. 26, 2 (June 1934): 135-49.

Fuess, Claude M. "Carl Schurz and Henry Cabot Lodge in 1884," *New England Quarterly*. 5, 3 (July 1932): 453-82.

Griffen, Clyde C. "Rich Laymen and Early Social Christianity," *Church History*. 34, 1 (March 1967): 3-23.

Hartman, William. "Pioneer in Civil Service Reform: Silas W. Burt and the New York Custom House," *New York Historical Society Quarterly*. 39, 4 (October 1955): 369-79.

Hays, Samuel P. "The Politics of Reform in Municipal Government in the Progressive Era," *Pacific Northwest Quarterly*, 55, 4 (October 1964): 157-69.

————. "The Social Analysis of American Political History, 1880-1920," *Political Science Quarterly*. 80, 3 (September 1965): 373-94.

Hirsch, Mark D. "The New York Times and the Election of 1884," *New York History*. 39, 3 (July 1948): 301-8.

Hixson, William B. Jr. "Moorfield Storey and the Struggle for Equality," *Journal of American History*. 55, 3 (December 1968): 533-54.

Hoogenboom, Ari. "An Analysis of Civil Service Reformers," *The Historian*. 23, 1 (November 1960): 54-78.

Huthmacher, Joseph. "Urban Liberalism and the Age of Reform," *Mississippi Valley Historical Review*. 64, 2 (September 1962). 231-41.

Kammen, Michael G. "Richard Watson Gilder and the New York Tenement House Commission of 1894,)) *Bulletin of the New York Public Library*. 66, 6 (June 1962): 364-82.

Karier, Clarence J. "Testing for Order and Control in the Corporate Liberal State," *Educational Theory*. 22, 2 (Spring 1972): 154-80.

Klebanow, Diana. "E. L. Godkin, the City, and Civil Responsibility," *New York Historical Society Quarterly*. 55, 1 (January 1971): 52-75.

Kurland, Gerald. "The Amateur in Politics: The Citizens' Union Greater New York Mayoral Campaign of 1897," *New York Historical Society Quarterly*. 53, 4 (October 1969): 352-84.

Lasch, Christopher. "The Anti-Imperialists, the Philippines, and the Inequality of Man," *Journal of Southern History*. 24, 3 (August 1958): 319-31.

McFarland, Gerald W. "Inside Reform: Status and Other Evil Motives," *Soundings*. 54, 2 (Summer 1971): 164-76.

————. "Partisan of Nonpartisanship: Dorman B. Eaton and the Genteel Reform Tradition," *Journal of American History*. 54, 4 (March 1968): 806-22.

————. "The Breakdown of Deadlock: The Cleveland Democracy in Connecticut, 1884-1894," *The Historian*. 31, 3 (May 1969): 381-97.

————. "The New York Mugwumps of 1884: A Profile," *Political Science Quarterly*. 78, 1 (March 1963): 40-58.

McPherson, James M. "The Antislavery Legacy: From Reconstruction to the NAACP," in Barton J. Bernstein, ed. *Towards a New Past: Dissenting Essays in American History*. New York: Random House, 1968.

Malin, James C. "Roosevelt and the Elections of 1884 and 1888," *Mississippi Valley Historical Review*. 14, 1 (June 1927): 25-38.

Mann, Arthur. "British Social Thought and American Reformers of the Progressive Era," *Mississippi Valley Historical Review*. 42, 4 March 1956): 672-92.

Mowry, George E. "The California Progressive and His Rationale: A Study in Middle-Class Politics," *Mississippi Valley Historical Review*. 36, 2 (September 1949): 239-50.

Muccigrosso, Robert. "The City Reform Club: A Study in Late Nineteenth-Century Reform," *New York Historical Society Quarterly*. 52, 3 (July 1968): 235-54.

Sherman, Richard B. "Charles Sumner Bird and the Progressive Party in Massachusetts," *New England Quarterly*. 33, 3 (September 1960): 325-40.

————. "The Status Revolution and Massachusetts Progressive Leadership," *Political Science Quarterly*. 78, 1 (March 1963), 59-65.

Skolnik, Richard. "Civil Group Progressivism in New York City," *New York History*. 51, 4 (July 1970): 410-39.

Swett, Steven C. "The Test of a Reformer: A Study of Seth Low, New York City Mayor, 1902-1903," *New York Historical Society Quarterly*. 44, 1 (January 1960): 5-41.

Terrill, Tom E. "David A. Wells, the Democracy, and Tariff Reduction, 1877-1894," *Journal of American History*. 55, 3 (December 1969): 540-55.

Thelen, David P. "Social Tensions and the Origins of Progressivism," *Journal of American History*. 56, 2 (September 1969): 323-41.

Welch, Richard E. Jr. "Motives and Objectives of Anti-Imperialists, 1898," *Mid-America*. 51, 2 (April 1969): 119-29.

Wood, Gordon S. "The Massachusetts Mugwumps," *New England Quarterly*. 33, 4 (December 1960): 435-51.

Index